CHURCH, STATE, AND EDUCATION IN AFRICA

Edited by

DAVID G. SCANLON

TEACHERS COLLEGE PRESS
TEACHERS COLLEGE, COLUMBIA UNIVERSITY
NEW YORK   1966

PREFACE

The controversy over church, state, and education is one of the most persistent problems in education throughout the world. It has been debated for centuries in Europe and continues to be a pressing issue in most countries. It is inextricably bound to politics, for rights of the state and rights of the church are resolved by political decisions.

Upon achieving independence, the majority of African countries found they had inherited an educational system that was managed by churches and missionaries. The decisions and allocation of rights and responsibilities in education had been reached through decades of consultation and heated debate by missionary groups and colonial administrators. With independence it was obvious that new negotiations would be necessary between an increasingly Africanized church and African political leaders. While this is a new dialogue with new participants in a new situation, the roots of the issue are found in past history. This book is intended as a series of introductory essays on the problem.

Each contributor was asked essentially to review the past patterns of church-state relations in education, analyze existing arrangements, and comment on what appear to be future trends. Two criteria were used in deciding which states should be included in this book. The first was representation of English, French, and Belgian patterns. Current arrangements and future changes can best be understood by a knowledge of the arrangements that existed at the time of independence; conditions were quite similar in all colonies held by a given authority. The second criterion was the willingness of known leading educators to take time from their schedules to contribute to this book.

However, if the British, French, and Belgian examples were to be included it appeared that attention should also be paid to

Africa's oldest independent country, Ethiopia, and to the peculiar problems of South Africa. Ethiopia, with its ancient Church, evolved a pattern unique in Africa. South Africa, with its policy of "apartheid," has developed its own model; the contributor of this chapter, Dr. Peter Hunter, has chosen to emphasize church-state relations since the Nationalists assumed office in 1948.

As students of African affairs are well aware, events move rapidly on that continent. Three of the chapters were completed in 1964, three in 1965, one in 1966. It was not possible to have all chapters end on an agreed terminal date. However, the background and perspective given in the chapters should enable the reader to interpret any current changes that occur.

It should also be stressed that the introduction was written by the editor without consultation with the contributors. It is intended as a guideline for the reader unacquainted with the problem in Africa and to provide a setting for the subsequent chapters.

The editor would like to thank the Institute for Education in Africa, Teachers College, whose grant helped make this study possible.

Orleans, Massachusetts
April, 1966

CONTENTS

I

INTRODUCTION

DAVID G. SCANLON

The editor is Professor of International Education and Coordinator for Studies for the Institute for Education in Africa at Teachers College, Columbia University. He has worked in West Africa for UNESCO and in East Africa for the Institute for Education in Africa. His publications include INTERNATIONAL EDUCATION: A DOCUMENTARY HISTORY; TRADITIONS OF AFRICAN EDUCATION; EDUCATION IN UGANDA; *and, coedited with* L. Gray Cowan *and* James O'Connell, EDUCATION AND NATION BUILDING IN AFRICA.

For Africa the closing decades of the nineteenth century were marked by two crucial events. The first was the well-known partition of Africa by European powers. As they moved in from the coast, the great central portion of sub-Sahara Africa was explored, mapped, and divided. Politically, old Africa was gone. The maps that appeared showed the familiar colors indicating the colonial holdings of metropolitan powers; the bright pink and dark green of Britain and France were to last until the 1960's. The administration of the territories under colonial rule, their structure and organization, have been discussed by many authors and do not need review here. Each country, as might be expected, ruled Africa according to its particular philosophy, in the case of England and France influenced very often by Asian experience. The establishment of government, the pacification of recalcitrant areas, the maintenance of law and order, and the attempt to build an economic system consumed the majority of time of most administrators.

But no European power would justify its existence purely on the basis of political advantage or economic gain. Underlying all government pronouncements regarding the colonization of Africa were professed statements of aid and assistance to the Africans. The echoes of Livingston's famous speech at Senate House, Cambridge, were still loud, and they were reinforced by the horrors of the slave trade described by Stanley and others. The press and the public in Europe and America were interested in Africa to a degree that was not matched until the past decade of our history.

Independent of the political action of the European powers was a second event that was to have a most profound effect on Africa. This was the great religious revival that swept the United

3

States, England, Scotland, and, to a lesser extent, the continent of Europe. The missionary movement had been smoldering for generations. Since the turn of the century British, French, and American missionaries had taken an active role in Sierra Leone, Liberia, and Senegal, following in the footsteps of Portuguese and Danish missions. Pockets of missionary activity could be found in East and Central Africa as well as at the older established stations in South Africa. The Portuguese boasted of a mission tradition that dated from the fifteenth century.[1]

By the 1870's the revival movement had begun; it was to reach its greatest heights in the period from 1890 to World War I. In the United States, Dwight L. Moody and his colleague Ira Sankey were electrifying their audiences with sermons that gave their listeners the simple choice of salvation or damnation. The success of the revivalist resulted in a more vigorous, active church that strengthened its many component parts—and one important part was foreign missions. Under the zeal of Robert Wilder, son of a missionary to India, the Student Volunteer Movement for Foreign Missions was organized at Northfield, Massachusetts, in 1886 and met with instant success. Speakers and organizers covered the United States, meeting with groups in colleges in every state and encouraging students to become missionaries. By 1894 three times as many men expected to be missionaries as in 1886, and by 1914 almost 6,000 had gone out as missionaries.[2]

Paul A. Varg, commenting on the effectiveness of the Volunteer Movement, wrote, "The Student Volunteers were the dynamo which set the whole organized denominational machinery of American Protestanism into motion in behalf of missions. It did far more than recruit missionaries; it was the chief promotional agency in the missionary movement. At the time of its organization, few ministers showed any enthusiasm for foreign missions,

---

[1] For a review of the earlier period see Gustav Werneck, *Outline of a History of Protestant Missions* (New York: Fleming H. Revell Co., 1901) ; C. P. Groves, *The Planting of Christianity in Africa,* Vols. I-III (London: Lutterworth Press, 1948, 1954, 1955).

[2] *Students and the World Wide Expansion of Christianity: Addresses Delivered Before the Seventh International Convention of the Student Volunteer Movement for Foreign Missions, Kansas City, Missouri, December 31, 1913, to January 4, 1914* (New York: Student Volunteer Movement for Foreign Missions, 1914) , p. 18.

the young people knew almost nothing about the enterprise, and laymen were almost wholly indifferent."[3]

The enthusiasm of the students was matched by financial support from the business community and churches scattered throughout the country. Business and professional men organized the Laymen's Missionary Movement in 1906, and a decade later, when the Laymen's Missionary Congress met in Washington, the editor of *The Missionary Review of the World* wrote that the delegates "were men of large influence and big business responsibilities; manufacturers, merchants lawyers, brokers, bankers, physicians, professors, editors and heads of corporations."

A second dimension was added to the blossoming missionary movement with the rise of Progressivism, with its concern for social reform and human welfare. The work of Jacob Riis and Jane Addams had popularized a sentiment of humanitarianism that was to gain national and international acceptance.[4] In religious groups the movement was represented by an emphasis on the "social gospel." The physical and social progress of man had always been a concern of missionaries, but this aspect of the mission movement was now reemphasized and those writers who stressed this aspect of missionary effort became the leaders of the effort.[5] While the missionary would always, of course, be concerned with personal conversion, he was now told in explicit terms to seek the social regeneration of society. Social reform became the hallmark of the overseas effort. This effort was summarized by one missionary leader who wrote in 1915,

One of the most marked changes taking place in the foreign mission propaganda during the last century has been the shift of emphasis from the individual to society. The social aspect of Christianity was not given due recognition at home or abroad a generation ago. It is not strange

[3] Paul A. Varg, *Missionaries, Chinese and Diplomats: The American Protestant Missionary Movement in China, 1890–1952* (Princeton: Princeton University Press, 1958) , p. 60.

[4] See Jacob Riis, *The Children of the Poor* (New York: Charles Scribner's Sons, 1902) ; Jane Addams, *Democracy and Social Ethics* (New York: The Macmillan Co., 1902) ; Stanton Coit, *Neighborhood Guilds* (London: S. Sonnenschein, 1891) .

[5] See for example James S. Dennis, *Christian Missions and Social Progress: A Sociological Study of Foreign Missions* (3 vols.; New York: Fleming H. Revell Co., 1897) ; Robert E. Speer, *Christianity and the Nations* (New York: Fleming H. Revell Co., 1910) .

therefore that while missionaries were promoting great, sweeping social movements, international in character and fundamental in reach, they did recognize them as such, but continued there as we did here to put supreme emphasis upon individual conversion.[6]

A religious revival, a concern for the social gospel, financial and moral support never before possible combined to make the years from 1880 to 1920 the golden period of missionary effort in Africa. It paralleled the period in which European powers were building, consolidating, and extending those administrative units that were to be foundations for colonial government. For the colonial powers, the expansion of missionary effort was fortuitous, as support of missions gave credence to the "civilizing" objective of colonialism. And it was done at remarkably low cost to the European powers. The mission hospital, printing press, and demonstration garden became a familiar sight at many mission stations. But such activities were to prove secondary to the most common and most effective service provided by the missions—the development of education.

From the time of the earliest Portuguese missionaries of the fifteenth century through the nineteenth century, Christianity and education had been inextricably bound together. Varying in degree from those who believed the most rudimentary knowledge was necessary for conversion to those who demanded as high an educational level as possible, agents of the church and the literacy movement marched in lockstep. In West, South, and East Africa, missions might forego many luxuries, but education was considered a necessity. Therefore, when the rapid expansion of missionary work in the 1880's began, it was only natural that education should be expanded. And added to the necessity of education for conversion was the new, powerful thrust of the social gospel. Education was the major means of alleviating the basic problems of health and poverty. There was no institution other than the school that could undertake this responsibility.

In supporting the role of the missions, the European colonial powers were relieved of a great deal of administrative and financial responsibility. Moreover, Europe was repeating in Africa what had become established policy in Europe. Patterns of support for

---

[6] James L. Barton, "The Modern Missionary," *Harvard Theological Review*, VIII (January, 1915), 6.

church-related schools in Europe had emerged through the centuries and were familiar to the European administrators and colonialists responsible for the organization and management of the colonies. Agreements that had been reached in the metropolitan power became the pattern for agreements overseas. African church, state, and educational policies became projections of the respective European models. To understand the emerging pattern in Africa it is essential to understand the home policy of the European powers, for there was little that occurred in the European countries that was not reflected in the approach used in the African colonies.[7]

In England the modern educational system which started in the early nineteenth century had its origins in religious groups and philanthropic organizations. In 1833 the government began a policy of providing funds to some voluntary schools. The Forster Act of 1870 established a national system of elementary schools that resulted in a "Dual System" of education.[8] Schools operated by religious groups were to be aided financially by the government and encouraged. However, to "fill the gaps" publicly supported schools were also established by local communities. The Balfour Act of 1902 made additional concessions to denominational schools by authorizing the use of local taxes for them. But the law also provided for control of the secular instruction in the voluntary schools by Local Education Authorities. From the passage of the Balfour Act until World War I the issue of church, state, and education provoked heated arguments and much public debate. "For the people of the British Isles the controversy provoked an emotional excitement not unlike that generated in France by the contemporaneous Dreyfus affair. The strife produced court trials, prison sentences, distraint of property, election issues, exchanges between opposing church leaders and negotiations in political

---

[7] For an excellent brief review of church, state, and educational patterns in world perspective, see *Religion, Government and Education* edited by William W. Brickman and Stanley Lehrer (New York: Society for the Advancement of Education, 1961), pp. 144–247.

[8] The bill caused much debate in England and was finally passed after thirty nights of controversial debate. For a review of the background and controversy see W. O. Lester Smith, *Education in Great Britain* (London: Oxford University Press, 1960), pp. 48–75. Nicholas Hans, in *Comparative Education* (London: Routledge and Kegan Paul, 1951), gives a penetrating analysis of the religious traditions of education. See Part II, pp. 85–174.

circles."[9] Despite the burning debates, charges, and counter-charges, the *status quo* remained.

The period between World Wars I and II saw a movement to strengthen religion in education but little to change the nature of the Dual System.[10] The comprehensive Education Act of 1944 gave official sanction and recognition to religious practices that had existed in most English schools. The act required that the school day in every county (nonreligious) school begin with "collective" worship and that religious instruction be given in every county school and in every voluntary school.[11] Turning to the Dual System, the Act continued the pattern of support for voluntary and Local Educational Authority schools. The voluntary schools were financed by the Local Educational Authority, which provided teachers' salaries, educational equipment, heating and lighting, and similar expenses. The Local Education Authority supervised the secular part of the curriculum.

The pattern of support by the government of religious or voluntary schools was and remains an integral part of the English administration and financing of education. It is therefore not surprising that when the colonial governments began to assume a more active role in education they turned to the existing mission schools and gave them financial support. With the opening of government schools a "Dual System" was created in Africa. However, there was a marked difference between England and Africa. The missions had near monopoly on the schools in most sections of English-speaking Africa. Moreover, the real organization of education by colonial governments did not occur until the close of World War I, and by this time the mission schools were in fact the overwhelming majority of schools in the African territories.

The same bitterness found in British church, state, and education issues from 1902 to 1914 plagued France for over a century and a half. The Roman Catholic Church held a monopoly on

[9] Benjamin Sacks, *The Religious Issue in the State Schools of England and Wales, 1902–1914: A Nation's Quest for Human Dignity* (Albuquerque, N. M.: University of New Mexico Press, 1961) , p. v.

[10] Religion was strengthened in the schools run by the Local Education Authorities (non-religious) by agreement on a nonsectarian outline of religious instruction. This "agreed syllabus" was first adopted in Cambridgeshire in 1924 and became common in most L.E.A. schools.

[11] See "Education Act 1944:7" (London: H.M. Stationery Office, 1944) .

education for centuries that was swept away by the French Revolution, regained some of its power under Napoleon, and by 1850 had completely regained its privileged position. However, by 1875 anticlericalism and secularism were on the rise in France. In 1882 the first law was passed aimed at secularization of the schools. Primary education was made secular and compulsory. Priests were not permitted to inspect, supervise, or direct public and private primary schools. In effect the law closed all primary schools to religious instruction; as a compromise the schools were closed one day a week in addition to Sunday to permit parents to arrange for religious instruction outside the schools.[12] By 1886 clergy were banned as teachers of secular subjects; by 1904 all members of religious orders were barred from teaching in any kind of school.[13] The final separation of church and state was promulgated by law on December 9, 1905.

However, within France the "wall" of separation between church and state education was never so rigid as it has been in the United States. Outstanding Catholic priests held chairs in state institutions of higher learning; poor children attending Catholic schools were granted financial aid and textbooks. The line of demarcation was therefore not between black and white but was a gray area that was constantly revised depending upon the political currents of Paris.

And if the separation of church and state in education was not always sharp in France, it certainly was less clear in the French African possessions. As Gerard Lucas documents in his chapter on the Republic of Congo (Brazzaville), official separation might be the law, but for the sake of extending French interests, colonial administrators were not reluctant to aid French Catholic missionaries and indeed supported them to an extent that would have been impossible in metropolitan France.

Under the Vichy regime (1940–1944), liberal concessions were made to Catholic schools. They received government grants, religious orders were permitted to teach in church schools free from government control, the teaching of religion was reintroduced in the public schools, and the government paid the salaries of school

[12] The full text of the law can be found in Robert Brichet, *L'Obligation Scholaire* (Paris: La Vie Communale et Departementale, 1946), pp. 53-59.

[13] Paul Foulquié, *L'Eglise et L'Ecole* (Paris: Editions Spes, 1947), p. 69.

chaplains. In the years following World War II, gradual concessions were made to Catholic schools. The *Loi Marie* and *Loi Barange* of September, 1951, permitted subsidies to children irrespective of the type of school they attended. The most recent crucial law was passed in December, 1959, and was a broad concession to Catholic schools. It provided for the payment of salaries of qualified teachers in private schools on the same basis as the public school teachers, gave communities the right to give assistance to any child despite the school he attended, but insisted that all schools receiving such aid be open to any child regardless of his religious beliefs. It was this approach or a revision of it, popularly called the "DeGaulle Plan," that was put into effect in the Congo and the majority of other French-speaking countries at the time of independence.[14]

In Belgium, as in France, the dispute over church and state is a long and bitter one. For over a century, clericals and liberals have debated, fought, and compromised over the issue of state support for religious schools.

The establishment of Léopold II's control over the Congo in 1885 occurred at a time when the Catholic Party had defeated the Liberals and had become the dominant party in Belgium, as it was to remain until 1914. Since gaining independence from Holland, the Belgians had been divided into two major groups, the Liberal Party and the Catholic Party. Under the Liberal ascendancy a beginning had been made in establishing state schools. In 1864 the *Ligue de l'Enseignement* had been founded, dedicated to free, compulsory, and "neutral" state education; its growth was phenomenal. The majority enjoyed by the Liberals in the election of June, 1878, encouraged the Liberals to create a State Ministry of Education; state schools grew rapidly and it was increasingly made clear that education was a state responsibility. This was a decided movement toward state rather than local control of educacation and was, of course, a direct attack on the church-run schools. While state schools continued to grow, the result of the reforms was to rally divided Catholic groups into unified opposition to the new educational program.

With the fall of the Liberals in 1884 the Catholic Party intro-

[14] See *Education in France*, No. 9 (New York: French Cultural Services, 1960).

duced reforms which strengthened religious schools, weakened the state system, and particularly emphasized the role of the community in determining educational policy. Opponents claimed the Catholic Party had a stranglehold on the schools; supporters claimed this increase in the power of the church was simply a reflection of the real desires of the people and pointed out the continual victory of the Catholic Party in elections to substantiate this claim. However, by the eve of World War I the Liberals and Socialists had strengthened their position and school reforms were considered a major political issue.[15]

World War I interrupted all major efforts at educational reform, but after the war Belgian politics was dominated by coalition governments until World War II. Compromise was necessary and the state education system in Belgium grew. However, the support of both the state system and the Catholic schools that became the pattern in Belgium was not felt in the Congo in the interbellum period. A clear Liberal or Socialist victory might have forced the issue, but as this victory was not forthcoming, the Congo continued under the status quo. However from 1945 on the Socialists and the *Ligue de l'Enseignement* repeatedly challenged the role of Catholic missionaries in the Congo and worked for state schools. As Richard Dodson indicates in his chapter, the exclusive position of the Catholic missionaries was broken when a Liberal minister (Godding) granted subsidies to Protestant mission schools. And it was under a Liberal-Socialist coalition that the first lay nonreligious schools were established in the Congo in 1954. The Congo was taking part in the political and religious controversy of Belgium.

Missionaries Viewed as Collaborators

There is little doubt that colonial governments viewed missionaries as collaborators in building a viable colony. And while all missionaries might be useful in this endeavor, Belgium and France gave ample evidence that they preferred missionaries who were also nationals of their own country. If France proclaimed as one

[15] For an excellent summary of the interrelationships of church, state, politics, and education see Vernon Mallinson, *Power and Politics in Belgian Education* (London: William Heinemann, 1963).

of her major reasons for being in Africa the extension of "civiliza-tion," this could most easily be done by those who were themselves part of French culture and could extend French "civilization." National missionaries, it was hoped, would have a greater sym-pathy for the political and economic objectives of France. And while all missionaries carried the "word of God," French colonial officials preferred to have the "word" spoken in French. Colonial officers in French-speaking Africa might be personally anticlerical, but ordinarily this did not blind them to the fact that the French missionaries were serving France as well as their religion.

Dodson points out that Léopold used early missionaries to occupy the Congo Basin and so present a greater claim for his sovereignty. But it was not enough to have just *any* missionaires engaged in this endeavor. Ideally, they should be Belgian. Hence Léopold's insistence on an Apostolic Vicariate for the Congo placed under the control of the Scheutist Fathers in Belgium, re-placing the earlier French and Portuguese Catholic missionaries. As British Protestant missionaries were considered more sympa-thetic to Léopold's avowed aims for the Congo, they were treated more favorably than nationals from France and Portugal whose governments had shown little enthusiasm for his plans. However, when Léopold's abuses in the Congo were publicly criticized by Protestant missionaries and these criticisms were later confirmed by the Report of the Commission of Enquiry (1905)[16] appointed by Léopold to investigate charges of maladministration, foreign Prot-estant missionaries were no longer considered "loyal" to the regime.[17] A concordat was signed with the Vatican in 1906 that in effect gave the Catholics a privileged position and officially marked the beginning of subsidized Catholic parochial schools. Protestant mission schools as described by Dodson were not subsidized until 1948, when all Christian missions were placed on an equal basis and could claim government support as long as they met official requirements. During the period from 1906 to 1948 Belgian mis-

---

16 *The Congo: A Report of the Commission on Enquiry Appointed by the Congo Free State Government* (London and New York: G. P. Putnam Sons, 1906).

17 The Catholic Party in Belgium criticized Léopold, and a leading Belgian Jesuit wrote a book attacking the Congo State Government. See Arthur Ver-meech, *La Question Congolaise* (Bruxelles: Charles Bulens, 1906) .

sionaries were considered particularly desirable in building a loyal educational system. After World War I, when the Belgian government reexamined its educational policy in the Congo, the report of its commission was appropriately entitled *Projet d'organisation de l'enseignement libre au Congo Belge avec le concours des missions nationales* (Plan for Organizing Free Education in the Belgian Congo with the Cooperation of the Belgian Missions).[18]

Professor Ed. De Jonghe, Director-General for the Ministry of the Colonies at Brussels, commenting on the cooperation of missionaries in 1931, wrote, "The Belgian missionaries especially render a most important service. Along with the light of the gospel they spread the love of Belgium, the influence of Belgium to the remotest corners of Central Africa."[19]

Compared with the colonies of France and Belgium, there was less identification of "national" missionaries in British Africa. It was in most cases easier for the foreign missionary to work in the British colonies and protectorates, and "national" missions were not stressed as much as they were in the other two colonial holdings. To be sure, in times of crisis national background would be important. The civil war between Catholics and Protestants that rent Uganda in 1892 was soon described as a battle between the French (Catholic) party and the British (Protestant) party.[20] But such occurences were unusual.

British administrators saw the value of the missionaries in undertaking the responsibility for building an educational system and were quick to emphasize their value in building a sound colony. Sir Harry Johnston (despite his own personal view of reli-

[18] See David G. Scanlon, ed., *Traditions of African Education* (New York: Teachers College Press, Teachers College, Columbia University, 1964), pp. 141–184. *Missions nationales* (Belgian missions) are defined as those missions which had their headquarters in Belgium, which were directed by Belgians, and which included a certain number of Belgians among their missionaries.

[19] Ed. De Jonghe, "Education in the Belgian Congo," in *Educational Yearbook of the International Institute of Teachers College, Columbia University, 1931* (New York: Bureau of Publications, Teachers College, Columbia University, 1932).

[20] The charge that the French Catholic missionaries were responsible for the war is dramatically presented in Ernest L. Bentley's *British East Africa and Uganda: A Historical Record* (London: Chapman and Hall, 1892). An answer to the charges was published by the Catholic Union of Great Britain in *Memorandum on the War in Uganda* (London: Waterlow and Son, 1894).

gion) and Lord Lugard were among the many administrators who emphasized the need for mission work in the colonies.[21]

Conflict of Missionaries and Administrators

If there was a recognized need for the missions, particularly in the field of education, there was also the fact that personality and policy clashes between the administrator and the missionary were not unusual.[22] Anyone who travelled in Africa before independence would invariably find the administrator whose view of the missions was far less complimentary than that of Sir Harry Johnston or Lord Lugard. This perhaps was inevitable. Against the African background were two groups of Europeans—the administrators and the missionaries—each dedicated to goals and policies that for the most part overlapped. But there were bound to be areas where the administrator and the missionary disagreed. The work of the Protestant missionaries in the Congo had contributed to the downfall of Léopold. A vigorous aggressive missionary such as Dr. John Philip in South Africa could rally support from followers at home that would cause serious embarrassment to the colonial government.[23] In a case of extreme pressure, the missionary did not hesitate to appeal to his home church for support and popular pressure on home governments by religious groups was not uncommon. The complaint by Professor A. J. MacDonald was undoubtedly shared by many administrators:

> Too long have the great missionary organizations regarded themselves as independent of imperial policy and activity . . . not until they and the church at home realize that the work of administrator and missionary have the same object in view will true imperial action and a true civilization in tropical and sub-tropical regions be possible.[24]

21 Sir Frederick Lugard, "Progress in Africa," in Edwin Smith, ed., *The Christian Mission in Africa: A Study Based on the Work of the International Conference at Le Zoute, Belgium, September 14th to 21st, 1926* (London: International Missionary Council, 1926). See for example Sir Harry Johnston's preface in A. J. MacDonald, *Trade, Politics and Christianity in Africa and the East* (London: Longmans, Green & Co., 1916) .

22 See for example Sir Harry Johnston, *British Central Africa* (London; Methuen, 1906) , pp. 77, 107–108.

23 See W. M. Macmillan, *The Cape Colour Question* (London: Faber and Gwyer, 1927) and *Bantu, Boer and Briton* (London, Faber and Gwyer, 1929) .

24 A. J. MacDonald, *op. cit.,* p. 56.

But despite the disputes the missionary work, particularly in education, proceeded. In fact, it was the very success of the missions in education that caused the church to turn to the government for financial help. By 1910 it was apparent to many missionaries that it would be impossible for missions to staff and finance the rapidly expanding educational system, and this problem was discussed at the famous Edinburgh Conference of 1910.[25] World War I delayed any direct action by governments, but the missionaries continued to insist that they needed aid. Many were concerned about the quality of education offered, for the comparatively rapid expansion of education had resulted in a number of poorly equipped schools staffed by individuals with little or no training. It was this sense of responsibility, concern over the continuing expansion, and worry about the ultimate consequences that led missions to press their demands for a review of education in Africa.

In the United States, the American Baptist Foreign Missionary Society recommended the establishment of a commission to study education in Africa. The Baptists sent their recommendation to the Committee of Reference and Counsel of the Foreign Missions Conference of North America. The committee, after finding that other denominational boards would cooperate, supported the recommendation and proposed Thomas Jesse Jones as chairman. The Phelps-Stokes Fund provided the funds and undertook the responsibility of forming the commission. The commission comprised Europeans, Americans, and James Aggrey from the Gold Coast.

The commission published its first report in 1922 and a second in 1925.[26] Both, particularly the first, were widely read and discussed in Europe. They came at a propitious time. The entire concept of European possessions overseas had been deliberated in the mandate debates of the League of Nations. Discussion of the duty of those supervising mandates emphasized once again the social responsibility of the colonial powers.[27] Whether the cause

[25] See *World Missionary Conference, 1910, Report of Commission,* III (New York: Fleming H. Revell Co., n. d.).

[26] See Thomas Jesse Jones, ed., *Education in Africa* (New York: The Phelps-Stokes Fund, 1922) and Thomas Jesse Jones, ed., *Education in East Africa* (New York: The Phelps-Stokes Fund, 1925).

[27] See Quincy Wright, *Mandates Under the League of Nations* (Chicago: University Press of Chicago, 1930).

was a new humanitarian wave sweeping Europe in the shadows of World War I or simply the fact that the colonies, as a result of selling new products during the war, had more money to spend on social services would be difficult to determine.

In any case, Britain, France, and Belgium established a more formal structure for dealing with education in Africa within their colonial departments in London, Paris, and Brussels. All three countries issued formal statements outlining their colonial policy for developing education in the African territories.[28] The British and Belgian statements made clear that voluntary or missionary effort would be encouraged. The policy of encouraging mission schools on the elementary and secondary level while opening a relatively few government schools became the basic approach in British Africa, while in the Congo missionary schools were, for all practical purposes, the only schools. The French, particularly in Muslim areas, extended government schools, but the old policy of non-official aid to missions continued.

Despite the stated objectives of developing education more rapidly and comprehensively, the worldwide depression of the 1930's made it difficult for governments to carry out stated goals. Enthusiastic supporters were agreed on the needs and objectives of education, but the decline in financial resources made it difficult in some areas to continue existing patterns; rapid expansion was impossible. World War II, like World War I, interrupted the development of education, and it was only after World War II that funds and men were available to undertake the task that had been designed in the 1920's. During the interbellum period governments had supported mission schools, and a pattern emerged of missions depending on government support and governments depending on missions for management and, in most cases, staff and partial financing. Missions would not have been able to expand their educational systems without the financial support of the government, but the government could never hope to replace mission schools with government schools if it had been so inclined, and there was no indication that this was ever a serious consideration.

After World War II, under grants from the British Colonial and Development Acts, the French Plan for Modernization, and

[28] For a general review of policy statements see Scanlon, *op. cit.*

the Belgian Ten Year Plan for Economic and Social Development of the Congo, the development of education in Africa was accelerated. Expansion of primary education and the growth of higher education were the hallmarks of British and French efforts, and Belgium began the process of a skeletal secondary educational system. In the decade before independence the majority of African countries went through an educational revolution. To be sure, much remained to be done, but the first thrust had been made and the desirability of the action is well documented by the emphasis placed on education by newly independent African nations.

At independence the majority of African countries found themselves with educational systems managed by religious groups.[29] But if there had been major political changes in Africa, there had been a parallel change in the churches. Increasingly the churches acquired an African identity. African bishops, elders, and lay leaders had replaced, in many areas, the "foreign" missionary. The Africanization of the churches had been going on for decades. The education of Africans for the clergy had been one of the objectives in establishing schools among the earliest missionaries, and many missionaries had demanded greater role for the African clergy. This was based upon the assumption that only when the church was Africanized could it be said to have real roots in the African environment. Otherwise, it was a grafted institution that would be blown away if the foreigners left. The Africanization of the clergy in all denominations has proceeded since independence at a rapid rate.[30] Among many religious groups the very word "missionary" is no longer in good repute but has been replaced by "fraternal worker."

But in spite of the Africanization of the clergy and the control of the church placed in the hands of nationals, there is still a

[29] In Kenya, for example, on the eve of independence there were eight government primary schools for Africans and 4,024 aided primary schools, the overwhelming majority managed by religious groups. There were no government secondary schools and 50 aided secondary schools. The great majority of aided secondary schools were managed by religious groups. *Ministry of Education Annual Summary, 1961* (Nairobi: Government Printer, 1962), p. 24.

[30] In some cases this may be as a result of governmental pressure. Sekou Touré in Guinea expelled the French head of the Guinean Catholic Church and demanded that he be replaced with a Guinean. See L. Gray Cowan, "Guinea," in *African One-Party States*, ed. by Gwendolen M. Carter (Ithaca: Cornell University Press, 1962).

dependence on overseas financial aid and manpower. If the control of the church is no longer exclusively in the hands of foreign mission boards, still there is a close association that helps bolster the African church. Doctors, teachers, agriculturists, and clergy sent by foreign mission boards strengthen the growing African church. Thus the foreign influence remains a strong factor.

Since independence the task of the government and the heads of religious groups has been to reexamine their respective roles in the new nations. Only one African country—Guinea—has nationalized the schools, excluding the churches from education. However, it should be pointed out that the role of Christian missions in Guinea had never been great; the majority of the people are Muslims. It would be far more difficult to replace the mission or church-related schools in areas where mission work has had a long tradition and has become a crucial factor in the educational system. In the Sudan the majority of Christian missions have been expelled, reflecting the decades-old political problem of North and South Sudan. In South Africa there has been direct confrontation between some church schools and the government over the issue of the Bantu Education Act, and this issue has been discussed by Peter Hunter in his chapter on South Africa.

Theoretically there are four possible variations in church-state-education relations in Africa. The first is to continue the present policy of supporting church-managed schools. This is what is occurring in most sections of Africa today. Responsibility for education is, of course, in the hands of the Ministry of Education, and inspectors determine whether or not the schools are meeting government requirements. The local administration of the school is left with a representative of the churches, and he may be aided by a local board of advisors or trustees. This arrangement permits the churches to continue their religious role in education and relieves an often short-handed government of administrative problems. However, since independence the expansion of government schools has been remarkable. This expansion has been possible because of the increased number of African college graduates and the number of teachers who have been recruited in Britain, France, and the United States by such agencies as the Peace Corps. This dual system of government-supported mission schools and purely government schools will probably continue.

A second variation would permit church-related schools to

continue but only at their own expense. If this scheme were put into effect, the majority of churches would be forced to close their schools, for government financial support has made possible the vast network of church-related schools throughout sub-Sahara Africa. Conversely, the responsibility in education undertaken by missions would be difficult for governments to assume at this time.

A third possibility would be to nationalize the schools and, following the pattern of Guinea, refuse the church the right to operate schools. Should substantial elements of the church-related schools appear disloyal to the existing regime, this is a possibility. However there is no evidence at the present time that this is seriously under consideration. Again, the very mechanics of operating the large church-related sector of the educational system would preclude this approach at the present except under the most extreme circumstances.

The fourth possibility is that state recognition and subsequent financial support would be given to only one religious group. This occurred in the Belgian Congo from 1906 to 1946, but there is no evidence that this approach will be used in any African country, that political leaders in sub-Sahara Africa would relegate all of their educational system to one religious group.

Practical considerations would suggest that variation one or two is the pattern that will be followed in the immediate future. In the majority of areas the continuation of the church-related schools under the close supervision of the government, with a growing number of government schools, seems to be the most efficient way to meet the educational needs of Africa. However, if there are government officials anxious to nationalize schools they would find support among some missionaries and church leaders who feel that the management of the schools is requiring too much time and use of limited manpower. This group would take the position that the role of the church in Africa is not simply to run schools and that it is being prevented from developing to its full potential because of its heavy responsibility in education. This argument would continue that the interest of the government in assuming full responsibility for education simply means that the church's contribution in this area is no longer necessary and it should assume other social responsibilities needed at the present time.

Such a view is by no means universal, and the majority opinion would undoubtedly support a continuation of government support for church-related schools. In attempting to define their role, many churches in Africa have reviewed their position and made explicit their responsibilities and rights in the field of education. While there are differences in emphasis, the delineation of the rights of parents, state, and the church are similar in the Catholic and Protestant points of view. Both recognize that (1) the right of the parents is primary in the education of children, (2) the state has the responsibility of ensuring that adequate facilities for the education of all its children and young people and indeed all its citizens are provided, and (3) the church as a religious society is entitled to see that her members are given a basic religious foundation. This task is aided by the establishment of denominational schools.[31]

The debt most African nations have to mission groups is well known and readily accepted by African leaders.[32] The criticism levelled at missionaries and churches in the past is accepted by leaders of the churches in Africa, and some of the critical analysis of greatest insight has come from missionaries and church groups. D. E. Baloji Idowu, Senior Lecturer in the Department of Religious Studies of the University of Ibadan, has said,

. . . most of African Christianity began as Christianity within colonialism. It was a religion associated with the ruling powers, and by some

[31] For the similarities and slight differences see Joint Pastoral Letter of the Nigerian Hierarchy, *The Catholic Church in an Independent Nigeria*, Oct. *1, 1960* (Ibadan: Claverianum Press, n.d.); The Archbishops and Bishop of Tanganyika, "The Catholic Church and Politics" (Washington, D. C.: African Research and Information Center, 1963); The Christian Churches' Educational Association, "Report from Executive Committee on 'Christian Education in Africa' " (Nairobi: The Christian Churches' Educational Association, n.d.); All Africa Churches Conference, *Christian Education for a Changing Africa* (London: Oxford University Press, 1963).

[32] See, for example, Alex Quaison-Sackey, *Africa Unbound* (New York: Praeger, 1963), p. 51. Mr. J. D. Otiene, Minister for Education, in a speech before the Christian Educational Association of Kenya, asked, "Is it too much to hope that the pioneering spirit which led your predecessors to establish the first schools in Kenya and thus to lay the foundation of our educational system of today will henceforth be directed towards serving the unity and progress of this young African Nation, by building up your schools to be models of what education should be, when it is rooted in the soil of Africa?" The Christian Churches' Educational Association, *Minutes of the First Meeting of the New Council of the Association* (Nairobi: The Christian Churches' Educational Association, 1963) pp. 3–4.

miscarriage of purpose, a form of imperialism operated in the church. Thus, the spirit of the church was so affected that it today suffers from spiritual infantilism. On the whole, the church did not quite know what it is to struggle for its life: so much was done for its benefit and to give it prestige by the ruling power.[33]

The confrontation of the church and its educational system with the dynamic social and political revolution sweeping Africa is being faced realistically by many leaders of the African church. Dr. Donald M'Timkulu, Director of the Planning Committee of the Salisbury Conference, has written,

The rise of new nation states, the tremendous force of nationalism seeking to weld together nations from what was heretofore a heterogenous assembly of tribes, makes demands on all to give their varying contributions to this tremendous task of nation building. Our willingness to make this contribution to the total life of the nation, or our failure to do so could mean the success or failure of all the well-laid schemes we have heard about.[34]

Dr. M'Timkulu's advice would be shared by many government and church leaders. In the drive for modernization, all schools of Africa will have to play an integral part. There is no other single institution that can be as effective, and it is doubtful if schools will be permitted to remain on the fringes of this massive social movement. How the church-related schools take part in this drive for modernization will undoubtedly determine their future role in African education. If they are viewed as an important sector of the *modernization* process, there is no reason to believe a "dual" system cannot work. However, if they are concerned simply with an extension of *westernization,* it is difficult to see how they can continue in the future in view of the political and social realities of modern Africa.

In the process of working out new church-state relationships there will undoubtedly be some conflicts. The church-state systems inherited by the newly independent countries from the former

---

[33] Dr. E. Bolaji Idowu, "The Selfhood of the Church," in *Forward From Kampala* (Kitwe, N. Rhodesia: All Africa Conference of Churches, 1963), p. 9. See also James Scherer, *Missionary Go Home* (Englewood Cliffs, N. J.: Prentice-Hall, 1964).

[34] Donald M'Timkulu, *Policy and Planning in Christian Education in Africa* (All Africa Churches Conference, Conference on Christian Education in a Changing Africa; mimeographed statement).

colonial powers were the results of centuries of European debate and dialogue. The transferred institutions will be reexamined in the light of existing African conditions and tested against a background of African needs. Education has been the core of Christian activity in Africa; education is considered by new African countries as the core for manpower development and political stability. The success of bringing these two imperatives together, of sharing a common concern for the building of modern Africa, will determine future relationships.

II

ETHIOPIA

RICHARD PANKHURST

Richard Pankhurst is Director of the Institute of Ethiopian Studies at Haile Selassie I University. His writings on Ethiopia include two books, AN INTRODUCTION TO THE ECONOMIC HISTORY OF ETHIOPIA *and* TRAVELLERS IN ETHIOPIA, *as well as several dozen articles in journals including the* JOURNAL OF AFRICAN HISTORY, *the* JOURNAL DE LA SOCIÉTÉ DES AFRICANISTES, PRÉSENCE AFRICAINE, *and the* JOURNAL OF ETHIOPIAN STUDIES. *He received his B.Sc. (Econ.) and doctorate from the London School of Economics.*

affection by the king, who, however, soon died, leaving his wife with an infant son as heir of the bereaved kingdom. The queen appealed to Frumentius and Aedesius to share with her the cares of government till her son should grow up. The young men agreed.

Frumentius meanwhile had sought out those of the "Roman merchants," i.e. Levantines or Greeks, who were his coreligionaries, and had urged them "to establish conventicles in various places to which they might resort for prayer." He provided them with "whatever was needed, supplying sites for buildings and in every way promoting the growth of the seed of Christianity in the country."

When the young heir came of age, Aedesius returned to Tyre, while Frumentius journeyed to Alexandria, perhaps the most important center of Christianity at the time, where he informed the great Patriarch Athanasius of the work thus far accomplished for Christianity in the Aksumite empire. He begged the Patriarch to look for some worthy man to send as bishop over the many Christians already congregated. Athanasius, having weighed and considered the words and deeds of Frumentius, declared in a council of priests: "What other man shall we find in whom the Spirit of God is as in thee who can accomplish these things? And he consecrated him and bade him return in the Grace of God whence he had come."

The young Syrian accordingly returned to the Aksumite empire as its first Christian bishop. He was renamed Abba Salama, or "Father of Peace," and is said to have initiated the people into the Christian faith by baptism, as well as by building churches and ordaining priests and deacons.

"These facts," says Rufinus, "I know, not from vulgar report, but from the mouth of Aedesius himself, who had been the companion of Frumetius and was later made a priest in Tyre." [2]

The above account, which is confirmed in its essentials by the traditions of the Ethiopian church as well as by archaeological evidence, would suggest that the Aksumite empire was converted to Christianity around the year 330 A.D.[3] About two centuries later

[2] E. S. Pankhurst, *Ethiopia, A Cultural History* (London: Sidgwick and Jackson, 1955), pp. 56–57. See also J. Ludolf, *A New History of Ethiopia* (London: Samuel Smith, 1684), pp. 250–251.

[3] R. K. P. Pankhurst, *An Introduction to the Economic History of Ethiopia* (London: Sidgwick and Jackson, 1961), pp. 33–35.

the Graeco-Egyptian author Cosmas Indicopleustes reveals that the empire was by then an integral part of the Eastern Christian world, declaring: "in Ethiopia and Axom [Aksum]" as well as in "Arabia and Palestine, Phoenicia, and all Syria and Antioch as far as Mesopotamia . . . there are everywhere churches of the Christians, and bishops, martyrs, monks and recluses, where the Gospel of Christ is proclaimed." [4]

The scanty records of the centuries which follow tell us nothing precise about the Ethiopian church's role in education, and we have indeed to wait until the nineteenth century for any description of traditional church schools. It is, however, safe to assert that the church in Ethiopia, as in other Christian countries, was traditionally the custodian of the nation's culture. It "provided elementary and intermediate schools, and Monastic Universities with branches devoted to theology, history, poetry, music, medicine and surgery, all of which function to this day, forming one of the oldest and most continuous systems of education in the world." [5]

Despite its undeniable cultural importance, the church never achieved anything approaching mass education. A large proportion of children in fact did not attend its schools, being merely brought up by their parents. Thus the nineteenth-century missionary Gobat, describing the youth of the peasantry, observed: "After the age of 6 or 7 years, the children are considered as servants. The boys are shepherds till the age of 14 or 15, and reside with their parents; but if their parents are poor, they leave them, by their own choice, at the age of eight or nine years, in order to get their livelihood by keeping cattle elsewhere. The girls are occupied in managing the little affairs of the house, and begin to fetch water, which is always at a distance, as soon as they can walk steadily: at the age of eight or nine years they begin to fetch wood from the mountains. They do not begin to grind till they are 13 or 14 years old."

Turning to education in this peasant class, he observed: "There are some fathers who send their children into convents, or

---

[4] J. W. McCrindle, *The Christian Topography of Cosmas* (London: Hakluyt Society, 1929), p. 120.

[5] E. S. Pankhurst, *Education in Ethiopia* (Woodford Green, England: New Times and Ethiopia News, n.d.), p. 29.

elsewhere, to have them instructed; but there are many who will not do this, lest their children should become monks: on this account many boys desert their parents, in order to seek instruction for themselves. Some enter the house of a priest or another teacher, as servants during the day, and they receive instruction at night: others go, after their lessons are over, to get food by begging. There are also some persons, in easy circumstances, who support those children who seek instruction without the help of their parents."

Education for the children of the aristocracy was, as might be expected, more important. "Nearly all the great men," Gobat said, "send their children into convents, to learn reading, and to repeat the Psalms from memory: this is all the instruction they receive." Women had fewer educational advantages. "The daughters of the higher class" says Gobat, "learn nothing but spinning and managing the affairs of the house: there are, however, a few ladies who can read." [6]

The Italian missionary M. de Jacobis, writing in the 1840's, noted that church education was "entirely gratuitous," as the up keep of the professors was the responsibility of their monastery. The student had to submit to almost incredible privations. "Without speaking of the personal service, often the most menial character rendered by the pupil to his master—a service, however, which their filial affection for their tutors seems to make sweet and easy to them—the student leaves his home and family, carrying on his back the sack of pease or meal which is his whole subsistence during his college term; and when that is exhausted, his only resource is to beg in order to live. Add to this, that the length of the course of study exacted is perfectly despairing." Seven years, he said, might be devoted to music and chanting, nine to Geez (the Latin of Ethiopia, also known as Ethiopic), four to poetry, and ten to the Old and New Testaments. Civil and canonical law, astronomy, and history could also be studied, but few students had "the courage to embark on them." Many a humble church teacher, he concluded, had nonetheless "more real knowledge than the most learned professors in our European Schools." [7]

[6] S. Gobat, *Journal of Three Years' Residence in Ethiopia* (London: Seeley, Burnside, and Seeley, 1834), pp. 312–313.
[7] Lady Herbert, *Abyssinia and its Apostle* (London: Burns, Oates, 1867), pp. 81–82.

A modern writer, the Rev. Douglas O'Hanlon, is one of very few observers to devote much attention to traditional church education, which of course continues to this day. He declares: "In the Christian parts of Abyssinia there is a church in almost every village. Every church has its school, which is an honoured institution." Describing a visit to Shoa, not long before the Italian invasion of 1935, he added: "Church schools are nearly always in the precincts of the church, generally within the outer wall of the church green.

"The impression on a stranger is that the average teaching priest is earnest and painstaking. The buildings are small and dark, and for the most part ramshackle, with no attempt at uniformity of design. The hours are long, writing materials, books and furniture scanty. Lessons, therefore, are largely oral and the degree of memorisation is high.

"Often the first sound that greets the visitor to an Abyssinian village is the chorus of voices raised in some jointly repeated lesson." [8]

C. H. Walker, sometime British Consul for Western Ethiopia, also described church education in this period. He said: "In a big town there may be 30 boys who are under three teachers, but in a monastery town there may be as many as a hundred, and at Zeig Amal and at Addis Ababa one may find a thousand. But the children of officers will learn at home, for an officer will build a hut nearby where the Confessor will teach them the alphabet, arithmetic and the Psalter."

Describing the traditional scene where many children went untaught, Walker observed: "A poor father will say, 'not even for myself and my boy have I money enough. How then can I enter him in the house of a teacher?' So he will leave the boy untaught, unless his god-father demand the lad and have him instructed." Turning to the traditional church schools, Walker added:

"The teacher may be a priest who is a Liq, or Professor, who knows much learning. . . . Or he may be an ordinary priest or even a scribe, though the scribe they praise not overmuch, for he may work cunning and wander here and there round the town. But the priest will sit quiet with his fly-whisk while the lad who was first

---

[8] D. O'Hanlon, *Features of the Abyssinian Church* (London: Society for the Promotion of Christian Knowledge, 1946), pp. 13–14.

instructed teaches the last comer. So the priest will sit as a judge and will punish the boy who errs, crying: 'Was that what I told thee yesterday?' pulling and twisting his ear, till he pours forth tears. Thus he will learn, perforce." [9]

Relations between teacher and student, nonetheless, were generally cordial. The French ethnologist Marcel Griaule described it as typical practice for boys in the province of Begemder to gather in the house of their teacher on a particular saint's day and to bring cake, roasted barley, and beer as gifts.[10]

The first stage of study consisted in the mastery of the Geez alphabet, or more properly syllabary, made up of twenty-six basic characters, each with seven forms, the vowels being combined with the consonants and indicated by signs attached to them.

The second stage, called the Apostle's Alphabet or *Fidel Hawaria,* comprised the memorizing of the first chapter of the first epistle general of St. John in Geez. The study of writing would probably begin in this stage, and particularly in more modern times some arithmetic would be added.

In the third stage, called *Gabata Hawaria,* the Acts of the Apostles were studied, being read aloud by the pupils and explained by the teachers. Certain prayers were committed to memory; writing and arithmetic would be continued. The children would now be able to serve as choristers, their voices contrasting with the adult voices of the *debteras,* or lay clerics, for much attention would have by now been devoted to singing.

The fourth stage, called *Dawit,* i.e. David, began with the reading of the Psalms of David. This stage was considered an important achievement in a child's education and would be celebrated by the parents by a feast to which the teacher, father confessor, relatives, and neighbors were invited. A boy who had reached this stage, moreover, would usually be able to write, and might be in demand as a letter writer.

After the Psalms had been read and studied, the *Qal Timhert,* or oral lessons, would start. The whole book of Psalms would be committed to memory, with proper stress and intonation. Other

[9] C. H. Walker, *The Abyssinian at Home* (London: Sheldon Press, 1933), p. 12.

[10] M. Griaule, "Les saints patrons en Abyssinie," *Orientalia* (1934), pp. 106–107.

work in this stage would be the study of the *Wadese Amlak,* or
Praises to God; the *Arganon,* or Praises to the Virgin Mary, arranged for each day of the week; the Song of Solomon; and the
Songs of the Prophets. All this Biblical material was often included
in a devotional manual written on parchment and enclosed in a
small parchment or leather satchel hung by a strap round the neck
of the pupil and carried by him to school.

At this stage, according to O'Hanlon, the average scholar
would leave school, perhaps at about the age of twelve, "having
learnt to read Ethiopic, though not to understand it, and also to
read his own language of Amharic and to write a little." [11]

Walker, who concentrated on these earlier stages of this education system, remarked: "If the teacher is firm and vigorous, in six
months he will make the pupil repeat his Psalter. . . . When the
boy has read it, the teacher will send to the father, saying ['Give
me the reward] of good news! Thy son has finished the reading,'
and the father will give him a cow or $15, and to the boy a horse
or a calf or a sheep. Also the boy will go round among his kin to
tell them of the good news, and to beg a dollar or half a dollar or a
sword.

"If his father or mother dies, he will write his Christian name
at the beginning and end of his Psalter, and whenever he finishes a
reading, he will say, 'Pardon for me the soul of my parent!' suppli-
cating God.

"When the pupils rise to go home, they will bless their teachers, saying, 'May God cause thy word to be heard and make thee to
arrive at earth in Debra Libanos and to be evergreen like the
cibaha. May He broaden thee as the sycamore and cause thee to
shine as the moon!' So the priest will bless them in turn and say
'Take care that ye come early tomorrow!' " [12]

The church also provided the most persevering students with
higher studies in such varied fields as church music, poetry, theology, history, philosophy, and manuscript writing. Each of the
main divisions had its own "school." The *Zema Bet,* or School of
Music, had three principal branches. In the first the students learnt
degwa, or church music, in the second *zemare* and *mewaset,* songs

11 O'Hanlon, *op. cit.,* p. 14.
12 Walker, *op. cit.,* pp. 12–13. See also E. S. Pankhurst, *Ethiopia, A Cultural
History,* pp. 232–282.

sung respectively at the end of the Eucharist and at commemoration services and funerals, and in the third *kedase*, prayers and chants studied only by priests and deacons.

The School of *Aquaquam*, which means literally "how to stand," gave additional training to students of any of the aforementioned branches of music, and dealt with beating of time and dancing. Two years or more might be needed to become proficient in any one of these branches of culture.[13]

The *Qené Bet*, or School of Poetry, was an important institution. Sylvia Pankhurst, describing this type of school as remembered by Ato Menghestu Lemma, a scholar of the present generation who himself went through it, observed: "The class usually assembles in the late afternoon or early evening, when the subject selected by the professor is studied and discussed until seven or eight p.m. The students then disperse to meditate on the appointed theme; many are already in the throes of composition during the long hours of the night. Early in the morning the youthful poet repairs to some solitary place where he may gain inspiration. ... Here he will endeavour to express in verse the subject selected for the poem of the day. . . .

"Towards evening they return to their teachers, to sing to him their compositions and to receive his criticisms and corrections. The Professor will conclude the session by reciting a poem of his own, composed in the space of a few minutes of silence—usually a remarkable illustration of the aptitude for verse acquired by long practice."[14]

After three or four years of the *Qené Bet* the students would be expected to compose a whole series of poems every day. When the professor considered one of his students sufficiently advanced for the examination, he would arrange for the youth to be invited to have a series of his poems sung in the church at the close of the service on a Sunday or other religious festival. "This," Menghestu Lemma said, "is a much prized honour, but also a considerable ordeal; if the student is nervous and diffident he may even decline it, but if he has courage he will rejoice at being chosen. On the day of the audition he will be treated with great respect. Should he accidentally let fall his tau-cross eager hands will raise it.

[13] E. S. Pankhurst, *Ethiopia, A Cultural History*, p. 244.
[14] *Ibid.*

"He will stand in the centre of a row of his fellow Debteras, for by the time he is chosen as the 'leader of the day,' he has generally been raised to their order. He will be placed in front of the Aleka who is the head of the Church. . . . In a low voice he will sing his poem, line by line. As he utters it, a fine singer, appointed beforehand, usually a fellow Debtera, whose voice is specially admired, will receive the words from his lips and sing them forth splendidly. If all goes well, if the youthful poet is fortunate, he will be gratified at the close of the ordeal by a chorus of 'Melkam!' the Ethiopian expression of praise.

"But if confidence or memory fail him, or if he pauses or stumbles in delivering a verse to the singer, some other poet, of greater self-assurance and experience may break in, and continue the series of poems in his own fashion. In such a case the trembling novice may protest, if he have spirit to defend himself, that had he not been interrupted he would have concluded his series in a manner resembling the interloper's interpretation, or he may protest with bitter indignation that verses vastly inferior to his own and out of harmony with his opening stanzas have been rudely interposed. The Professor, no less than the vanquished poet, will be much discomforted by the misfortune of his pupil. It may happen on some occasion that a youthful aspirant for poetic laurels, though he allowed no loophole for an interloper to intervene during his recital, fails, nevertheless, to receive the hoped-for praise. Silence, instead of 'Melkam' may greet his effort, or from some quarters at least, sharp criticism may be voiced alleging defects either of form or of content in the quality of his verse . . . debate may ensue among such experts in the art of poetry as are present in the church at the young man's initiation."[15]

The last main type of traditional school was the *Masahaf Bet,* or School of Reading, which would be divided into classes for the Old and New Testament, the Fathers, and special books on monastic life. O'Hanlon, who says "such schools are to be found all over the country," describes one in which "the Liq, or Professor, sat on a raised dais, his pupils, about 20, on mats on the ground."[16]

Such traditional schools, being attended by only a minority of the population, never achieved anything like mass literacy. Go-

---

[15] *Ibid.,* pp. 245–246.
[16] O'Hanlon, *op. cit.,* p. 19.

bat, for example, thought that only one-fifth of the male population in Amharic-speaking and one-twelfth in Tigrinya-speaking areas could "read a little." The lower figure for the region speaking Tigrinya was due to the fact that the language was not at that time written, literacy in that part of the country presupposing knowledge of a nonvernacular language, i.e. Amharic.[17] Other early nineteenth-century travellers took a more or less similar view of the extent of literacy. Blondeel, a Belgian observer, thought that the population able to read and write was about the same as in Western Europe,[18] which might be taken to mean about 25 per cent,[19] while the English traveller Henry Salt wrote a more depressing account, stating that at Digsa, in Tigre, he met "only a few persons" who could read the Bible and that "not one in twenty could write the characters they read."[20]

The disturbed conditions of the mid-nineteenth century may well have resulted in a significant retrogression in education and literacy in certain areas. This at least was the opinion of the British consul, Walter Plowden, who in a report for 1854 observed: "the number of persons that can read is diminishing daily."[21] The illiteracy of the mass of the population is underlined in the memoirs of several later nineteenth-century travellers. Mansfield Parkyns, asking the question: "who can read?" in Tigre, replied, "some, but not all of the priests, the scribes, and a very few men of the highest rank."[22] Waldmeier, discussing the situation in Begemder, observed that in general "people do not know how to read or write; this is an art known only to the priest or debterra."[23]

Literacy at the end of the nineteenth century was still by no means extensive. Vanderheym, a French traveller writing of Shoa, observed that the nobles were usually illiterate and obliged to

[17] Gobat, *op. cit.*, pp. 312–313.

[18] E. Blondeel, *Exploration en Abyssinie* (Bruxelles: Ministère des affaires étrangères, 1842) , p. 64.

[19] Estimate by Surendra Patel, late of the Economic Commission for Africa, in "Educational Distance Between Nations: Its Origin and Prospects," *Indian Economic Journal* (Bombay University) , July-September, 1965.

[20] George, Viscount Valentia, *Voyages and Travels to India, Ceylon, the Red Sea, Abyssinia and Egypt* (London: Rivington, 1811), II, 487–488.

[21] *Correspondence Respecting Abyssinia* (London: H. M. Stationery Office, 1868) , p. 110.

[22] M. Parkyns, *Life in Abyssinia* (London: Murray, 1853), I, 139.

[23] T. Waldmeier, *Autobiography* (London: Partridge, 1887), p. 16.

employ youths educated in the church to look after their correspondence.[24] This view was shared by a British official, Major Austin, who wrote in 1900: "one could not help being struck with the comparatively few officers of rank we met who were capable of either reading or writing their own language."[25] Four years later the linguist Armbruster made the following significant comment on a visit to Gojam: "I have met with a great many individuals who could read and write Amharic after a fashion, but with comparatively few who could read it fluently, and only three or four who could write it without continually making gross mistakes in spelling."[26]

The gravity of the position in the early twentieth century may be seen from the remarks of Dr. Mérab, a physician long resident in Addis Ababa, who expressed the view that there was only 10 per cent literacy among the Amharas. As for the government itself, he said he had reason to believe that only half the Council of Ministers could read and write with ease, that three could do neither, and that two others knew no more than how to sign their names —though this was not important, as seals at this time were invariably used instead of signatures. Among the womenfolk, apart from the princesses, those who could read and write in 1913 could be counted on the fingers, constituting in fact no more than perhaps 1 in 1,000.[27]

Though the church prior to the twentieth century was the only source of schooling within the country, a number of Ethiopians in one way or another succeeded in obtaining education abroad. Their importance was out of all relation to their number—a clear indication that church schooling, though invaluable in preserving the country's traditional culture, was inadequate when it came to either undertaking foreign relations or entering modern walks of life.

The first significant Ethiopian to travel abroad was perhaps Abba Gregorius, a seventeenth-century monk who made his way

24 J. G. Vanderheym, *Une expédition avec le négous Ménélik* (Paris: Hachette, 1896), pp. 120–121.

25 United Kingdom, Foreign Office, 403/299, Austin, 7/7/1900.

26 F.O., 401/11. "General Report on Mr. Armbruster's Journey to Abyssinia."

27 Docteur Mérab, *Impressions d'Ethiopie* (Paris: Vigot, 1921–29), III, 343–347.

to Rome and thence to Germany, and greatly assisted the German scholar Job Ludolf in writing the first important history of Ethiopia as well as several major linguistic works.[28] Another early expatriate was Abi Ruch, a monk who accompanied the eighteenth-century Scottish traveller James Bruce to Alexandria and later translated the New Testament into Amharic for the British and Foreign Bible Society.[29]

It was not, however, until the second half of the nineteenth century that foreign-educated Ethiopians played any significant role in their country itself. The first of any importance was a young man of Tigre called Mahedere Qal, who was taken to Paris in 1843 by the French traveller Théophile Lefebvre. Mahedere Qal, whose patron was the Foreign Minister, M. Guizot, was placed in a Jesuit establishment, the Collège Henri IV, where he remained three years before entering a Protestant college in Malta. He then went to England where each week he visited his old frind Guizot, by then an exile as a result of the French Revolution of 1848. In 1852 Mahedere Qal left Europe for Egypt, where he continued his studies with a Mr. Lieder in Cairo; he did not return to Ethiopia until about 1856, just after the coronation of the Emperor Theodore (1855–1868), who made him his interpreter.

Mahedere Qal served the Emperor loyally throughout his reign, but was later quoted as saying that Theodore should not have stayed in Magdala on the approach of the British expedition of 1867–68, but should have taken to the country and harassed the invader as Abdel Kader had done in Algeria; "not a single Englishman," he said, "would have escaped, everyone without exception would have found their grave in our country."

Mahedere Qal subsequently passed into the service of the Emperor Yohannes (1871–1889), for whom he conducted important business. General Gordon, who found the interpreter difficult to deal with, once referred to him as "a great scamp."[30]

Two foreign-educated half-castes were also prominent during the reign of Theodore and subsequently during that of Yohannes. Mercha Worqe was the son of an Armenian by an Ethiopian mother and was educated at the Rev. Dr. Wilson's Missionary Es-

28 Ludolf, *op. cit.*, Preface.

29 K. Luthi, "Athiopisch in der Schweitz," *Schweitzerisches Gutenbergmuseum* (1930), p. 100.

30 H. Dufton, *Narrative of a Journey Through Abyssinia* (London: Chapman and Hall, 1867), pp. 79-81; F.O., 407/14, Malet, 12/29/1879.

tablishment at Bombay; he spoke Hindustani as well as English. Besides interpreting for diplomatic missions to Ethiopia, he was sent by Yohannes on a two-man mission to England.[31]

Mercha's brother, Burru, who was born in 1832, went to England where he spent three years in the house of a Norfolk clergyman. Fully conversant in English and Arabic, he acted as interpreter for both Theodore and Yohannes and was well known to most of the important foreign visitors of the period.[32]

During Theodore's dispute with the British much use was also made of Samuel Ali, an Ethiopian Christian convert from the Shoho tribe, who before finding service with the Emperor had travelled widely, according to Rassam, in India, Egypt, and Syria.[33]

Increased contacts between Ethiopia and the outside world during the reign of Theodore resulted in a limited amount of foreign study. Several young Ethiopians went abroad in the late 1860's. The Emperor's son, Alemayehu, who had been born in 1860, was taken to England by Lord Napier and was looked after by Queen Victoria, but died at the age of 18. A handful of youngsters were also taken to Europe by Protestant missionaries. Waldmeier, writing in 1869, said that there were then eight boys in two missionary schools in Jerusalem, and several more at the Chrischona missionary institute and other schools in Switzerland, the total of students being perhaps just over a dozen.[34]

The students at Chrischona comprised six converted Falashas or Ethiopian Jews, as well as a couple of Ethiopian Christians. The Falashas, most of whom had earlier been at Bishop Gobat's school at Jerusalem, were looked after at the expense of an Englishwoman, Mrs. E. Potts of Chester, while the remainder were supported by Gobat. All were more or less under the guardianship of the missionary Martin Flad, who taught them German at his home in South Germany before their arrival in Switzerland.[35]

The most important of the missionary-educated boys of this

[31] E. A. De Cosson, *The Cradle of the Blue Nile* (London: Murray, 1877), II, 55; G. H. Portal, *My Mission to Abyssinia* (London: Arnold, 1892), p. 156.

[32] Earl of Mayo, *Sport in Abyssinia* (London: Murray, 1876), p. 40.

[33] H. Rassam, *Narrative of the British Mission to Theodore* (London: Murray, 1869), I, 258.

[34] T. Waldmeier, *Erlebnisse in Abessinien* (Basle: Spittler, 1869), p. 140.

[35] J. M. Flad, *60 Jahre in der Mission unter den Falaschas in Abessinien* (Basle: Brunner Verlag, 1922), *passim*.

time was Gabru Desta, a Christian youth of Begemder, who had been with the Protestant mission to the Falashas and was taken to Gobat's school in Jerusalem, on which account he was sometimes called Gabru Gobat. Later, in 1873, he went to Basle, where he stayed until 1878 when he returned to Gobat's school as a teacher; he later joined a group of missionaries stationed at Zanzibar and was also for a time attached to the British Keith Falconer medical mission in Aden. On hearing of the Italian occupation of the Red Sea port of Massawa in 1885, he determined to return home to assist the Emperor Yohannes in the period of difficulty ahead. "The Emperor," we are told, "received him somewhat coldly" because of his strong distrust of missionaries, "and even suspected him of being an agent of the Italians, but Gabru finally won his confidence and was charged with several important missions."

On the death of the Emperor, Gabru went to the city of Harar, where he distributed scriptures on behalf of British and Foreign Bible Society and was later appointed chief of police. Not long afterwards the Emperor Menelik (1889-1913) summoned him to Addis Ababa and made use of his services there for many years. After the Emperor's defeat of the Italians at the battle of Adowa in 1896, Gabru was responsible for looking after the Italian prisoners, at which time he explained to Menelik the diplomatic importance of treating them with every care. He was later appointed *Kantiba,* or Mayor, of Gondar, and in 1898 was entrusted with the task of negotiating with the Kalifah in the Sudan. He later represented Menelik at the coronation of King Edward VII in 1901. Gabru incurred the displeasure of the French Legation, which conspired actively against him. A British report for 1902 noted that he had "suffered confiscation of his property and was imprisoned for several years owing to French intrigues against him on account of his English sympathies." He later became interpreter to the German Legation. After World War I, he was chosen by the Ethiopian Government to visit London and Washington to congratulate the Allies on their victory. With the formulation of the Emperor Haile Selassie's first constitution in 1931, Kantiba Gabru was appointed Vice-President of the Senate.[36]

[36] *New Times and Ethiopia News,* April 17, 1937; January 27, 1945. F.O., 403/274, Cromer, 6/16/1898; Rodd, 9/16/1898; 140, Harrington, 8/8/1902; 401/13, Harvey, 7/29/1909.

Another remarkable Ethiopian taken abroad at the time of the Magdala expedition who subsequently became important was Hakim, or Doctor, Worqneh, also known as Doctor Martin. Born in 1863, he was found on the battlefield of Magdala by the British troops, who, thinking him an orphan, took him to India. There he was christened Charles Martin after two of the officers who had befriended him. He was later handed over to the Punjab Central Mission School and went in due course to the Lahore Medical College, from which he graduated in 1882. He was then, at the age of 22, appointed assistant surgeon under the British Government in India, but he resigned his appointment in 1889 and took ship to England to continue his medical studies. Having secured his diplomas in Edinburgh and Glasgow in 1890, he was given the position of a District Medical Officer and Civil Surgeon in Burma. Several years later, on learning that the Italians had invaded his native land in 1895–96, he obtained three and a half months' leave and rushed off to Aden and thence to the Somali port of Zeila— only to be stopped by the British District Commissioner, John Harrington, who told him that on account of the war he could not allow him to proceed, and that in any case it would take six weeks to reach Addis Ababa. Grievously disappointed, Martin was obliged to return to Burma, his savings exhausted. His effort was not, however, wasted, for Harrington was shortly afterwards appointed British Agent in Ethiopa and on meeting the Emperor Menelik told him of the young Ethiopian doctor who wished to see him. The Emperor thereupon asked the envoy to arrange for Martin to come to Addis Ababa. The invitation was accepted with alacrity.

The young doctor was soon presented to the Emperor, who asked him to remain permanently in the country and succeeded in discovering his relatives. Menelik meanwhile arranged with the British for Worqneh to obtain leave of absence for a year, informing them that he would himself pay for the young man's services. Worqneh urged the Emperor to open schools, and Menelik agreed, but so much opposition was encountered from the church that no progress was made. The young man therefore asked the Emperor's permission to depart, but Menelik refused, promising him to put down the opposition. Worqneh meanwhile was working continually as a physician and surgeon. He was, however, by no means in a satisfactory position. He found it very difficult to obtain any remuneration, though the Emperor finally agreed for him to be given a modest salary. The French and Russians, who were very jealous of him, intrigued against him, claiming that he was a British spy. He nevertheless remained in Addis Ababa until 1901.

After going back to Burma he returned to Ethiopia in 1908, being appointed medical officer to the British Legation. He served in that capacity for five years and then after a brief spell in Burma returned once more to his native country in 1919. Zealous as ever to assist his country, he undertook medical work, ran farms and flour mills, developed the capital's hot mineral springs, helped in the establishment of a school and a hospital, and initiated a cooperative society and a school for freed slaves.

In 1927 he went to the United States on behalf of the Ethiopian Government in an attempt to negotiate for the building of a dam on Lake Tana. In the following year he was appointed president of the special court to try cases involving Ethiopians and foreigners, and he later travelled to India to arrange for the employment of teachers and technicians. After the Emperor Haile Selassie's coronation in 1930, he was appointed governor of the province of Chercher, and set to work building a reservoir and a system of piped water as well as constructing roads, bridges, and government buildings; he also reformed the government coffee farm, developed cotton and sugarcane plantations, and opened a dispensary. In 1933, he was appointed governor of the Dankali province, and finally, in 1935, he became Ethiopian Minister in London, a particularly important post because the Italian invasion was then imminent.[37]

Efforts to send other Ethiopians abroad were made by a number of foreigners during the reign of the Emperor Yohannes. One was Lord Napier of Magdala, who wrote to the British Foreign Office in 1884, urging that it would assist British relations with Ethiopia if "a moderate number of young Abyssinians" could be taken abroad for education, possibly in Bombay or Madras. The

[37] R. Pankhurst, "The Foundations of Education, Printing, Newspapers, Book Production, Libraries and Literacy in Ethiopia," *Ethiopia Observer*, VI (1962), 251–253.

Foreign Office seems to have been unwilling to spend the funds required, but it later agreed that one young Ethiopian should be entrusted to the care of an English clergyman.[38]

The second sponsor of foreign study was a Russian adventurer, Nicholas Ashinoff, who took two young Ethiopians, a boy and a girl, with him to Russia. The outcome of the plan, which was connected with his ambition of arranging an alliance between the two countries, is shrouded in mystery, but was probably not very successful as the boy seems to have been very headstrong. To quiet him the Russian Minister on one occasion arranged for him to be taken for a drive in a St. Petersburg tram. The British Ambassador, who learned of this from the Foreign Minister, reported that the youngster was travelling in the vehicle when "a respectable Russian citizen turned round to his neighbor and said, 'That is a negro' upon which the young Abyssinian, who is only twelve years old, flew at the burgher's throat and declared in excellent Russian: "Tu m'appeles nègre: toi-meme tu n'es qu'un cochon Russe,' at which his excellency chuckled a good deal."[39]

Foreign missionaries were also active in taking students abroad. Monseigneur De Jacobis is said to have taken twenty-three Ethiopians to Rome as early as 1841, while a further eighteen young men, mostly Galla, were installed around 1869 at a Capuchin institution, St. Michel College at Marseilles. One of these students, Yosef, was subsequently prominent in Menelik's service and acted as a liaison with foreigners.[40]

The Swedish Evangelical Mission also educated a handful of students abroad. The first was a Galla called Nesib who was rescued from the hands of Arab slavetraders; he was sent to Sweden in 1873 to equip himself as a translator of the Bible and was in due course ordained. He returned in 1904 to the country from which he had been captured as a boy and worked there as a missionary for about a quarter of a century. Four students from the nearby Italian colony of Eritrea were also sent to Sweden in the eighteen-eighties.[41]

The foreign-oriented also included by this time a number

[38] F.O., 1.30, Napier, 1/2/1884; F.O., 1/31, 9/6/1886, 9/19/1886.

[39] F.O., 403/89, Morier, 3/10/1887.

[40] P. G. Gimilac, "Le vicariat apostolique d'Abyssinie," *Revue d'Histoire des Missions* (1932), pp. 131, 139.

[41] Luthi, *op. cit.,* pp. 109, 111.

of professional interpreters. Foremost among them in the eighteen-eighties were Peter Bru Werqe and his three sons. A British traveller, Captain Wellby, who saw one of them at the turn of the century was quite impressed. "Mr. Beru," he recalls, "was the first Abyssinian I had ever seen, and my first conclusions with regard to these people led me to believe that they were of a very different class to the ignorant barbarians they had been generally depicted, and that they were, in fact, quite civilised and up-to-date."

Other foreign-educated Ethiopians of the time included Walde Haymanot, who had been educated at the Swedish Mission and later in Jerusalem and Cairo, and Mikael Hailu, who studied at Bombay and subsequently went to Alexandria and Naples, where he wrote several articles on his native country.[42]

Though the Emperors Theodore and Yohannes had, as we have seen, both made significant use of the handful of Ethiopians who had happened in one way or another to obtain education abroad, neither of these rulers had taken any action to sponsor such training. It was left to the great modernizing Emperor Menelik to send students abroad at Government expense. The Emperor's motive was explained long afterwards by Ashaber Gabre Heywot, the son of one of the youths educated at this time. "We need educated people," the Emperor is reported to have said, "in order to ensure our peace, to reconstruct our country, and to enable it to exist as a great nation in face of the European powers."[43]

State-sponsored foreign education may be said to have begun in 1889, the year of Menelik's coronation as Emperor, when this reforming sovereign saw a young Ethiopian artist, Afewerk Gabre Yesus, painting in the church of St. Mary's at Entoto and asked the Italian representative, Count Antonelli, to take him to Italy for further study. The young man was dispatched to Europe and in due course enrolled in the Academy Albertino in Turin.

A few years later two other young Ethiopians, Gugsa Darge and Kelew Zamanuel, were sent to Switzerland with Menelik's Swiss adviser Alfred Ilg. The youngsters subsequently made their way to Turin with Afewerk Gabre Yesus and were in Italy through-

[42] M. S. Wellby, *'Twixt Sirdar and Menelik* (London and New York: Harper, 1901), pp. 10–11; Mikael Hailu, *L'Etiopia descritta da un etiope* (Naples: Cosmi, 1891), *passim*.
[43] Achaber Gabre Hiot, *La Vérité sur l'Ethiopie* (Lausanne: Freundweiler-Spiro, 1931), p. 32.

out the period of Italo-Ethiopian hostilities in 1895–96. This unfortunate circumstance later caused them to be somewhat reluctant to return home, as they feared they would be considered to have been disloyal to their country.[44]

Not long after these students left for Switzerland, a further six were dispatched to Russia, a country much favored at this time because of its Orthodox Christian faith. The group comprised two students of medicine, Gizaw and Dagne, two students of literature, Azmach Genno and Samu Negus, and two students of military science and engineering, Takla Hawariat and Haile Mariam Wonde.[45]

At least two other students, Tesema Eshete and Astatke Wolde Tsadik, were later sent in 1908 with a German, Herr Holtz, to study motor mechanics in Germany.[46]

Several of these students subsequently played a significant role in their country. Afewerk Gabre Yesus became an important author, writing among other things a history of the Emperor Menelik as well two works on linguistics, and much later on was appointed Ethiopian Minister in Italy. Gizew and Dagne, the two medical students who had gone to Russia, were employed in the first hospital that Menelik established in 1910, while Takla Hawariat, who stayed seventeen years in Russia, later held a number of important positions including those of Minister of Finance and Minister to France.

Menelik's interest in foreign education was recorded by the first United States envoy to Ethiopia, Robert Skinner, who relates that he spoke to him in 1903 of the possibility of sending young Ethiopians to American schools and colleges, whereupon Menelik replied, "Yes, that will come; our young men must be educated."[47]

The first significant steps in modern education in the country itself were not taken until the beginning of the twentieth century. In the first years of the century the Emperor established a school in the palace. Young courtiers, according to the German envoy

[44] Vanderheym, *op. cit.*, p. 138; Count Gleichen, *With the Mission to Menelik* (London: Arnold, 1897) , p. 154; F. Martini, *Il Diario Eritreo* (Florence: Vallechi, 1949), I, *passim*.
[45] R. Pankhurst, "The Foundations," p. 257.
[46] *Ibid.*
[47] R. P. Skinner, *Abyssinia of Today* (London: Arnold, 1906), pp. 101–102.

Rosen, were there instructed in good manners as well as a number of more academic subjects, including reading and writing, calligraphy, religion, Ethiopian history, law, and Geez.[48]

Presumably aware of the inadequacy of this first school, as well as of the old church schools, the Emperor some years later decided to import teachers from abroad. He faced strong opposition from the church, above all from Abuna Matheos, its Egyptian head.[49] To overcome this opposition the Emperor arranged that the proposed teachers should be recruited from among the Copts of Egypt. In 1906 some ten Copts arrived and were stationed at the capital, Harar, Ankober, and Dessie, under the general direction of one of their number, Professor Hanna Saleb Bey.

The first modern school, the Ecole Imperial Menelik II, was opened by the Emperor in October, 1908. It was directed by Hanna Saleb, assisted by some of the above-mentioned Egyptian teachers —who were associated with it until Mussolini's war. It offered courses to about a hundred children of the best families. Teaching included French, English, Italian, and Amharic, mathematics and science, physical training and sports. The language of instruction was French, which was also the most popular subject with the students. Board and tuition was entirely free. On July 16, 1911, after a public examination, prizes were awarded.

The Phelps-Stokes mission, which visited the school in 1924, recorded that 20 per cent of the Menelik's school's students had four or more years of schooling, but that though the school was completely free attendance was described as "the worst in the world." Entry was at that time open to anyone who could speak and write Amharic, and there was no age limit, many students indeed being married. It was reported that no fewer than 3,000 students had passed through the school in the two and a half decades since its inception. Most of them had entered government employment as interpreters, accountants, and secretaries, while some had been trained as teachers "with satisfactory results."[50]

The beginnings of modern education in the provinces, as in

[48] F. Rosen, *Eine deutsche Gesandtschaft in Abessinien* (Leipzig: Veit, 1907), p. 267.

[49] Mahtama Sellassie, *Zekra Neger* (Addis Ababa: the author, 1942 [Ethiopian calendar]) , p. 616.

[50] T. J. Jones, *Education in East Africa* (London: Edinburgh House Press, [1925]), p. 326.

the capital, may be said to date from 1908, when Menelik established a primary school in Harar. In the following year, Hanna Saleb was officially appointed Ethiopian Director of Education.[51]

Various missionary societies were also active in this period. In October, 1907, about a year before the opening of the Menelik school, the French community established an Addis Ababa school for Ethiopians which was run by the Brothers of St. Gabriel in a small hut. A similar school was set up in Dire Dawa at about the same time. Both schools, which were conducted in French, were taken over by the Alliance Française in 1910. The Addis Ababa school, the Ecole Française, was later reorganized and formally opened in Addis on November 24, 1912. It was run by the Brothers of St. Gabriel under the guidance of a local committee. Entrance to the school was free, so students came from all classes. They studied reading, writing, arithmetic, French language and grammar, hygiene, geography, chemistry, physics and natural science, drawing, music, history, accounting, geometry, algebra, and moral instruction, and devoted an hour a day to Amharic. The Phelps-Stokes mission reported that by 1924 this school had 150 students, all male, of whom 100 were boarders, and that a further 1,400 students had by that time graduated. Graduates mainly entered government service or became interpreters.[52]

The excitement with which the few enlightened Ethiopians greeted the opening of these schools may be seen from an anonymous essay of this time. Its author, who argued that "the construction of schools is more important than anything else," employed much rhetoric, demanding, for example: "Do you think that it is ignorance which has constructed for man's advantage, cannon, aeroplanes, telegraphs, railways, submarines, and which has extracted from wood and earth the different kinds of drugs that there are in the world?"[53]

Foreign missionary activity expanded considerably after World War I, with the result that missionary education was soon considerably more widely diffused than government education. The latter was, however, of higher quality and in greater vogue in government circles. Ashaber Gabre Heywot notes that the mission boys

[51] E. S. Pankhurst, *Ethiopia, A Cultural History*, pp. 534–535.

[52] A. Zervos, *L'Empire d'Ethiopie* (Alexandria: the author, 1936), p. 439.

[53] J. I. Eadie, *An Amharic Reader* (Cambridge: University Press, 1926), pp. 110–111.

seldom rose above the level of clerks and interpreters, and were frequently almost devoid of patriotic feeling.[54]

The Phelps-Stokes mission of 1924 learned that besides the Addis Ababa and Dire Dawa schools of the Alliance Française, which have already been mentioned, there were "a considerable number" of Roman Catholic "small out-schools" in the interior, most having only fifteen to twenty pupils. There were, however, larger schools for children of both sexes at Addis Ababa, Harar, Dire Dawa, and Sofi, as well as a handicraft school at Dire Dawa.[55]

Traditional schools also flourished in the capital. Dr. Mérab, writing at the end of World War I, reported that about a hundred primary schools had sprung up in the city, with the result that elementary education was beginning to be relatively widely diffused, very many children being taught at least to read and write. Such schools were almost invariably of traditional type, and were usually held in the open air with the students sitting on the ground on sheepskins which they brought every morning and took away in the evening. There were also a few boarding schools. In either type of school the teacher would be surrounded by some thirty students whose primer was usually the *Dawit,* or Psalms of David. Instruction was free, the teachers being paid sometimes by the government, sometimes by the church, and sometimes by a rich or pious philanthropist. The teacher, who was usually an old priest and, according to Mérab, sometimes could not even write, would normally receive no more than six or seven Maria Theresa dollars (one Maria Theresa dollar being worth about $2.60–$2.80 American) a year besides his food and clothing. Self-respecting parents who could afford to do so usually employed their own teacher, who would be treated as a member of the family.[56]

State education, which had been initiated by the Emperor Menelik, took a significant step forward during the regency of Ras Tafari Makonnen, the future Emperor Haile Selassie. The Regent, who had himself attended Menelik's old school, showed considerable interest in the development of education. He allocated funds for the establishment of schools, expanded the foundations of state education, and encouraged missionary activity pro-

---

[54] Achaber Gabre Hiot, *op cit.,* pp. 61–62.
[55] Jones, *op. cit.,* pp. 327–328.
[56] Mérab, *op. cit.,* II, 127–128.

vided it was primarily concerned with education rather than with conversion.

An important step on the road to modern education was taken on April 27, 1925, when the Regent opened the Tafari Makonnen School despite opposition from traditionalists which had delayed the project for two years. In his opening speech he declared that the time had passed for mere lip service to their country. The crying need of the people, he said, was education, without which they could not maintain their independence. The proof of real patriotism was founding schools and forwarding the cause of education in every way. Progress had to be made little by little. He declared that he had built the school as a beginning and as an example, and appealed to the wealthy among the people to follow.[57]

The Tafari Makonnen school, which is said to have cost 300,-000 Maria Theresa dollars and a further 130,000 for the dormitory building, was spacious and much more modern than the old Menelik school. It had well-lit classrooms, a library, a laboratory, refectories, dormitories, ample gardens, and recreation grounds. Its curriculum was also more modern and included French, Arabic, English, mathematics, chemistry and physics, history, geography, gymnastics and sports, as well as Amharic. Education differed from that given in the old Menelik school in that it was much more French-oriented. Not only was instruction given in French, but the school had a succession of French principals. Pupils of the school went to the French Legation annually to sit for the examination which qualified them for the French Government's certificate of competence in primary studies.[58]

The school was supervised in the early years by the aforementioned Dr. Worqneh Martin. Some fifty students were enrolled on the opening day, but this number increased later in the year to 184, and reached 300 by 1931–32. The number of boarders always tended to exceed that of day boys. A rough idea of the cost of the school can be seen from the fact that expenses at this time averaged 83,310 Maria Theresa dollars a year.[59]

[57] C. F. Rey, *In the Country of the Blue Nile* (London: Duckworth, 1925), p. 210.

[58] Zervos, *op. cit.*, pp. 223–224; E. S. Pankhurst, *Ethiopia, A Cultural History*, pp. 535, 586–589; E. J. Bartleet, *In the Land of Sheba* (London: Cornish Brothers, 1934), pp. 48, 57.

[59] E. S. Pankhurst, *Ethiopia, A Cultural History*, pp. 586–593.

The British traveller Charles Rey, who visited the school in 1926–27, says that boarders paid only nine Maria Theresa dollars a month, though the poorer students were educated and fed entirely at the founder's expense. The same observer added that the students were keenest on languages (French and English). It is recorded that in 1928–29 124 students were attending classes in French, 76 in English.[60]

The country's educational system began to take shape after the Emperor Haile Selassie's coronation in 1930. At that time a Ministry of Education and Fine Arts was established.[61] A plan was later drawn up by the Emperor's American educational adviser, Ernest Work, formerly of Muskingum College, whereby there was to be a system of six years of primary education, six years of high school education, and four years of university education. Special attention was to be paid to teacher training and agriculture. The basic problem, Work explained, was that there were no teachers to implement the plan.[62] Notwithstanding the immensity of the problem, significant advances were made in the next few years.

In 1930 the Lycée Haile Selassie I was founded. It was designed to give technical and linguistic training to about one hundred students. Instruction was in French, and the curriculum included mathematics, physics and chemistry, civil engineering, veterinary science, and modern languages.[63]

In 1931 the Empress Menen founded the first girls' school, which bore her name. The students followed their courses in French and had a succession of French headmistresses; pupils studied science and mathematics as well as drawing, dressmaking, household management, and physical training; they sat annually at the French Legation for the examination qualifying for the French Certificate in Primary Studies. By the time of the Italian war the school was attended by some 80 girls.[64]

The importance of this girls' school may be seen from the fact that it was established in the face of significant opposition to women's education. Thus Mérab had noted a few years earlier, in 1928, that very few even among the rich were willing to employ a priest

60 Rey, *op. cit.*, p. 30; E. S. Pankhurst, *Ethiopia, A Cultural History*, p. 590.
61 Zervos, *op. cit.*, p. 223.
62 W. J. Makin, *War over Abyssinia* (London: Jarrolds, 1935), p. 104.
63 Zervos, *op. cit.*, p. 241.
64 *Ibid.*, pp. 224–225.

to educate their daughters. The popular opinion, he says, was that an educated woman would not look after the house, while the popular prejudice was that the husband of a wife who could read would never live long, as his spouse would resort to curses and other wicked practices to kill him. Mérab, on asking one of his Ethiopian friends why he did not educate his only daughter, received the following reply: "Where have I the money to pay a priest or *debtera* to educate my daughter, and to buy a eunuch to supervise the priest or *debtera?*"[65]

Several other schools were also established in the capital in the years immediately before the Italian war. St. George's School, situated near the cathedral of the same name, was opened in September, 1929, under the direction of a Swiss; it had five teachers and about 200 pupils; it was entirely free of charge. Instruction was in French and Amharic, the subjects of study including science, mathematics, shoemaking, blacksmiths' work, and other trades.

A teacher-training school was established in 1934 to provide teachers for provincial schools. A Boy Scouts' school was also founded in 1934. Instruction was given in French and included all primary subjects as well as the special activities of Boy Scouts.

The Imperial School of Art was established under the direction of Ato Agañew Ingida, who had studied in Paris at the Academie des Beaux Arts.

All together some 4,000 children were at school at the time of the Italian war.

The foundations of primary education were also being laid in a number of provincial towns, where fourteen primary schools were set up between 1928 and 1935. Eight of them, at Makale, Adowa, Gondar, Debra Markos, Lekemti, Gore, Jiggiga, and Asba Tafari— all places on the periphery of the Empire—gave instruction in English; five, at Harar, Dessie, Jimma, Ambo, and Salale—more in the heart of the country—used French, while one at Dire Dawa used both languages.[66] Orders were also given in this period that all soldiers should be taught to read and write and that the priests should instruct the youth.[67]

While these developments were taking place in the country

[65] Mérab, *op. cit.*, III, 347.

[66] Zervos, *op. cit.*, p. 230.

[67] General Virgin, *The Abyssinia I Knew* (London: Macmillan, 1934), p. 54.

itself, some of the most promising students were also being sent abroad by the government or encouraged to go at their own expense. Some went to schools and colleges in three Middle Eastern countries, Egypt, Lebanon, and the Sudan, from which a considerable proportion went on to universities in Europe and America; others went directly to such countries as France, Britain, Italy, Germany, Switzerland, Belgium, and the United States. Though complete statistics are not available, it is known that at least twenty students went to Egypt, a further twenty to Lebanon, and six or more to the Sudan. The largest number of students, some sixty, went to France, about twenty to Britain, ten (five of them girls) to Switzerland, nine to the United States, another nine to Italy, and two each to Germany and Belgium. In addition to these students, who were mainly sent by the Government, about forty students, many of them from the adjacent colony of Eritrea, went to the Vatican under Roman Catholic auspices; twenty-five Falashas were sent under Jewish auspices to various parts of Europe, where some took Rabbinic studies and others a wide range of practical subjects, including medicine, printing, weaving, carpentry, and mechanics.[68]

All in all, almost two hundred students left for study abroad between 1918 and 1935. Their return was significant, for they included students of all the disciplines required for the creation of a modern state, such as medicine, veterinary science, engineering, law, pedagogy, economics, literature, painting, journalism, and aviation, as well as military subjects, no less than thirteen of the students having been attached to the French army school at St. Cyr.[69]

The 1920's and especially the early 1930's seem to have witnessed unprecedented advances in basic literacy as well as education. Sandford claims to have discerned a steady rise in literacy in this period. "It was quite remarkable to a resident of many years' standing" she notes, "that whereas in 1920 the boy on his household staff who could read and write was a notable exception, in 1935 among the same society there were few young men and boys who had not the Amharic script."[70] This statement was confirmed by a British report of 1932 which commented that the level of

68 R. Pankhurst, "The Foundations," pp. 277–278.
69 C. Sandford, *Ethiopia under Haile Sellassie* (London: Dent, 1946), p. 69.
70 *Ibid.*, p. 67.

education, though "not high," was nevertheless "higher than usual" in countries in a similar stage of evolution.[71] A Swedish missionary, Eriksson, also writing in 1932, agreed that "the number of people able to read is definitely increasing."[72]

Though Ethiopia's traditional church schools have continued uninterrupted to the present day, modern education was brought almost to a complete halt by the Italian invasion of 1935. The policy of the Italian Fascists was, generally speaking, strongly opposed both to the creation of an educated African elite and to any kind of training which would enable "natives" to compete with "nationals," i.e. Italians. The philosophy behind this attitude was stated by Mussolini in an official Italian publication of 1938, in which he declared that the problem of race had "a definite relation to the conquest of the Empire, because it is necessary to realise that the Empire is conquered by the sword but is held by prestige. To maintain prestige we must have a strict and clear racial consciousness, which will stabilise not only the difference of race but also our absolute superiority." The application of this thesis was expounded by Guiseppe Fabbri, the editor of the publication, in an article in which he argued that when of old Agricola had educated the native chiefs of Britain he had "betrayed Rome"; to prevent a similar fate befalling Mussolini's empire in Africa, he urged that the "natives" be excluded from any kind of contact with government activity:

"We abhor the invasion of the colonial office by officials who employ natives, because that constitutes a formidable danger. The mentality of the natives is spoilt; they believe themselves equal to us when they see themselves invested with functions we are accustomed to fulfil. Moreover, the native mass tends always to admire this kind of aristocracy of their race; to foment this evil germ is to destroy our empire.

"The office and the administration should seem mysterious to the native, a place where white people stay as at the altar; the documents locked in the cupboards should have the odour of sacred papers which natives must not touch. It is when natives are put in

---

[71] G. Mackereth, *Economic Conditions in Ethiopia* (London: Department of Overseas Trade, 1932), p. 17.

[72] O. Eriksson, "Education in Abyssinia," *Africa* (1932), p. 342.

contact with such instruments of civilisation that they cease to be sensible of the difference between themselves and us. It initiates, in fact, a gradual process of assimilation, which finally develops consequences grave, if not fatal, to our supremacy, because in order to retain our natural race superiority and to preserve it from being undermined we must maintain our prestige."[73]

Schooling in accordance with this policy was severely restricted during the Italian occupation of 1936 to 1941.

After the liberation of Ethiopia in May, 1941, the country faced immense economic and administrative difficulties. Efforts were, however, soon undertaken to reopen the Government schools, most of which had been closed for over five years. Some were opened in the latter months of 1941—only a few months after the end of the fighting and before the official resumption of Ethiopian Government in February of the following year.

Throughout this period the Emperor Haile Selassie displayed a great interest in the speedy establishment of schools. A Ministry of Education was almost immediately established, but the funds at its disposal were inevitably small. Popular desire for modern education was, however, immense. Foreign observers of this time were impressed by the tremendous desire for education among Ethiopian youth, and report that young people at the roadside would cry "School! School!" when they saw the Emperor or any of the ministers or government officials approaching; some even threw themselves into the road, at the risk of their lives, to bring to a halt the car of any person to whom they could make their appeal for a place in school. Many children tramped great distances to the capital in the hope of going to school.[74]

The immediate postwar years witnessed immense difficulties: administrative chaos and shortage of funds, teachers, textbooks, and other equipment.[75] Several new government schools were, however, established in the capital in the next few years, including three secondary schools, the Haile Selassie I Secondary School, the General Wingate School, and the Medhane Alem School. Other schools set up at this time included a teacher-training school, a

[73] Quoted in E. S. Pankhurst, *Ethiopia, A Cultural History*, pp. 691–693.
[74] *Ibid.*, p. 552.
[75] Girma Amare, "Government Education in Ethiopia," *Ethiopia Observer*, VI (1963), 336–337.

commercial school, a technical school, a handicraft school, and a school for children of the patriots who had taken part in the resistance struggle of 1935–1941. Many provincial schools were also established. By 1949—seven years after the resumption of Ethiopian rule—there were 52,965 pupils in 600 government schools throughout the country.[76]

The foreign personnel utilized in the establishment of these schools were drawn from many parts of the world. Foreign teachers included French Canadian Jesuits, most of them at the Tafari Makonnen School; Swedes, mainly at the Haile Selassie I Secondary School; English men and women, particularly but by no means exclusively at the General Wingate Secondary School; Americans, notably after 1950; and Indians, who were very numerous in the provinces. Certain schools were for a time more or less run by one or other of these groups; but there were changes from time to time, with Ethiopianization of personnel becoming increasingly important after about 1955.

Considerable efforts were also made, as before the war, to send students abroad, at first for secondary level studies and later, as education developed, for university work. By 1949, seven years after the reestablishment of the Ethiopian Ministry of Education, 229 students were studying abroad under government auspices. This figure grew rapidly in the next decade. Statistics compiled in March, 1958, for example, indicated that there were then 832 students abroad, 217 of them in United States and Canada together, 128 in Egypt, 88 in Lebanon, 83 in Italy, 80 in Germany, 77 in Great Britain, 35 in India, 33 in France, 27 in Israel, 19 in Sweden, and 11 in Mexico, as well as smaller numbers in eleven other countries, Greece, Australia, Switzerland, the Sudan, Norway, Denmark, Finland, Nigeria, Uganda, Tanganyika, and Belgium. Of these students, 197 were in the social sciences, 143 in engineering, 102 in the medical sciences, and 81 in education, while a further 134 were pursuing secondary school courses. An additional 354 students had by then returned from foreign study, 99 of them in the social sciences, 98 in engineering, and 42 in the medical sciences.[77] Such returnees were by then doing much to meet the most pressing shortages of trained personnel.

[76] E. S. Pankhurst, *Ethiopia, A Cultural History*, pp. 566–652.

[77] Ministry of Education, *Directory of Ethiopian Students Abroad and Returned* (Addis Ababa: The Ministry, 1958), pp. 1, 3, 4.

Academic education in the country itself, which had been envisaged but never attempted before the war, had meanwhile been inaugurated. Ethiopia's first institution of higher learning, the University College of Addis Ababa, was established by the government in the later months of 1950 and officially inaugurated on February 20 of the following year. The institution was modelled more or less on the American University pattern. From the outset it issued its own degrees and ran an Ethiopian School Leaving Certificate examination.

Five additional colleges were set up by the government in the next five years. They were a College of Engineering, a Building College, and a Theological College, all in the capital, as well as a College of Agriculture and Mechanical Arts at Harar, and a Public Health College at Gondar. Four of these institutions gave degree courses from the outset; the fifth, the Theological College, had substantially lower academic standards and did not issue its first degrees until 1964.

The development of higher learning was formalized by the establishment on December 18, 1961, of the Haile Selassie I University, which was housed in the Emperor's former palace and brought the above six institutions under central control. Since that time the University College has been divided into three separate Faculties, of Arts, Education, and Science, and several new institutions have been inaugurated, including Colleges of Law, Business Administration, and Medicine, a School of Social Work, and an Institute of Ethiopian Studies.

Foreign personnel in the various colleges that eventually made up the university were, as in the schools, very international. In the University College there was at the outset a predominance, though never more than that, of French Canadian Jesuits, as well as a number of displaced persons from Eastern Europe. Later, however, two of the college's three constituent faculties had Israeli deans, while the third dean was an Ethiopian. The Engineering College was run at the beginning by an American, but later by an Israeli dean. The Agricultural College, which was assisted by the United States government, had a contract relationship with the Oklahoma State University, with the result that its personnel were all American. The Public Health College, which was assisted by the United States government as well as by WHO and UNICEF, was also largely staffed by Americans. The Theological College had at one time an Armenian and at another time an Indian dean, as well as a number of Indian members of staff. The Law School staff at its inception was entirely American, while the College of Medicine, also a new institution, was largely British.

The development of education in this period may be illustrated by the fact that by 1963 949 Ethiopian degrees and diplomas had been awarded. These included 190 degrees in agriculture, 100 in education, 86 in public administration, 68 in engineering, 60 in economics, and 53 in building.[78]

An interesting development by the academic year 1958–59 was the institution of Ethiopian government scholarships to enable students from other parts of Africa to come to its schools and colleges. By 1963 a total of 99 such students had come to attend college courses. The largest number of the students came from Kenya and Tanganyika, which contributed 32 and 18 respectively; fourteen other countries were also represented, namely Uganda, Nyasaland, the Sudan, Nigeria, Ghana, Southern Cameroons, Egypt, Liberia, British Somaliland, Zanzibar, Northern Rhodesia, Southern Rhodesia, Gambia, and Basutoland.[79]

Academic education was supplemented in the postwar period by specialized training. In this connection it is necessary to mention the establishment of the Military Academy at Harar and the Naval College at Massawa, set up with the aid of Indians and Norwegians respectively, the Air Force School at Debra Zeit, better known as Bishaftu, and the Abba Dina Police Staff College at Gulele, both of which were instituted with the help of Swedes.

The educational position in Ethiopia in the second half of the twentieth century reflects the developments outlined in this chapter. The traditional church schools still account numerically for a large proportion of the country's entire student body. There are believed to be some 17,000 or so Ethiopian Orthodox churches in the country, which has led some writers to guess that there are as many as 10,000 church schools, with perhaps one hundred thousand or more pupils. The Ethiopian Church Office, on the other hand, had record of the existence in 1963–64 of only 1,557 church

---

[78] Central Statistical Office, *Statistical Abstract* (Addis Ababa: The Office, 1964), p. 146.
[79] *Ibid.*, p. 147.

schools with a pupil attendance of 53,902.[80] This figure, however, may not be complete, especially as much teaching is carried on in an informal manner. The education given by such schools is almost entirely traditional and, apart from imparting a knowledge of reading and writing, makes little contribution to the needs of the modern world.

A far more important contribution to education is being made by the state schools, whose pupils, if we can believe the statistics of the Church Office, greatly exceed those in the traditional schools. The state schools have the advantage of employing modern teaching methods and following a modern curriculum, thus enabling their graduates to find employment in a developing society. Statistics for 1962–63—the latest available at the time of writing— indicate that there were 701 government schools in the country with 5,086 Ethiopian and 570 foreign teachers and a student enrollment of 212,002, including 52,505 girls. Of this number, 198,-595—50,775 of them girls—were in primary schools, i.e. in the first eight grades of schooling; 7,927—933 of them girls—in academic type secondary schools, i.e. in the ninth to twelfth grades; and a further 4,439—739 of them girls—in technical and vocational schools. There were in addition 1,041 students, including 58 girls, enrolled in the various institutions of higher learning.[81]

Missionary education carried out by both Roman Catholic and Protestant groups, though not negligible, was in comparison with state education by no means important. Thus in 1962–63 there were 199 mission schools, with an enrollment of 30,029 pupils, as against 701 government schools with an enrollment of 212,-002. Missionary education in Ethiopia, unlike that in many other parts of Africa, was largely restricted to the primary level, though the country's sole missionary secondary school had 778 pupils, in contrast to the 7,927 in government secondary schools.[82]

The initiative in education, started at the beginning of the century by the Emperor Menelik, is thus in Ethiopia still firmly in the hands of the state. The immensity of the task before it is apparent from the fact that Ethiopia, which covers an area as large as France and Spain combined, has a population estimated by the

---

80 "Education Report," *Ethiopia Observer*, V (1961), 61.
81 *Statistical Abstract*, pp. 142, 145.
82 *Ibid.*, p. 143.

Ministry of Education at perhaps 21 million, of whom it is thought 4½ million are aged from 7 to 14 and hence of school-going age. Less than one in twenty of these children are yet in government schools.

Modern education has, however, made very significant progress. It has created a cadre of skilled personnel that every year is playing a substantially greater role, reinforcing or replacing the traditionally trained generation in government, and rendering less essential the employment of foreigners in the specialized or technical fields. A measure of the progress already achieved was that Ethiopia, during the crisis in the Congo in 1960, was able to export trained soldiers and technicians to that war-torn land.

The task confronting the relatively tiny Ethiopian elite is nonetheless immense, entailing as it does the acceleration of the country's entire economic, social, and political development. One of the foreign-educated of recent years summed the matter up when he declared: "The standard of living, health, education and culture of our country is rising, but it must rise higher still before Ethiopia can truly claim equality with the really advanced countries of the world."[83]

[83] Quoted in E. S. Pankhurst, *Ethiopia, A Cultural History,* p. 715.

III

CONGO—LEOPOLDVILLE

RICHARD DODSON

Richard Dodson is Program Officer, African Graduate Fellowship, African-American Institute. From 1953 to 1956 he was Principal of a school in Coquilhatville and from 1957 to 1959 he was School Inspector of Bomongo Territory. He was Dean of the Union Theological Seminary at Elizabethville from 1959 to 1961 and Study Secretary for the Congo Protestant Council, Léopoldville, from 1962 to 1964. He received his B.A. from Transylvania College, B.D. from Lexington Theological Seminary, and doctorate from Teachers College, Columbia University. In 1952–53 he studied at the Colonial School, Brussels.

A basin suggests an arena, and the Congo basin's geographic situation has provided an arena for the encounter of three great religious faiths—all three of which were dealt with during the early history of Congo by a masterly political force in the person of King Léopold II of the Belgians. These three religious forces are Islam, Roman Catholicism, and Protestantism.

The Congo Independent State, which existed from 1885 until 1908, was ruled by King Léopold II. Léopold's administration of the Congo Independent State was as direct as communications of the period permitted. Especially at the beginning of his reign, Léopold's policy was the result of what appeared to be years of his own planning for getting control of the Congo basin. His actions were not delayed by the need to consult parliamentary institutions or subject to policy changes from legislative bodies. His personal diplomacy as King of the Belgians and his personal direction of the Congo basin exploration through the International African Association became a personal government for the Congo Independent State when in August of 1885 he notified the signatory powers of the General Act of Berlin that he was sovereign of the Congo Independent State.

Léopold's power alone was not adequate for the development of the Congo Independent State. He needed financial help as well as international approval and collaboration for his projects in the country. This was demonstrated in the way he dealt with the major non-Bantu religious force which his explorers and administrators found in the Congo basin: Islam. The Islamic religion was brought into the Congo by the Arabs, who had penetrated the basin to establish trade in slaves and ivory. Early explorers reportedly found Koranic schools among the Arabized populations when

61

they first arrived in the eastern part of the Congo basin.[1] Islam itself did not constitute an immediate problem for Léopold II, but the Arabs who had brought it did, and he concentrated on getting rid of them. To do so, he called on the support of the antislavery sentiment and movements that existed on the Continent, in the British Isles, and in America. This support meant money as well as encouragement and approval for his internal military and administrative campaign against the slave-traders, and Léopold was concerned with this campaign during most of his reign over the Congo Independent State.

While the slave-traders were in the Congo, they converted enough of the indigenous population to Islam in the northeastern part of the country for the Belgian colonial administration to deem it advisable to provide a limited special school program over the years for some of the children of "Arabized" Congolese. The number of "Arabized" people in the permanent population has never been great, and the pressure of Islam on the education system in the Congo has been of no general consequence to date.

The other two chief religious forces to come into the Congo basin in modern times, Roman Catholicism and Protestantism, penetrated the country with King Léopold's explorers and administrators. In some places, the missionaries did the exploring and charting—even at times being charged with governmental administrative responsibilities. Léopold saw the missions as either potential collaborators or opponents for his ambitions in Congo. When the General Act of Berlin's creation of the Congo Independent State in 1885 finally made it possible for him to have a country to claim and defend, he was more interested in the nationality of missionaries than he was in their confessional affiliation.

Although it was not long before Léopold saw the importance to his plans of the kind of *education* given by missionaries of one nationality or another, his first concern was for the contribution missionaries might make through their *occupation* of the Congo Basin. He wanted it occupied by people loyal to his projects and to Belgium.

Catholic missionaries from Portugal first arrived at the mouth of the Congo River late in the fifteenth century. However, there

---

[1] O. Liesenborghs, "L'Instruction publique des indigenes du Congo Belge," *Congo*, I (March, 1940), 235.

was very little trace of the four centuries of their declining occupation when two Baptist missionaries from England landed there in 1878—the year following the arrival of Henry Morton Stanley at the Congo's mouth after he had crossed the middle of Africa from the east coast. The first Protestant missionaries came chiefly from England, but it was not long before American and Swedish missionaries joined them. The first Catholic missionaries to come back to this area were French, and their work was under the jurisdiction of an Apostolic Vicariate controlled by the Portuguese. Léopold II became more concerned over aid the Catholic missionaries might give to French and Portuguese competition to his ambitions in the Congo basin than he was over British Baptist missionaries, who were in fact favorably inclined toward his projects at the outset. He took personal steps to stimulate Belgian Catholic mission interest in the Congo basin and to promote diplomatic action with the Holy See in Rome; in 1888 an Apostolic Vicariate was created for the Congo Independent State and put under the control of the Scheutist Fathers in Belgium. Once Belgian Catholic missionaries were responsible for the Congo Vicariate, Léopold was able to obtain the departure of the French Catholic missions, except for the educational work begun on the extreme eastern border of the Congo by Cardinal Lavigerie's White Fathers with priests recruited by their order in Belgium.

The missions were ahead of the government in opening schools. Protestant missionaries found the teaching of reading necessary to their methods of evangelism. They wanted people to be able to read the Bible for themselves, and translation of it into the vernacular was begun as soon as contact was well enough established with the local population to permit the learning of their language. Some of the pioneer Protestant missions even required ability to read as one of the conditions for baptism. Teaching people to read formed the basis of early classes, where they were taught writing and the rudiments of arithmetic as well. The missionaries had to rely on local people to teach reading and writing in the outlying village centers of evangelism that began to develop, and a school for training evangelist-teachers was soon established on almost every newly opened mission station. Circumstances dictated that such central training programs be for older children and young adults, which they largely were in the development over the first half-century of Protestant mission work. The pioneer missionaries also saw the need for a more general type of primary education for children, and wherever they settled they began a primary school for children from surrounding villages. As the missions erected buildings and added other services to their program, they needed skilled workmen, which moved them to begin early the establishment of simple trade schools. This "industrial training" was later developed in some missions as a means of serving the general economy. Once they saw what the situation was, the majority of Protestant missionaries strove to provide as much education as their time, personnel, and finances permitted.

The first Catholic missionaries to return to the mouth of the Congo River were the Holy Ghost Fathers, who founded a school at Boma in 1880. That same year, the White Fathers opened their first mission station on what was later to become the eastern border of the Congo Independent State. From the very first the Catholic missionaries opened schools wherever they established themselves. Whereas the Protestant missionaries were moved to educate people because of the need they saw, or because it was necessary to their method of evangelization (for many of the Protestant pioneers favored a program of rapid extension motivated by the call to preach the Gospel everywhere to hasten the second coming of Christ), Catholic missions saw the development of schools as the main means of the solid and progressive establishment of their church in the Congo. Once King Léopold II was able to convince the Belgian Catholic missions that they should work in the Congo, they began creating a network of schools there in collaboration with the government that kept them following the expansion of Léopold's Congo administration. They began with orphan colonies and primary schools, but they were soon opening trade schools, teacher-training schools, and minor seminaries. The spirit of competition also contributed to expansion of both Catholic and Protestant educational programs.

An explanation of the religious situation in Belgium is necessary to any further description of the relationships of the church, the state, and education in the Congo. Modern Belgium is a predominantly Catholic country; the proportion of Protestants in the population is less than 1 per cent. Although Léopold I, whom the Belgians called to be their king when they obtained their own constitution at the beginning of the nineteenth century, was a Protestant, it was required that every future king adhere to the Roman Catholic faith. Anticlericalism among Catholics, agnostics, and nonbelievers forms a much stronger opposition to the Catholic Church in Belgium than that of Protestants themselves. The Catholic Church backs the major political party (the Christian Socialist Party) and a labor union. It takes a coalition of the Socialists and the Liberals to gain a majority over the Catholic party in parliament. Quite naturally, the civil service in both Belgium and its Congo administration has been composed largely of Catholics. As for Belgian Protestants' influence on the mission situation in Congo, their lack of numerical strength and available missionary personnel reduced their role to a minor one until the last decade of the Belgian colonial administration, so that over the years the reference to "national" (meaning Belgian) missions in the colony has in effect meant Belgian Catholic missions.

From the very beginning of the Congo Independent State, Léopold and his Congo administration were bound by international law in their attitude toward the missions. The General Act of Berlin, which created the Congo Independent State, stipulated that there should be freedom of worship, that the missions had the right to create institutions for the "teaching and civilization of the natives," and that the Government should favor and protect missions and philanthropic organizations. Léopold always respected this law, but it did not hinder him from aiding as he wished those missions that were favorable to his plans for the Congo. Not only did he personally invite every Belgian Catholic mission that came to the Congo, but he aided them whenever possible with transport, administrative facilities, land concessions, and financial assistance.

At the same time that Léopold concluded his diplomatic arrangement with the Holy See to have apostolic jurisdiction for the Congo placed in the hands of Catholic missions in Belgium, he arrived at a way within the Congo itself to control further the amount of non-Belgian influence on the missions. In a decree of December 28, 1888, he stated that only those missions and philanthropic organizations that had a legal identity within the Congo itself would be dealt with as legally responsible organizations. Each mission that wanted such a legal identity had to apply for it on the basis of a request made by missionaries residing within the territorial limits of the Congo Independent State. In addition to this, the person chosen by a mission to be its legally recognized representative could function as such only as long as he resided in the Congo. The limit that this decree put on foreign mission boards and their executives is obvious. These stipulations for the granting of legal identity to a mission or a charitable association were maintained by the Belgian colonial administration and have been kept in force to date by the independent Republic of Congo.

The traditional educational systems within the cultures of the people in the Congo basin were intended to prepare each new generation to fit in with the one that preceded it rather than to prepare people for participation in a modern, technologically oriented economy and society. Participation (at least as skilled auxiliaries) was what Léopold needed from the people of the country if the Congo were to be a politically and economically worthwhile venture. It would have been economically and logistically impossible to import and maintain all of the skilled and trained workers necessary for the development of the Congo's economy to more than that of an exchange of imported manufactured goods for exportable raw materials. A system of education had to be set up within the Congo to provide the necessary skilled labor, military, and clerical personnel to advance the exploitation of the country's natural resources. Léopold decided in 1890 to create educational colonies to be run by his administration. Three of these schools were soon opened at Boma, Moanda, and Nouvelle-Anvers. Their objective was to turn out candidates for the National Guard, teachers for the military camps, and auxiliaries for the civil administration. Most of the schools created on this pattern were soon passed over to one Catholic teaching order or another for their operation. At the time of the establishment of such schools, responsibility for education in the Congo was carried by the judicial section of the administration.

The Protestant missionaries who came to the Congo were all from churches that believed in the total separation of church and state. Yet they were able to modify their attitude before the realities of the situation in the Congo, learning to accept both the responsibilities and the favors which the administration gave them from time to time. They continued the development of their schools and began to feel the obligation to furnish whatever the administration could not furnish among the people they served. However, the contrast between their position and that of the Catholics was set out sharply by the signature of a convention between the Congo Independent State and the Holy See in 1906. The prelude to this convention was Léopold's last round of political and administrative efforts to guarantee his claim to the whole territory of the Congo Independent State and to allay criticism of abuses committed by agents of his administration and the rubber concession companies. To forestall any linkage of the Congo to the German Lutherans and the Anglican missions on the east, he had witheld permission for any Protestant mission to establish new stations in the eastern part of the Congo. It was thus that the British Baptists were halted at Stanleyville in their hopes to establish a chain of stations across the interior of Africa. At the same time, he promoted the settling of the Premonstratentian and Sacred Heart Fathers in the northeastern part of Congo as a buffer against Anglican influence from Uganda.

Protestant missions lent their support in varying degrees to the international criticism of abuses by certain administrators during the latter part of Léopold's reign over the Congo Independent State. This caused Léopold to have further reservations about the Protestant missions and to seek the support of Catholics in both England and the United States. As a part of his campaign to win public opinion, Léopold persuaded the English Catholic missionary society at Mill Hill to send missionaries to Congo. He had the Mill Hill Fathers locate near the equator in the same area as the outspoken British Protestant critics of his policy, the Congo Balolo Mission. Meanwhile, the Belgian Catholic missions were being criticized for not having spoken out about the abuses in the Congo. They defended themselves by saying that they had not been located in the areas where the abuses were committed. Just the same, they were annoyed with Léopold because their close association with his administration in Congo had put them in a bad light. In addition to rectifying his administration in order to prove his good intentions, Léopold needed to make amends to his Belgian Catholic missions and to give them firm guarantees of their prerogatives in the Congo if he was to count on their support of his point of view. Thus it was that the signing of a convention with the Holy See was a propitious act for both Léopold and the Catholic missions.

The "Convention Between the Holy Apostolic See and the Independent Congo State," which was signed on May 25, 1906, began with the following statement:

> The Holy Apostolic See, concerned with favoring the methodic diffusion of Catholicism in Congo, and the Government of the Independent State, appreciating the considerable share of Catholic missionaries in its work of civilization in central Africa, have come to an agreement between them and with the representatives of the Catholic missions in Congo, in view of further assuring the realization of their respective intentions.

The convention goes on to say that each Catholic mission station, which was allotted a concession of from 100 to 200 hectares of land for an indefinite length of time, would within the limits of its resources create a school for the instruction of the indigenous population. According to the terms of the convention, the program of courses was to be submitted to the Governor General for approval. Periodic reports on the schools' operations were to be sent to the Governor General. This was not an uneconomical arrangement for the Government, for it was spared the expense and trouble of recruiting and maintaining Belgian lay teaching personnel in the Congo. Two years before the signing of the convention, the *Official Bulletin* of the Congo reported that Catholic schools already numbered 75 on the primary level, 3 on the secondary level, and 440 on the elementary level, where native instructors taught the elements of reading, writing, and arithmetic. Catholic missionaries totalled 384, and 72,382 Christians and catechumens were reported for the Catholic missions.[2] Protestant mission statistics were not reported in the *Official Bulletin* at that time.

King Léopold II hoped that the policy he had established toward the Catholic missions would be continued. In his will leaving the Congo to Belgium, which appeared in the *Official Bulletin* of June, 1906, he recommended to the "General Secretaries" who were responsible for the Congo administration that they continue to facilitate the work of the Catholic missionaries. Belgium finally annexed the Congo on October 18, 1908. On the same day, the

---

[2] *Bulletin Officiel*, Etat Indépendant du Congo, June 19, 1904.

Parliament voted the *Colonial Charter,* or "The Law of October 18, 1908, on the Government of the Belgian Congo." This law assured the complete freedom of education in the colony (Article 2). Article 5 of the charter took up the policy of the General Act of Berlin toward missions and philanthropic organizations in the following text:

> He [the Governor General] is to protect and favor, without distinction of confession or nationality, all religious, scientific or charitable institutions or enterprises created toward these ends [that is to say toward the ends of material or moral progress] or tending to instruct the natives and to make them understand and appreciate the advantages of civilization.
>
> Christian missionaries, scholars, explorers, their escorts, belongings and collections are the object of a special protection.

Arguments had already begun to rage over the terms "favor" and "protect," and Léopold asked in 1906 that an international group of jurists decide on the interpretation of the terms. He felt that as long as he favored and protected all such organizations as directed in the Act of Berlin he was justified in giving additional material assistance to particular missions and associations as he saw fit. The interpretation given to the jurists' decision by the Belgian administration was that "favor and protect" were matters of international law, but that particular material assistance given to certain works was a matter of internal politics.[3] Over the years, Belgian Catholic missions came to look on the assistance at first as a favor, then as common sense, and finally as an obligation of the Government. The Christian Socialist Party and partisans of confessional national interest in Belgium saw it as a utilitarian policy. Non-Catholic non-Belgians saw such a selective material assistance as contrary to the Colonial Charter and to the rights of the Congolese who were denied such assistance for confessional reasons. The issue was not resolved, and each side retained its own interpretation.

World War I brought about greater awareness of international problems, reflected on the next occasion when the terms "favor" and "protect" were treated in relation to the Congo. This occa-

[3] De Jonghe, "Les Missions religieuses au Congo Belge," *Congo,* I (January, 1933), 13.

sion was the signing of the convention at St. Germain-en-Laye, on September 10, 1919, revising the General Act of Berlin and the Declaration of Brussels of July 2, 1890. Article 3 of the convention at St. Germain-en-Laye gave an international flavor to the guarantees which the Belgian Government had provided in the *Colonial Charter*. Article 3 was specific in saying that the freedom, favor, and protection in the Congo applied to missions and scientific organizations from all countries that signed the convention and from member nations of the League of Nations.

The pattern and strength of the forces that developed in the Congo educational system from 1908 until the colony gained its independence in 1960 carried over into the independent republic. From the very start, religion and education were closely involved in the politics of Léopold II and the Belgian governments that followed him in administering the Congo. A major aspect of the church's educational role in the Congo has been essentially political. Even the two confessional bodies of Protestants and Catholics were dealt with largely in political terms. Due to the numerically weak Protestant influence in Belgium and to the Belgian identity that Léopold II had succeeded in giving Catholicism in Congo, it was generally possible to make political distinctions along confessional lines dealing with missions in Congo. During the entire period of its colonial administration, Belgium's external political attitude concerning the Congo was the principal factor in its treatment of missions. It became important to give a Belgian identity to the Congolese people as well as to the country, and until the latter part of the colonial administration, the effort to do this was channeled chiefly through Catholic-operated schools. Whenever Belgian internal politics spilled over into the Congo, the political distinctions followed confessional lines. The Christian Socialist Party was the defender of Catholic mission interests, while the Belgian Socialist Party and the Liberal Party felt help for their anticlerical position might be gained by showing some solicitousness for Protestant aspirations—at least until their parties could establish a foothold for government nonconfessional schools in the colony.

All of this is not to say that respective doctrinal positions on the relation of church and state and on the nature and function of Christian education were not a factor in what has taken place in the Congo. They cannot be ignored any more than can the unique geographical and national circumstances of the chief religious protagonists there. The Roman Catholic missions were not prevented by their doctrine or by the religio-political situation in Belgium from being closely identified with the state in the Congo; on the contrary, they often promoted that identity. As has already been pointed out, the Protestant missionaries to the Congo came from free-church backgrounds advocating the separation of church and state. Nor did they have the Catholic's desire to educate their children in confessional schools—at state expense, if possible—rather than in a public school open to people of all religious convictions. Their Christian social doctrine was also more subject to the influence of modern thought. So it was that their humanitarianism enabled them to respond to the need that they saw for schools, and the theological ferment of the period (the "social gospel" was coming in vogue in American Protestantism, and British free-church people were often social-reform-conscious) made them sensitive to social injustices and to international political opinion on social conditions.

The period from the time of the signing of the convention by the Congo Independent State with the Holy See in 1906 until after World War I and its resultant treaties was a time for the expansion of Catholic mission educational activities in collaboration with the government on the terms of the convention. In 1912 the government's expenses directly related to education accounted for only 0.85 per cent of the colonial budget, or 402,300 francs (the franc was worth about 20¢), with 50,000 francs of this going for subsidies to Catholic mission schools. There was another annual obligation in the budget related to the convention with the Holy See, a category called "culte" that consisted of financial aid to Catholic missions. This item amounted to 600,000 francs for the same year of 1912.[4] The subsidy allowed for Catholic mission schools in the annual budget went down to 31,000 francs from 1914 through 1918, but it was up to 72,150 francs for 1919.[5] The opening of new stations was facilitated for Catholic missions by the clause enabling a large concession of land to be granted. A

[4] Liesenborghs, *op. cit.,* p. 266.
[5] *Ibid.,* p. 244.

school was sure to be opened with each new station because it was the determining condition for granting the concession.

It was during this period that the government confided its trade and clerical training schools to the Catholic teaching orders for operation. Such schools were not subsidized but were rather financed directly by the government from the education part of its budget. These schools were called "official congregational" schools, and their type of administrative status has been maintained to the present. With the advent of this arrangement, the government began to call on religious orders that specialized in teaching. Men trained by one or another of the Catholic teaching orders have been the main source of skilled workers in the Congo. By 1920 there were nine of these "official congregational" schools, whose accent was on technical and professional training, with 1,861 pupils enrolled in them. At this same date, the number of subsidized Catholic schools had risen to 120, with 20,311 pupils reported attending.[6] Elementary education continued to expand through the use of indigenous teacher-catechists, and some Catholic missions had begun to give a higher-level program for more than just teacher training. The secondary schools they had established were now opening the way for the training of an indigenous clergy.

Protestant missionaries moved ahead to open stations in previously unoccupied areas once Léopold II's restrictions on expansion had been lifted. Though their main educational emphasis was on the primary and elementary level, they began to see the need for higher training for teachers and evangelists. By the end of this wartime period there were several Protestant normal schools functioning. "Industrial training" given by the Protestant missions continued to expand, although it was by no means so extensive as that given by the Catholics teaching with government help. The more established Protestant missions began to show a concern for the quality as well as the extent of their educational work, and by 1921 they had formed an interdenominational committee for education. All of their continued work, expansion, and improvement, of course, was carried on without government assistance. The annual report made by the Colonial Administration to the

[6] *Rapport sur l'Administration du Congo Belge,* présenté aux Chambres Legislatives, 1920.

Belgian Parliament in 1920 showed that there were then fifteen Protestant missionary associations in the Congo, with 392 missionaries, as compared to twelve Catholic associations with 374 missionaries.[7]

In 1920, responsibility for official and subsidized education still rested with the judicial section of the colonial administration. Matters relative to it appeared in annual reports under the heading of "public instruction." The administration was beginning to have time after the long period of preoccupation with World War I to examine its own effectiveness in Congo. It seemed particularly more sensitive to educational needs and to all the factors involved in the presence of Christian missions in the colony. The Minister of Colonies at that time, Louis Franck, visited the Congo in 1920 and took particular pains to visit both Catholic and Protestant missions. A Phelps-Stokes commission on education had visited Africa at about the same time and made recommendations for the Congo that included the nomination of a director of education, with a budget for his department. The Phelps-Stokes report also suggested that the government encourage the improvement and multiplication of mission schools.[8]

The provincial Governors in the Congo must have been reading reports or articles of one sort or another about education in their country—or else their possibly having entertained the Minister of Colonies or the members of the Phelps-Stokes commission during their visits drew the matter to their attention—for they almost all had remarks to make about the scholastic situation in their respective provinces when writing their part of the Colonial Administration's annual report to the Belgian Parliament for 1921. Their recommendations centered on some kind of uniformity being given to what was taught in all the schools and on giving a utilitarian orientation to the curriculum.[9] During this time, Governor General Lippens made a speech to the Antwerp Chamber of Commerce in which he outlined a firm Belgian nationalistic policy in the Congo.[10] The outcome of all this was that the Minister

[7] *Ibid.*

[8] "L'Education des Nègres," Rapport de la mission d'études du Phelps-Stokes Fund, par Jesse Jones, *Congo,* II (July, 1921), 171.

[9] *Rapport sur l'Administration du Congo Belge,* 1921.

[10] "Allocution du Gouverneur Général Lippens à la Chambre de Commerce d'Anvers," *Congo,* I (May, 1921), 768–771.

of Colonies named a special commission to determine colonial educational policy. In a later protest made by the General Secretary of the Congo Protestant Council, it was pointed out that in spite of the importance and extent of Protestant mission-operated schools in the colony no representative from them was named to the commission or even consulted by it.[11] The protester took some satisfaction in remarking that the curriculum decisions of the Franck commission generally coincided with what the Protestant schools had been doing for some time and consequently saw no pedagogical motive for excluding Protestants from the commission.

The two principal aspects of the decisions of the Franck commission were a policy of collaboration with "national" missions and the adaptation of the curriculum to the native milieu. A mission was considered "national" if it had its headquarters in Belgium and if two-thirds of its missionaries in the Congo were of Belgian nationality. Consequently, the mission of the Montfortain Fathers, whose headquarters was in France, was not considered a "national" mission, but the mission of the Mill Hill Fathers from England and Holland was assimilated into "national" status because of the special consideration they had been given personally by King Léopold II. In consultation with the Catholic missions, the government drew up regulations in 1924 establishing the conditions for subsidization to be applied to schools operated by "national" missions. These regulations were called the "Project for the organization of free education in the Congo," and on the basis of them the Catholic missions began signing scholastic conventions with the Congo government in 1925.

In addition to the stir of comments made on the clearer articulation of the Belgian national position in the Government's redefinition of its educational policy through the new program, there was also considerable support given to relying on evangelization by the Catholic missions as the best way of enabling the people of the Congo to participate in modern civilization. Governor General Rutter referred to the newly defined government policy in a speech at Liège in 1924 in these terms:

[11] "Memorandum adressé à Son Excellence le Ministre des Colonies par le Conseil Protestant du Congo au Sujet de la Politique du Gouvernement Belge envers les Missions," February 14, 1933, p. 16.

To go clear to the full extent of my thought, I would say that we have every interest to favor evangelization by the missionaries. To deprive ourselves of this means of raising the black race would be a folly which we will not commit.[12]

From the time colonization of the Congo began to be taken seriously, evangelization was seen by the colonial administrators as a means of social stabilization. The assumption was that Christianity gave the Congolese people beliefs and practices to replace those they were losing through the rapid social evolution caused by the opening up of the country and way of life to influence from the outside. That this Christian evangelization should be done in Congo exclusively by Belgian Catholic missions was sometimes used later as a combined confessional-national argument by defenders of Catholic mission interests against official recognition of Protestant schools in Congo or against efforts to establish government lay schools. A quotation referring to the decisions of the Franck commission in an article published in 1947, at the time when a Liberal-Socialist coalition Government in Belgium was revising the educational policy that had prevailed in Congo since 1924, contains the essence of the Belgian Catholic attitudes over the whole colonial period:

It [the commission] esteemed it as opportune to confide the black children to organizations which would base moral education on religious principles. In short they were inspired by a very legitimate patriotic concern.[13]

Over the years, the argument was given by Catholic missions in Congo that it was in Belgium's own best interest to entrust the whole educational program to them.

Protestant educational work in the Congo was not coordinated by any unity of doctrine or administration. However, the missions did need to consult each other on many aspects of their work. They also saw the need for a unified representation before the Government. Unity developed in general conferences caused them to form a Congo Protestant Council with a full-time General Sec-

[12] *Problèmes d'Afrique Centrale* (issue devoted to teaching), Bruxelles (1957), p. 128. Translation throughout the chapter by the author.
[13] G. E. Jambers, *L'Enseignement au Congo Belge* (Léopoldville: Imprimerie du "Courrier d'Afrique," 1947), p. 17.

retary. To celebrate fifty years of Protestant mission work in the
Congo, the General Secretary of the Congo Protestant Council,
the Reverend Emory Ross, was able in 1928 to combine the tenth
general mission conference for the Congo with a West African
mission conference at Léopoldville. At this meeting it was evident that at least for the participating missions there was now an
effort to provide a varied schooling of good quality which responded to the needs of the Congolese. There was evidence in
the speeches and reports that this kind of education was seen as
a part of evangelization and the Church's moral responsibilty.

Although the Congo missions represented at the conference
reaffirmed their fidelity to the Belgian administration, one speech
by an American Baptist, Dr. P. H. S. Lerrigo, reflected how strongly
the current Protestant theology led them to feel about the extent
to which the kind of education the Congolese received would determine their future. At one point he said, in reference to the
Government's need for Congolese auxiliaries in commerce, administration, medicine, and the military:

> The Government says: "We must have a system of education which
> produces them." Besides, the villagers see that the situation of these edu-
> cated workers is better than theirs. And they also in their turn want to be
> taught. From this comes the necessity for some kind of instruction. Who
> will give it to them? The State? It is not likely that it can do it for the
> moment. The increasing forces of Catholicism? It's possible; but if that
> is so, they won't train a true native elite, but rather a subservient class
> useful to the dominant race. The Congolese don't want that, and they
> must fall back on the evangelical missions for the training of the leaders
> they need and which they will not otherwise find.[14]

Other references in the conference were made to Belgium's
international responsibility for the Congo, and publication of the
conference report provoked Belgian Catholic reaction over the
non-Belgian identity of the Protestant missionaries in Congo that
had not yet subsided twenty years later. The Catholic bishop at
Elizabethville, Monseigneur de Hemptine, wrote in a reaction to
the conference report that there was an identity between the polit-

---

14 H. Anet, *Vers l'Avenir*, Rapport de la Conférence jubilaire des Missions
protestantes du Congo et de la Conférence missionnaire de l'Afrique occidentale,
Léopoldville-Est, 15–23 Septembre 1928 (Léopoldville: Conseil Protestant du
Congo, 1929), p. 94.

ical program of the American missions and that of Moscow.[15] In reaction to what Dr. Lerrigo spoke about training leaders, he said:

The leaders trained by the evangelical missions will shake the yoke of the dominant race; they will claim that emancipation which certainly, no native graduating from the national schools will ever claim.[16]

If Protestant unity was beginning to make itself felt, Catholic lines of administration were strengthened, too, for in 1930 the Holy See sent its first Apostolic Delegate to represent it in the Congo. The office of Apostolic Delegate was retained in Léopoldville until it was replaced by a Papal Ambassador to the Republic of Congo in February, 1963.

Government inspection and guidance of official and subsidized education were taking on a more effective administrative form as well. Provision for a Government inspection service (still in the judicial department) had been made in the 1924 regulations. The inspection service was organized and functioning by 1927. It provided for a chief inspector and an assistant for each of the principal regions of the country. In addition, each Catholic diocese was to have a subsidized missionary-inspector. By 1933 the school inspection part of the judicial service was transferred into a separate administrative unit called the "Education Service." It began its new identity with four official inspectors, who were assisted by twenty-nine Catholic missionary-inspectors.

Increasing numbers of Catholic missions had been signing the scholastic convention with the government since 1925 and were accordingly making an effort to bring their schools up to the required standard to qualify for subsidy. Even though they were not eligible for subsidies, Protestant missions continued to improve their schools and tried to bring them up to government subsidy standards. The ninth Protestant general conference for the Congo in 1924 had already gone on record with the following recommendation of principle:

Christian education is such a vital form of our missionary activity and so essential to the future extension of our work that it is to be hoped that this Conference will make a new resolve to check upon all its educa-

[15] Msgr. de Hemptine, *La Politique des Missions Protestantes au Congo* (Elisabethville: Editions de l'Essor du Congo, 1929), p. 29.
[16] *Ibid.,* p. 5.

tional work, to resolve highly to cooperate with its educational committee in its plans to unify our work and to bring it up to some standard of attainment which we will not be ashamed to exhibit not only to one another but to the Government.[17]

The Protestants wanted recognition for their work, especially official recognition of their schools' certificates and of their Congolese teachers. In the next two decades they gave even more attention to their teacher training and sent more of their missionaries for study in Belgium.

On the official side, the general government in Léopoldville was glad to deal with the diverse administrations of Protestant missions in the country through the Congo Protestant Council. The General Secretary of the council took advantage of this to press the government for recognition of Protestant school work. Through his contacts with authorities both in the Congo and in Belgium, he began to place official requests for recognition and to make protests of discrimination and abuses. The internal as well as the international import of the information presented in the General Secretary's actions was not lost on the opposition to the Christian Socialist Party in Belgium, and it was a factor in the final official recognition of Protestant school work after World War II.

One of the things which the Protestant missions hoped to obtain was official inspections, as at least a step toward recognition of their work, even though it might not be subsidized. However, this was difficult to do; the General Secretary of the Congo Protestant Council complained to the Minister of Colonies in 1933 that he had never been able to obtain a copy of the 1924 Government school regulations through official channels, that there had never been an answer to his official requests for Government inspection of Protestant schools, and that students of Protestant schools were told by authorities and by Catholic missionaries that their status was unrecognized and unofficial.[18] The spirit of competition, a

[17] *Congo Missionary Conference, 1924,* a report of the ninth "Conférence générale des missionaires protestants du Congo," September 25-October 2, 1924, held at Léopoldville-Est, p. 121.
[18] "Memorandum addressé à Son Excellence le Ministre des Colonies," *op. cit.*

sense of national prerogative and doctrinal rightness, plus the circumstances of a colonial administration among an impressionable people who were usually insulated from outside observation, naturally led to abuses or exaggerations related to Catholic mission activities in education. Although the civil administrators from Belgium were predominently Catholic and subject to subtle pressure on their professional advancement, they very often did their best to be fair in their treatment of Protestant missions. Yet in the general pattern of administration, actions and interpretations favoring Catholic mission schools were given beyond the requirements of regulations. Over the years the Protestant Congolese were subjected to a build-up of Catholic prestige and predominance in educational matters and public administration that has carried over into the independent republic.

Sections from two letters of the Protestant Council's General Secretary, reporting to member missions about Protestant difficulties, are illustrative of conditions during the period in question:

Most of the time the priests are allowed to tell the Natives openly and in defiance of the law and the truth that the Catholic schools are all state schools and that as such it is to them all children must be sent. Not infrequently that statement is made to assemblies of Natives in the very presence of officials, when uncontradicted, it naturally goes as an official pronouncement; and sometimes government officials themselves are so worked upon by the Catholic priests that they personally make such lawless statements, both verbally and in writing, to Natives under their rule. Travelling government doctors and sanitary agents are reported as used for the same purpose, having soldiers under their command seize scores of children and herd them off forcibly to Catholic religious schools. Missionaries tell us of priests who themselves go into Protestant village schools and actually pull little children out by their ears or arms or necks and personally drive them into Catholic schools, threatening them and their families with the most dire governmental vengeance if they dare to return to the school of their choice.[19]

Certain officials have a settled policy of ignoring completely Protestant schools. They visit Roman Catholic institutions with great pomp and Natives, Protestants and pagans as well as Catholics, are officially and unofficially gathered in from all about to witness such visits. Nearby

---

[19] Letter from Emory Ross, General Secretary, to member missions of Congo Protestant Council, April 21, 1931.

Protestant establishments are not visited. To the Native community the inference is obvious.[20]

The administration was increasingly sensitive to the numerical and strategic importance of Protestant mission schools and in 1934 began to include them in the scholastic statistics reported annually to the Belgian Parliament. Inspectors also made informal visits to Protestant schools. But all this did not bring the important help of recognition and subsidies to Protestant school work. On July 6, 1935, the Protestant Council's General Secretary wrote to the Governor General of the Congo protesting the injustice of paying subsidies exclusively to Catholic schools from government funds when Protestant Congolese were contributing to those funds. The letter pointed out that heads of Protestant Congolese families were helping through their taxes to pay for an educational program from which their own children could not benefit without having to change their religion. It went on to suggest government subsidy for both Catholic and Protestant schools and the establishment of a policy allowing for provision of education for minority religious groups that respected their faith. The letter assured the Governor General that children going through Protestant subsidized schools would be loyal to Belgium.[21] The argument was being made more frequently that, aside from the question of the non-Belgian nationality of the Protestant missionaries, the Protestant Congolese should enjoy equal rights with the Catholic Congolese and not be treated as second-class citizens of the Congo.

By this time, newspapers in the Congo were taking up the issue, which was becoming oriented more and more to Belgian internal politics than it was to the international aspect it had when representatives of King Léopold II and the Belgian Government were at the treaty tables. An article that appeared in Léopoldville's *L'Avenir Colonial Belge* in 1935 reflected the anticlerical, anti-Christian Socialist Party position of the newspaper in commenting on a visit to the Brussels Exposition. It pointed out the discrepancies between what the Government did for Catholic schools in Congo and what it did for Protestant schools. Beginning its argu-

[20] Letter from Emory Ross, General Secretary, to member missions of Congo Protestant Council, June 8, 1932.

[21] Letter from H. Wakelin Coxhill, General Secretary of the Congo Protestant Council, to the Governor General of the Belgian Congo, July 6, 1935.

ments on the obvious difference in cost between the simple Protestant and the extravagant Catholic educational displays at the exposition, the article went on to say:

> Let us suppose just the same that the government doesn't make a budgetary difference like that between the Catholic missions and the Protestant missions because the latter are for the most part of foreign origin.
>
> When it is a matter of doing good, of raising a whole population to the level of Christian principles, it is only the result of that evangelization which must count in a country whose Constitution establishes no differences among religions.
>
> When Mr. Tschoffen [the Minister of Colonies] said to the Senate: "You have your choice between the missionary school and ignorance," didn't he mean the Catholic missionary school by that? The context of his speech leads one to believe so.[22]

The colonial administration report to Parliament for 1935 showed the following statistics for schools operated by Catholic missions:[23]

	Schools	Pupils
Subsidized schools for European children	14	920
Official schools for Congolese children	11	5,691
Subsidized schools for Congolese children	4,654	214,311
Nonsubsidized schools for Congolese children	7,500	222,000
Minor seminaries	19	989
Regional seminaries	3	109
Non-African teaching personnel—880		

Protestant schools, none of which were subsidized, were reported as follows for the same year:

	Schools	Pupils
Central primary schools	160	27,359
Outlying branch schools	8,480	219,409
Trade schools	24	623
Normal schools	35	890
Non-African teaching personnel—396		

By 1939 3.06 per cent of the Congo budget (22,310,000 francs) was devoted to education; of this, 13,200,000 francs was subsidy to

[23] *Rapport sur l'Administration du Congo Belge,* 1935.
[22] "L'Enseignement au Congo et les Missions," *L'Avenir Colonial Belge* (daily newspaper, Léopoldville), September 25, 1936.

Catholic schools. The balance went to official schools, most of which were operated by Catholic teaching orders. In addition, the "culte" section of the 1939 budget paid out 3,798,500 francs to the Catholic missions for their religious services.[24]

The postwar period brought a liberalizing change of politics in Belgium and a new sensitivity to international concern for Belgium's administration of the Congo. Oddly enough, the first educational change was instituted in the school program for non-African children—an indication of the growing influence of Belgian internal politics on school policy in the Congo. In 1946 the government opened three official schools for European children and staffed them entirely with lay teachers who were employed directly by the government. Up until this time the Catholic missions had held a complete monopoly of official and subsidized education for European children.

But the more radical change was in the government's attitude toward Protestant mission schools. In February, 1946, the Belgian government decided that all Christian mission schools should be put on equal footing as long as they could meet government requirements. As for the question of "national" and "foreign" missions, the emphasis was to be put upon the nationality of the missionary himself, Protestant and Catholic alike, rather than on the nationality of the mission. One provision made immediately by the government was that all non-Belgian missionaries who were to be accredited for teaching in a subsidized school in Congo had to spend a year in Belgium making contact with the country's people, culture, and institutions. During this time they were to improve their use of the French or Flemish language, study Belgian pedagogy and school organization, and successfully pass a course organized by the Ministry of Colonies in matters related to their work in the Congo.

The new school regulations, which appeared in 1948, were called the "General Dispositions of the organization of subsidized free education for natives with the cooperation of Christian missionary societies." The general objectives of its policy were: 1) to provide instruction and education for the native youth; 2) to educate in such a way as to enable the native people to live by their own genius either in their ancestral environment or outside of it;

[24] Liesenborghs, *op. cit.*, p. 266.

3) to provide an educational program that would prepare a future elite group—and do all of this in keeping with the necessity of adapting the program to the conditions of the Congo milieu and to the exigencies of colonization as well as to the legitimate aspirations and possibilities of the natives.[25]

Each mission that wanted to be subsidized according to the new regulations was to sign the scholastic convention with the general government in Léopoldville. These original contracts for school subsidy have been maintained to date by the government of the Congo Republic, although the curriculum requirements have since been modified. Independence changed some of the conditions, such as residence requirements in Belgium for non-Belgian missionaries, but they are awaiting official modification as the educational ministry of the independent government organizes itself. By 1949 eighteen Protestant missions and all the Catholic missions but one had signed the new scholastic convention. The government educational service, to encourage rapid improvement and extension of the educational program, was very generous in granting subsidies to many schools in both Catholic and Protestant missions that did not meet requirements at first and allowed all missions a period of three years' grace to bring their schools up to subsidy standards. In 1948 and 1949 the government had twelve and then twenty official inspectors both to help with and to check on the application of the new regulations.

All of these developments reflected the postwar economic recovery and advance. The government could afford to be generous in budget allowances for increases in its own personnel and program as well as for subsidized school work. School subsidies in 1949 amounted to 117,109,658 francs for Catholic missions and 8,488,942 francs for Protestant missions, with a total education budget of 237,369,000 francs.[26] The following year the regular educational budget was up to a total of 279,060,000 francs, but alongside this was an exceptional budget category of direct expenses and subsidies for buildings amounting to 688,931,000 francs. Statistics for school enrollment that year came to a total which was nearly equal to half the school-age population.[27]

[25] *Rapport sur l'Administration du Congo Belge,* 1948.
[26] *Ibid.*
[27] *Ibid.,* 1950.

Now that subsidization of their work had become a real possibility, Protestant missions were called upon to decide what their doctrinal tradition on the relationship between church and state would allow them to do with this new opportunity. The missions that had sought subsidy in the first place saw that the circumstances which caused the development of their tradition did not necessarily apply in the Congo, and they did not want to deprive the Congolese Christians of the benefits which subsidies would bring to their schools. Some of the more conservative groups doctrinally were reluctant to change their position, but many of them gradually began to accede to the requests of their Congolese constituency for better educational opportunities. Perhaps one of the most radical changes the new regime brought about in Protestant missions was the proportion of missionary personnel assigned to educational work. The government requirement for accredited missionary school directors caused many of the missionary societies to send a large portion of their personnel for the required year's residence in Belgium and to put men who had been intended for pastoral and evangelistic work into the administration of schools. The consequent personnel shortage in the church oversight and evangelistic program had not been resolved by the development of a well-trained indigenous Protestant clergy in adequate numbers by the time the Congo gained its independence, and the current need for missionary teachers in Protestant secondary schools in particular has prolonged the question of priority in the placement of missionary personnel.

Continued postwar prosperity and a rise in the investment of European capital in the Congo caused by the Korean conflict maintained an economic situation which permitted the last maneuvers in the formation of the Congo educational structure by the rival Belgian factions before the rather sudden granting of independence to the country. All of this was generally limited by the budget and policy factors of a ten-year plan for economic and social development of the Congo. However, the Belgian political forces in control during each four-year period between elections were able to turn the budget resources and administrative nominations to their advantage. The fact that local consultation of representatives of all elements of the population in the Congo was being practiced on an increasingly extensive scale by the government only augmented the rivalry of the two Belgian factions to win favor there.

The return to power of the Christian Socialists in 1950 enabled them to turn the previous liberal decisions concerning education in the Congo and the budgetary benefits of the new prosperity to their advantage as much as possible. Two of their particular projects were the development of a university center, which had been moved to Kimwenza (Léopoldville) and operated under the tutelage of the Catholic University at Louvain, and the expansion of a general education program for Congolese in the "official congregational" schools by the opening of new Catholic-operated "groupes scolaires" on a direct support basis from the government. The "extraordinary" budget (nonrecurring expenses, such as building) for education reached a never-again-attained peak of 952,587,000 francs in 1953, while the "ordinary" education budget for that year amounted to 678,868,000 francs.[28] A revision of the "General Dispositions" was published in 1952, and under it subsidized confessional schools were allowed to begin employing a certain percentage of lay teachers at the rate of pay for government lay teachers.

Back in power once more in 1954, the Liberal-Socialist coalition set to work at once to extend its program of official lay schools to the Congolese population as well, and there was talk of reducing the budget allocations for subsidized schools. At about this same time there were Catholic riots in Belgium over the Liberal-Socialist school policy there. In response to the Liberal-Socialist Congo action, the Apostolic Vicars of the Congo said they would close all the Catholic-operated schools (which would have included the "official congregational" schools) , thus affecting about 70 per cent of the country's school population, unless the government modified its intended policy. The cuts in subsidy were not made, but four lay schools for Congolese were opened in 1954. To counteract the Catholic effort to sway public opinion against them, the schools were made as appealing as possible. The curriculum was as nearly as possible like that offered to European children, and the language of instruction was French from the very beginning.

Although the establishment of lay schools in Congo was a reflection of the Liberal-Socialist position in Belgium, there were

28 *Ibid.*, 1953.

local reasons for their popular acceptance by a segment of the
Congolese population. In practice, a very small portion of official
and non-Protestant private education had been in lay hands before
that time. Other than the lay schools begun for European children
in 1946, the only other official schools completely operated by lay
staff had been the training program of the government medical
service and the National Guard's school for noncommissioned
officers and technicians. Not until the 1950's did the government
begin developing training schools for its own employees, such as
those in the postal and telegraphic services. The large private
concession companies have always had some employee training
programs in order to keep supplied with skilled Congolese workers,
but most of them were largely dependent upon the "official congregational" trade schools, or they hired Catholic lay brothers to
do the teaching for them. As for the private primary and secondary
schools for employees' children that were located on concession
property, one of the conditions of the concession grant had been
that such school be operated by Catholic missions if not by company personnel. (This latter condition has been especially liberal-
ized since 1960, and there is a desire on the part of the concession
companies to see their schools become a part of the subsidized
school regime.) Government farm-school training programs, as
many as fifty of them at one time, were given to Catholic missions,
while no Protestant mission could qualify for the "national" status
that would allow it to receive a large enough land grant to permit
it to develop even one comparable farm school. The Government
also underwrote the expenses of special higher-level medical and
agricultural training and research programs at centers operated by
organizations called CADULAC and FORMULAC, which were
special agencies of the Catholic University at Louvain. In addition
to this, Protestant missions were simply too short of qualified personnel to greatly extend their secondary school program. What it
all amounted to was that many Protestant and other non-Catholic
Congolese parents had little choice but eventually to place their
child in a Catholic-operated school, and many Congolese youth
had to consider seriously the probability of becoming at least
nominal Catholics in order to advance in their vocations or careers.
The value of remedying such a situation was seized upon by the
Belgian Socialist Party, which in its "program of action" outlined

in July, 1956, listed as one of its points the development of an extensive system of lay schools in order to make the freedom of choice of school effective.[29] A few months earlier that year, the Christian Socialist Party, which was out of power at the time, had published a manifesto on the Congo saying that at the moment when Congo's educational needs called for an urgent response, a plea for help should go out to all possible sources—but that this had been the moment when the government (Liberal-Socialist) chose to export Belgium's internal political differences in order to try to paralyze the private (Catholic mission) initiative which had been called to fulfill the greater part of the Congo's educational task.[30]

Since their own missions and churches could not furnish adequate educational facilities for their children, many Protestant parents would have been happy to see the government open good-quality, confessionally neutral lay schools for them. Some Congolese had even officially expressed their desire for this, but it was not given much publicity during the years the Christian Socialists were in power. The parents' concern for a certain amount of religious training for their children in their own faith could be satisfied in a lay school, because up to five hours of religious training per week was provided for by law in all primary schools. Religious training for a shorter length of time has also been provided in the school program on the secondary level. The pupil or student in a lay school has his choice of a Catholic or Protestant religion course or of a confessionally neutral "moral" course. Regulations have required that the same possibilities for religious instruction be provided for pupils in "official congregational" schools, and the new post-independence regulations stipulate that such a choice be provided for in all subsidized schools. Application of the latter regulation has not yet achieved its ideal. Teachers of religion on the secondary level in official schools of all kinds are even paid for their work by the state. There is a current willingness in part of the population to see the expansion of the lay school program, just as the situation ten years earlier saw a certain amount of popular sentiment ready to welcome the opening of lay schools. The

[29] *LeProgramme d'Action du P.S.B.*, July 1–2, 1956, p. 5.
[30] *Le Manifeste du P.S.C. sur le Congo*, February 26, 1956, p. 4.

schools were popular from their inception, and their development was only limited by their resources and available personnel.

Protestant mission reaction to the lay schools was mixed. When the lay schools opened, they were greeted with relief by those missions that had been working under the pressure of inadequate staff and resources. Yet the opening of the lay schools worked a hardship on some of those same missions when their Congolese teachers were recruited by the government. Protestant schools suffered the most from the financial adjustment necessitated by the opening of the lay schools. The peak of the prosperous economy had been reached, and some kind of terms had to be agreed upon for the proportional use of credits in the "extraordinary" budget. A consultation by the Minister of Colonies in 1956 with the General Secretary of the Congo Protestant Council and the President of the Catholic Bureau of Education resulted in 45 per cent of available funds being allocated to lay schools, 45 per cent to Catholic schools, and the remaining 10 per cent to Protestant schools.

University-level education was subject to the same political-confessional factors as the rest of education in Congo, although its very uniqueness subjected a university's internal affairs to so much external view that its confessional attitudes toward students were bound to be more nearly neutral. Budgets, assistance grants, and professorial nominations, however, were more subject to the usual pressures. Consequently four years of a Christian Socialist Government in Belgium enabled the Catholic University of Lovanium to to open its doors at Kimwenza in 1954. On the basis of a convention which the "university center" signed with the government on March 11, 1950, Lovanium was to accept students of any religious confession.[31]

There was genuine regret at the cost involved in the opening of an official state university at Elisabethville in 1956, two years after Lovanium had begun its classes. The Liberal-Socialist coalition government had acted this time partly to satisfy the disappointment of those who had hoped that what was now Lovanium might have been a neutral, state university. But their action was chiefly to counteract the influence of Lovanium on the Congo. Elisabethville's official university was sponsored by all four of the

---

[31] *Rapport sur l'Administration du Congo Belge,* 1950.

Belgian universities. Since the university of Elisabethville was an official institution, it was also at the mercy of Government budgetary legislation, and when the Christian Socialists came into power once more in 1958 they reduced the budgetary support for its projects.

Both Lovanium and the official university have of necessity offered an introductory year of pre-university classes. By 1959 the combined pre-university and regular enrollment amounted to 361 students at Lovanium and 219 students at Elisabethville. The official university suffered academically and administratively from its location in Katanga during the period of that province's secession after independence, but it is now being reintegrated into the Congolese central government administrative structure. Foundation grants and foreign technical assistance are largely responsible for keeping the two universities operating today. Belgian technical assistance alone (through its payment of professors' salaries, scholarship grants, and contributions toward the operating expenses) amounts to the equivalent of one-third of the operating budget for each of the two universities. Congolese and international Protestant initiative channeled through the Congo Protestant Council has brought about the establishment of a third university in the Congo. The institution was recognized by the Congo government, and the Minister of Education, Colin, secured international recognition for it at the Conference of African Ministers of Education at Abidjan in February, 1964. Named The Free University of Congo, the school began a "propendentique" year at Stanleyville in October, 1963. It was materially impossible to hold classes at Stanleyville during the rebel occupation, and classes are presently being held by the Free University of Congo on the Lovanium campus at Léopoldville. Such an undertaking appears contrary to the tendency in newly independent African countries to establish secular state universities. Emotional support for a nonconfessional university established on Protestant initiative is strong among Protestant Congolese parents, more so than among some of the Protestant missionaries. The apparent explanation for the strong Congolese Protestant sentiment is that they would like to be sure there is a place for their children to be educated for future roles of leadership in the life of the country. Their experiences to date have been that both Lovanium and the official university at Elisabethville have been subject to the subleties and fortunes of Congolese and Belgian politics. The expressed intention of those promoting the project for a third university was to found an institution that is neither financially nor academically dependent on any one sector of national or international political or confessional opinion.

In the few years just before the Congo became independent there was little change in the relative positions of the three principal types of schools in the Congo. Part of this was due to the beginning of a decline in Government budget resources, and part was due to Belgian hesitancy to extend its investments in the country. Building projects for schools were particularly cut back. The principal changes were ones made by the Government in its approach toward education for the Congolese. A new vocabulary came into use for referring to the indigenous people. Reports and official documents had not referred to schools for non-Africans as "school for white children" since World War II, although the revision of the "General Dispositions" made in 1952 still referred to the program for Congolese as "education for natives." By 1956, selected Congolese children began to be admitted to schools intended only for Europeans. Their proportion increased each year after that. Whereas the two types of education programs had been referred to as "education for Europeans" and "education for natives," they began in 1957 to be referred to as "metropolitan regime" and "Congolese regime." The last reform before 1960 was the proposed changeover of all schools to a "metropolitan" (Belgian) regime, in which the instruction was to be given in French. The new program was to begin with the first grade of primary school in September, 1959. Another class was to have been added each year until the changeover was complete. A special team of pedagogues was put to work in Léopoldville hastily preparing the lessons before the school year opened, and the mimeographed lesson sheets were sent out along with teachers' instructions as the school year progressed.

Reports for the year 1958 indicated a total school population for the Congo of 1,500,000 pupils and students. They were divided proportionally among the different schools systems as follows: government lay schools, 4 per cent; Catholic (including "official congregational") schools, 76 per cent; Protestant schools, 19 per cent; and private company schools 0.7 per cent. These proportions were maintained for the following school year. At this time, 119 Catholic and 28 Protestant mission groups had signed the scholastic convention with the Government.[32] Population figures at that time listed the Congo as having nearly 14 million people. Of these, approximately 2½ million were Protestants and 5½ million were Catholics. There has been no official census taken since independence, but the proportions have probably remained about the same.

Subsidized educational programs had increased so much for Protestant schools that the Congo Protestant Council finally engaged a full-time educational secretary early in 1959 to deal with the educational services of the general government in Léopoldville on behalf of its member missions. Responsibilities for education in the Protestant Council have now been given to a department called the "Protestant Bureau of Education," which parallels the long-existent Catholic Bureau of Education. However, Protestant diversity has often caused missions and churches to be slow or disorganized in their dealings with the government. The council has also been reduced in its effectiveness by inadequate financial resources. These factors must be taken into consideration in comparing the educational influence of Protestantism in the Congo to that of a Catholic educational system that is efficiently organized and well staffed.

It will be necessary to wait to see what the definitive position of the government of the now independent Republic of the Congo will be on relations between church and state. The Congolese parliament has not yet voted a constitution for the republic, the apparent reason for delay being a reluctance to vote for a constitutional structure before the national parliament is sure of an acceptable arrangement for the division of authority between the central government and the provincial governments. In the meantime, the Congo government has based its authority and actions on a "Fundamental Law" which was prepared on the eve of independence to serve until a constitution could be adopted.[33] This "Fundamental Law" has at times suffered refusal by provincial authorities to abide by it and even temporary secession.

Two different provisional projects of a constitution for the

[32] *Ibid.,* 1958.

[33] *Moniteur Congolais,* "Loi Fondamentale du 19 mai 1960 relative aux structures du Congo," May 27, 1960.

Congo have been drawn up by special commissions of jurists. The first project set out preliminary principles which included the neutrality of the state toward all religions; that is, there would be no official religion. The second consultative group, which had been organized by the United Nations, prepared a commentary on their project[34] which stated that the elaboration of basic principles such as had been stated in the previous project should be left to the legislative body charged with the adoption of a constitution. However, both projects included detailed sections on human rights, where religious freedom and the right of parents to educate their children according to their religious beliefs were guaranteed. It remains to be seen what form these religion clauses will have when they are finally adopted. Meanwhile, the official attitude toward the Church which prevailed before independence has largely applied until now.

The predominance of Catholics among the Belgian technicians and the Congolese in the Government services and the national and provincial ministry staffs and the majority of Catholics among those nominated for ministerial posts quite naturally favors advancement of Catholic programs and projects, particularly in education. One of the educational reforms in process when independence came was a decentralization of the administration. Responsibility for primary and secondary schools has been placed in the hands of the provinces, of which there are presently twenty-one; and, as well as it can be established, each of the current provincial ministers of education is at least a nominal Catholic. The large proportion of Catholics in the civil service, in administrative posts, and in political leadership is to be expected on the basis of the confessional aspect of the pre-independence system of education.

Independence affected the mission structure as well. For the Catholic missions there had already been a move to consecrate Congolese bishops as the heads of the different dioceses. There are still a number of Belgian bishops within the Congo, yet the identity of the ecclesiastical hierarchy has become increasingly Congolese. The missions, movements, and agencies of the Catholic Church have the same efficient coordination that they did before independ-

[34] Groupe de Jurisconsultes Constitutionnels, "Avant-projet de Constitution Fédérale, Mémoire Explicatif," Léopoldville, 1963.

ence. This has been especially evident in the press, so that newspapers and other publications which have either direct or indirect connections with the ecclesiastical structure give the names of Congolese editors and staff on their mastheads but at the same time reveal a continuity of point of view that is not uniquely Congolese. Competition for the support of public opinion has been a major preoccupation of the Catholic press in the unstable years since independence, and the problems of education have had an important share of space devoted to them. By way of contrast, a secular, opinion-forming Protestant press is non-existent.

For Protestant missions, independence coincided with a hasty and often incomplete development of autonomous responsibility for the churches which were born from the evangelistic efforts of the various missions. Although the granting of legal identity for the autonomous churches by the government has been slow, partly because it has inherited the Belgian administration's inability to comprehend the diversities and indirectness of administrative lines of Protestantism in the Congo, the indigenous churches are now largely responsible before the government for Protestant schools. The Congo Protestant Council itself has a Congolese pastor as its General Secretary, and its Protestant Bureau of Education is headed by a Congolese school director. However, it will be some time before the transition from mission to church is complete and the Protestant churches of the Congo give a structure to their council that more completely responds to their internal needs.

A religious group that calls itself Christian, but that insists on not being identified with either the Protestants or the Catholics, has begun to receive Government subsidy for its schools since independence and has been granted a legal identity by the government. This group is known as "The Church of Christ on Earth by the Prophet Simon Kimbangu" or simply "Kimbanguism." Most of its adherents live in the "Lower Congo" region, which is between Léopoldville and the Atlantic coast. The church is a prophet movement that sprang up in the early nineteen-twenties around a Congolese Protestant catechist named Simon Kimbangu. The group of followers that developed around him was considered a threat to the Government administration and to public order, and Simon Kimbangu was finally put in prison for the rest of his life in another part of the country. His known followers who persisted in their practices were relegated with their families to isolated detention camps at great distances from their home regions. Yet the movement thrived. It also developed xenophobic overtones that probably would have disappointed Kimbangu himself. To counteract a possible later resurgence of the movement, the authorities placed Kimbangu's sons in Catholic boarding schools and surrounded the area of his origin with Catholic primary schools.

In 1958 there was a softening in the attitude of the Belgian government toward the Kimbanguists. It began repatriating the hard-core elements that had been relegated to isolated regions, and in December, 1959, it granted the status of a legal identity to the church that had been formed, recognizing the eldest son of Simon Kimbangu as its spiritual leader and legal representative. On January 4, 1960, the Kimbanguists began a rapidly expanding program of opening schools of their own. Their decision to undertake this action was reputedly based on complaints of Kimbanguist parents that their children were put out of or refused admission to Protestant, Catholic, and official lay schools.

None of the other religious sects have yet been recognized by the government. Some of the sects, such as the Kitawala—which has an historical connection with the Jehovah's Witness movement—are often anti-government as well as xenophobic in their attitudes. As more and more nontraditional religious groups come into existence, and perhaps as Islam becomes stronger, the government will be faced with the choice of which groups to give official recognition for school subsidy purposes.

Post-independence talk of nationalization of the educational program led to considerable apprehension on the part of Catholic school authorities. These were two aspects to the expression "nationalization": nationalization of the curriculum and nationalization of the administration of all schools. Only the passage of time made it clear that the government was limiting itself to the curriculum question for the moment. First reactions of some school people were that the government would want to take over the operation of all schools. The government pronouncement that was published in 1961 showed a nationalistic concern for the curriculum. It declared that Congolese children and youth should receive an education based on their identity and needs as modern

Africans rather than one preparing them for successful performance on the passage or leaving examinations of schools in Europe,
whose curriculum was determined by the economic and social
needs in one European country or another. Universal application
of the new national curriculum was required in the 1963-64 school
year. The practical implications of what is needed for the realization of this ideal (new programs, competent teachers, adequate
and rapid communications) are immense, but this is only one of
the problems facing the burgeoning educational system.

Administrative nationalization appeared to be a threat immediately after independence, but it now appears less imminent.
Continued confusion and anarchy in the general administrative
situation of the Congo showed that the government was at the time
incapable of an administrative nationalization that meant government operation of all schools. The possibility did remain, though,
that the government might decide to deal more directly with the
confessional schools by abrogating the scholastic convention terms
and dictating policy and administrative procedures to them. To
forestall such action, and to make the Catholic Church's position
clear to the government, the plenary session of Congo bishops in
December, 1961, published the concrete conditions by which they
could participate in a national education program.[35] They declared that a national education system acceptable to them was one
that respected the rights of parents. Furthermore, they considered
a state's requiring its youth to be educated exclusively in public
schools as contrary to the Declaration of Human Rights. On the
other hand, they saw as perfectly acceptable a national education
system that, in order to organize an efficient national program, not
only accepted but solicited the collaboration of competent organizations that have been properly accredited by it. They went
into considerable detail about the internal administrative rights
of a school which must be respected by any arrangement for national control of confessional schools, particularly: 1) the engage-
ment and dismissal of the director and the teaching staff; 2) the
choice of textbooks; 3) the admission of pupils, taking into account
the principle that education is open to all; and 4) the expelling of
pupils. For external relationships, they would require that their

---

[35] Martin Ekwa, S. J., *Pour un Enseignement Catholique National* (Léopoldville: Bureau de l'Enseignement Catholique, 1963), p. 27.

confessional schools be given equal treatment compared to all other schools in matter of: 1) the material and social situation of the teaching corps; 2) state support of operating expenses; and 3) access to the school open to all children. The conditions set down by the bishops for a confessional collaboration in a national educational system are parallel to what Protestant school leaders have expressed at different times concerning internal authority and equal status with other schools.

A few month later, a Catholic journal for lay action published an article defining the role of the church, the family, the school, and the state in education.[36] It pointed out that the church counted on the school to complete the education given to a child by his family and that in the school the conscience of the child should be developed according to the norms determined by the faith of his parents. Toward this goal, the church should organize schools with a "climate" where truly human and Christian education could take place. Many Protestants in the Congo would express the same attitude, although they do not categorically reject public lay schools. They would even in many instances welcome the services of a well-disciplined lay school where they could supplement the moral training of their children by religion courses in the school and by other Christian training activities outside the schools. Recent interviews with Kimbanguist educational leaders reveal that their views are similar, although they would prefer to operate their own schools where they could require their own particular moral disciplines of teachers and pupils alike.

The latest official Catholic statement of the role of the state in education has been published in a brochure entitled *For a Catholic National Education Program*. It is written by the president of the Catholic Bureau of Education, Father Martin Ekwa, a Congolese Jesuit priest. After defining what he sees as the difference between a nation (an entity of peoples bound together) and the state (which is to serve the nation), Father Ekwa sees the role of the state in education as essentially technical and coordinative between the different educational systems and confessions. He concludes his analysis of the present situation by saying:

[36] *Documents pour l'Action*, Bibliothèque de l'Etoile, Léopoldville (1961–62), p. 100.

Thus we conclude these reflections in remarking that, if we free ourselves from certain reflexes conditioned by European situations, if we truly sympathize with the real feelings of the Congolese people, if we are attentive to the researches of the legislative powers, if finally we notice that the episcopal declarations were well received in all segments of the population, we are necessarily led to think that the CONGO is far from preparing an impoverishing nationalization of its education system; on the contrary, we discover that our National Education will like be *an education which will harmonize the riches of a broad pluralism in the bosom and in the service of a same country*.[37]

Evidences of unrest and dissatisfaction from time to time show that the preceding idyllic analysis does not always apply. Attacks on Catholic schools at different periods of political unrest reveal a discontent with the close association between Catholic clerics and both the previous colonial administration and certain presently predominant political elements. The declarations of the bishops were not well received in absolutely all segments of the population, and emotional reactions led some people to call for a neutralization or nationalization of all confessional schools. During a June, 1963, meeting (at an open-air bar in Léopoldville) of teachers from all types of schools, the General Secretary of the Confederation of Free Labor Unions spoke out for what he called the "socialization" of the country's educational system. By "socialization" he meant that missionaries of all confessions should be put in the role of technical assistants rather than that of "boss" in the schools. One extreme speaker at the meeting said that if the missionaries refused to accept national control of their schools, a call for help would go out to no matter whom—to other "African friends," if necessary.

It would be physically and economically impossible to completely nationalize the Congo educational system under present circumstances. There are not enough personnel for present needs, let alone for replacement of the numerous religious personnel. The national education budget continues to be drastically inadequate for expenditures under the comparatively economical arrangement of subsidized confessional schools, so that it would be far beyond the government's resources to nationalize the mission schools and pay the teaching and administrative staff at official lay salary scales. Since most of the men in present legislative and

[37] Ekwa, *op. cit.,* p. 28.

administrative leadership can be qualified as "believers," they would not be likely to nationalize the country's educational system, except in temporary spite. The political and economic evolution of the next few years will be the determining factors. Catholic predominance in every aspect of the Congo's life, if tempered with the new ecumenical spirit, might be able to resist the erosion or direct thrusts of rising secularism on the nation's schools.

Since independence, nonconfessional education in official schools has expanded the most on the secondary and post-secondary levels, largely because of UNESCO's Congo program and foreign technical assistance programs. In an effort to improve the social situation of unoccupied youth as much as to give direct educational aid, UNESCO furnished teachers to help the government open an extensive network of first-year secondary school classes in 1961. In a situation where private estimates put the proportion of school children in the hands of confessional schools as high as 90 per cent, the first year of the UNESCO secondary program raised the proportion of students in official lay schools to 30 per cent of the total secondary school enrollment.

Specialized post-secondary training schools are operated for the Government by UNESCO and foreign technical assistance, and they are almost entirely staffed by non-Congolese personnel. These schools are training secondary school teachers as well as civil servants for judicial, administrative, meteorological, public works, and other technical services. The student body of the government teacher-training school in particular has been characterized as a hotbed of Communism, but part of the criticism of the school may stem from confessional reluctance to see the Government become satisfied with official schools of this type.

UNESCO aid with secondary teachers has also been extended to confessional schools. The teachers are divided among the schools according to a proportion agreed upon by the Ministry of National Education. For the 1962-63 school year, a total of 554 UNESCO teachers were furnished to the Congo, with 371 of them placed in official lay schools, 150 with the Catholic Bureau of Education, 29 with the Protestant Bureau of Education, and 3 in the Kimbanguists' only secondary school. Within their quota, churches and missions are allowed to recruit their own professors and submit them as candidates to UNESCO for hiring.

Belgian technical assistance since independence has given a gradually increasing number of school teachers to both subsidized and official schools. For the year before independence, there were 2,000 Belgian lay teachers in the Congo. Half of them were supplied to subsidized schools, almost entirely Catholic, and half of them were supplied to official schools, both "lay" and "congregational." After independence, only 800 Belgian teachers came back to the Congo the first year. The following year, the number went up to 1,100; in September, 1962, there were 1,200 teachers, enabling the Belgian technical assistance program to supply 600 of them to subsidized schools and 600 to official schools. According to the information supplied by the Belgian Embassy in Léopoldville, there was no indication of the proportion of teachers furnished to lay and congregational schools within the quota allotted to the official schools. It is understandable that all the Belgian technical assistance and scholarship grants offered to the Congo must take confessional opinion back in Belgium into consideration. The Christian Socialist Party has been in power there since 1958. The "scholastic war" over the conflict between official and subsidized education that has plagued Belgium still makes itself felt in the independent Congo.

Technical assistance programs from countries other than Belgium are not totally exempt from religious conditions. This is especially so in the scholarship programs. No United States money can be given for technical assistance or scholarship grants if the program involves the teaching of religion or appears to contradict the separation of church and state as set out in the Constitution. So the AID regional scholarship program in Africa specifically does not accept students in theology, while the French Government has a standing offer of scholarship grants each year for students in Congo who want to study theology or prepare for the pastoral ministry. Ten of the eleven scholarships offered through the Ministry of National Education to Congolese students by the United Arab Republic for 1963-64 were for the El Azhar University and are restricted to students of the Moslem faith. Private scholarship offers from church agencies show Catholic students, both clerical and lay, going chiefly to Belgium, Rome, and Germany. According to the scholarship secretary of the Catholic Bureau of Education, 20 per cent of the new students in clerical studies in

Rome in 1962 came from the Congo. Private Protestant scholarship students have gone mostly to the United States. Léopold II's ambitious diplomacy and politics have left their heritage even in the realm of scholarships.

The 1962–63 school year was a lost one in many ways for a large portion of the primary school population. Because of a crippling teachers' strike which began in May, some schools simply did not finish the year. Except in the city of Leopoldville and the South Katanga province, salary payments for teachers were as much as a year late. Teachers in subsidized schools suffered the most, but the official school system was not exempt from the dislocation of credits. There was a limit to the credits which the central government could transfer to the provinces, and the provincial authorities appeared to spend the money for everything but teachers' salaries. Those school systems able to bring the most pressure to bear on the authorities were the first to receive some relief since the unpaid teachers went on strike. The strike itself pointed up one more contrast within the confessional educational systems. The Catholic-oriented labor union, which changed its name from "Union of Christian Workers" to "Union of Congolese Workers," has a section for school teachers. Through its operation of school systems and its organizational activities in labor, the Catholic Church has placed itself on the side of both employer and employee. A secular teachers' union came into being, but it did not attract many Catholic teachers. Protestant teachers found themselves reluctant to join either the radical secular union or the Catholic union. Too weak to form a union of their own, they have been obliged to join one union or the other to obtain some kind of economic satisfaction, but most of them cannot agree completely with the policy of either union.

The crisis over the nonpayment of teachers, the shortage of finances, and the Belgian technical assistance program's reservations on the national emphasis in the secondary curriculum reform are causing apprehension in all sectors of the school system. Subsidized confessional schools are the most vulnerable, and the politically weaker of them still more vulnerable. Post-1960 analyses place the Congo statistically at the forefront in educational progress for developing countries, with 59 per cent of the school-age population enrolled in school. Forty-nine per cent of the national budget is allotted to education; 25 per cent is generally the highest figure hoped for in other countries. In a speech in July, 1963, the Minister of Education said that if the rate of expansion at that time could be maintained (a matter which has had to face mounting technical difficulties and instability caused by rebellions) in a secondary education program which saw the total number of students jump from 29,000 to 70,000 in two years—and an expected secondary enrollment of 85,000 in October, 1963—there would be 70,000 graduates from the country's secondary schools in 1967.[38] The number of secondary school teachers required from outside the country by that time would be 7,000. Add to this the professors needed for universities and special higher education, and it is quite apparent that the Congo will be dependent on external help in education for many years until it can train its own leadership for the positions now filled by foreign teachers and technicians.

Accurate statistics for any school year after 1959–60 in the Congo are impossible to obtain. Except for the increase in the proportion of students in official lay secondary schools and the establishment of Kimbanguist schools, the percentage among pupils in Protestant, Catholic, and official schools that obtained at independence would still apply. Lovanium and the official university at Elisabethville are reported to have had respectively 650 and 160 Congolese students for the 1962–1963 academic year. Enrollment for Catholic secondary schools was 44,846; there were 4,370 in the Protestant schools and 22,807 in the official schools. Primary schools statistics show 1,340,446 pupils in Catholic schools, 380,000 in Protestant schools, and 89,325 in official schools. Catholic educational interests have a strong enough voice in public opinion and a large enough educational organization to give weight to their negotiations with the government. Official lay schools depend upon those within the administration (aided for the moment by some of the technical assistance programs) who support their cause to promote the interests of lay public education. Protestant educational interests are still trying to find their voice and influence in national educational matters in proportion to their relative importance in the total population. Kimbangu-

---

[38] "Allocution du Ministre Michel Colin de l'education Nationale du Gouvernement Central, Léopoldville, le 17/7/63."

ism is struggling to advance on the basis of its foothold of the official recognition it has now achieved.

Christianity feels itself menaced more and more by secularism and non-Christian ideologies in equatorial Africa. In addition to this there is a growing indifference to the church and to Christian doctrine among believers themselves. The Catholic Church is active on all fronts to try to head off and counteract the trend. It counts heavily on its whole system of education (which is not limited to institutions of classical instruction, but has many ramifications and programs not reported here) to do this. The immediate problem for the Catholic Church is to keep even its own members in the government from going along with the secular movement. In spite of differences with Protestantism in the Congo over the years, Catholicism's leaders are beginning to make a plea for Christian unity and to change their previously competitive attitude to one of a common defense of Christianity in Africa. It was in this spirit that Father Ekwa concluded his brochure on a national Catholic educational system by saying:

> Finally, a last suggestion: if we at other times have opposed our own educational system against that of the Government or of the Protestants, or even of that organized by industrial groups, we must now search for paths of a complete collaboration.
>
> The question is delicate and one could establish a long list of the difficulties. Let us try to convince ourselves from now on that the formula of a National Educational system is not a formula of the easy way by suppression or ignoring contradictions and divergent points of view! It is rather a formula which requires that all teachers be more Christian, that they display an oversight which is more ingenious and more humble. Isn't this, for the good of the country, a form of apostolate that God is right in expecting of his faithful? [39]

Such an appeal as this will not immediately penetrate all of Catholicism or Protestantism in the Congo, but it merits consideration. Protestantism shares Catholicism's concern for the fate of Christianity in the Congo and a number of gestures and attitudes on the part of Catholic educational authorities have begun to prepare the way for a Protestant response to Father Ekwa's appeal.

Christian education as such in its national perspective will

[39] Ekwa, *op. cit.,* p. 36.

increasingly have to justify its methods and correct itself when necessary. Christian Congolese youth have begun to wonder about the motives of missions and have asked if their country has been "colonized" by the Gospel. The reply that the Gospel itself does not "colonize" but that those who proclaim the Gospel bear the burden of responsibility for their method of proclaiming it should be addressed first not to the Congolese youth but to those responsible for their education.

This chapter on the Congo was originally written in August, 1963. The rebellion in the Kwilu province of the Congo broke out the following January, and whole schools were often destroyed during rebel attacks. Some expatriate teachers in mission schools were killed or fled. Almost all were soon evacuated. Although Congolese teachers were also attacked or driven away, a general attack on them as "intellectuals" who stood in the way of popular revolution had not yet been thoroughly sloganized to the extent it was later on in the rebellions to the east and north.

The attacks were not motivated by basically antireligious or anti-Christian feelings, and this is essentially true as well of more recent and larger rebellious movements in the whole eastern half of the Congo. In one instance, a pietistic-natured rebel of Protestant background reportedly had his group stop to pray before they set fire to a building at a palm oil extracting plant. But Catholic and Protestant missions and their schools were seen as being favorable to the central government in Léopoldville and as agents of foreign governments that were assumed to be opposed to local nationalistic ambitions.

The rebel attacks were motivated by local dissatisfaction and organized and promoted by politically ambitious or jealous men who had been put out of power. Personal and tribal grievances also contributed to the choice of both individuals and groups who were the object of rebel attacks. This also applied in later rebellions, and many times false information was given on an individual or an institution to settle a grudge held by the informant.

Expatriate personnel began to resume their school programs in the Kwilu a few months after the rebellion had begun, but some of the schools operated by independent Protestant missions in isolated areas have been abandoned.

During the later rebellions in the Eastern Congo, there was

a concerted attack on educated people, chiefly school teachers and civil servants, who were characterized as "intellectuals" opposed to the masses obtaining what was due them. They were the only people, other than the political leaders, who were in any way able to obtain enought to eat and wear, and their situation was noticeably superior to that of the general population. The intent of those promoting the attack on intellectuals was to rid any locality of persons who might be loyal to the Léopoldville government, who might be personal or tribal enemies, or whose presence contributed to continuing local economic and administrative stability.

The attack on "intellectuals" as elements of enemy stability diminished with the passage of time and with the distance of any given locality from the areas of violent combat or from the source of fanatical propaganda inciting people to attack. Instances are reported where schools continued to operate, or resumed operation, during rebel occupation. Rebel militants often harassed the teachers in these instances by extorting or stealing their money and possessions. Such teachers were often tried by "peoples' courts" and high sums of money were demanded to ransom them from threatened execution. These exceptional instances do not temper the catastrophic effect of the rebellions on educational progress for the whole area.

Again, the rebel leadership in the Eastern part of the Congo has not shown itself fanatically opposed to Christianity, to missions, or to missionaries as such. The opposition has been to Americans and to suspected agents or agencies representing "imperialist" governments. One of the rebel leaders, Christophe Gbenye, was known to demonstrably practice his Catholic faith long before so much international attention was drawn to him. He and other leaders have at times forced missionaries to continue the operation of their schools, while at other times they have used them as white hostages or let them be murdered.

The rebellions still prevent any complete reporting of educational statistics for the whole of the Congo as a national unit. The basic situation has changed little since this chapter was first written. The training of indigenous teachers and administrators for the secular and confessional school systems has continued, and church institutional relations with the state have increasingly come under the influence of internal politics and tribalism as indigenous leaders have assumed responsibility, but the sources of external economic and technical support in education still have a preponderant influence on church-state relationships. As for the future, even the rebel groups have now shown themselves willing to utilize confessional school personnel and facilities when necessary, and a complete nationalization of the Congo's educational system under any government would be unlikely in the near future.

Bibliography

OFFICIAL PUBLICATIONS

Recueil Usuel de Legislation de l'Etat Indépendant du Congo. Annual volumes from 1876 to 1910.

Bulletin Officiel, Etat Indépendant du Congo. Annually bound volumes for 1890, and 1897 to 1906.

Rapport sur l'Administration du Congo Belge (pendant l'année . . . .), présenté aux Chambres Legislatives. Annual volumes from 1915 to 1958.

Dispositions Générales, organisation de l'Enseignement libre subsidié pour indigènes avec le concours des sociétés de missions Chrétiennes, Service de l'Enseignement, Congo Belge. 1948, 60 pp.; 1952, 116 pp.

Moniteur Congolais, "Loi Fundamentale du 19 mai 1960 relative aux structures du Congo." 1ère année, No. 21 bis, May 27, 1960.

BOOKS

Braekman, E. M. *Histoire du Protestantisme au Congo.* Bruxelles: Editions de la Librarie des Eclaireurs Unionistes, 1961. 392 pp.

Carpenter, George W. *Highways for God in Congo, Commemorating Seventy-Five Years of Protestant Missions 1878–1953.* Leopoldville: La Librarie Evangélique au Congo, 1952. 83 pp.

Halewyck, Michel. *La Charte Coloniale, Commentaire de la Loi du 18 octobre 1908 sur le Gouvernement du Congo Belge,* Vol. I. Bruxelles: M. Weissenbruch, 1910. 322 pp.

Kitchen, Helen (ed.). *The Educated African, A Country-by-Country Survey of Educational Development in Africa* (compiled by Ruth Sloane Associates). New York: Frederick A. Praeger, 1962. 542 pp.

Office de l'Information et des Relations Publiques pour le Congo Belge et le Ruanda-Urundi, *Le Congo Belge,* Vol. I. Bruxelles: Office de l'Information, 1958. 535 pp.

Piron, Pierre, and Devos, Jacques. *Codes et Lois du Congo Belge.* Bruxelles: Maison Fernand Larcier, 1954. 1694 pp.

Slade, Ruth. *English-Speaking Missions in the Congo Independent State*, Vol. XVI, No. 2. Bruxelles: Académie Royale des Sciences Coloniales, Classe des Sciences Morales et Politiques, 1959. 432 pp.

Stonelake, Alfred R. *Congo Past and Present*. London: World Dominion Press, 1937. 202 pp.

ARTICLES AND EDITORIALS IN THE PERIODICAL CONGO APPEARING FROM 1920 TO 1940

"Programme de l'Ecole Coloniale Supérieure d'Anvers (Arrêté royal du 11/1/1920)" (April–May, 1920), p. 137.

"Allocution du Gouverneur Général Lippens à la Chambre de Commerce d'Anvers" (May, 1921), pp. 768–771.

"L'Education des Nègres," Rapport de la mission d'études du Phelps-Stokes Fund, par Jesse Jones (July, 1921), pp. 165–171.

De Jonghe. "Les Missions religieuses au Congo Belge" (January, 1933), pp. 1–24.

Azed, M. "Les Missions protestantes au Congo" (March, 1938), pp. 288–296.

Liesenborghs, O. "L'Instruction publique des indigènes du Congo Belge" (March, 1940), pp. 233–271.

OTHER PERIODICALS

Carpenter, George W. "Church and State in Africa Today," *Civilizations* (a publication of the International Institute of Differing Civilizations, Brussels), Vol. III, No. 4 (1953), pp. 519–538.

Davis, Orval J. "Educational Development in the Belgian Congo," *The International Review of Missions*, Vol. XLIII, No. 172 (October, 1954), pp. 421–428.

Problèmes d'Afrique Centrale (issue devoted to teaching) (published in Brussels), No. 36, 2nd semester (1957).

Documents pour l'Action, Bibliothèque de l'Etoile, Léopoldville, Nos. 1–8 (January–February, 1961–March–April, 1962).

ARTICLES, REPORTS, AND BROCHURES PUBLISHED PRIVATELY

Anet, H. *Vers l'Avenir*. Rapport de la Conférence jubilaire des Missions protestantes du Congo et de la Conférence missionaire de l'Afrique occidentale (Léopoldville-Est, September 15–23, 1928). Léopoldville: Conseil Protestant du Congo, 1929. 111 pp.

Bureau de l'Enseignement Catholique. *Ou en est l'Enseignement au Congo?* Léopoldville: The Bureau, 1960. 31 pp.

Congo Missionary Conference, 1924. A report of the ninth "Conférence générale des missionaires protestants du Congo," September 25–October 2, 1924, held at Léopoldville-Est.

Ekwa, Martin, S. J. *Pour un Enseignement Catholique National.* Léopoldville: Bureau de l'Enseignement Catholique, 1963. 64 pp.

"L'Enseignement au Congo et les Missions," article published in *L'Avenir Colonial Belge* (daily newspaper, Léopoldville), September 25, 1936.

de Hemptine, Msgr. *La Politique des Missions Protestantes au Congo.* Elisabethville: Editions de l'Essor du Congo, 1929. 32 pp.

Jambers, G. E. *L'Enseignement au Congo Belge.* Léopoldville: Imprimerie du "Courrier d'Afrique," 1947. 72 pp.

Ligue de l'Enseignement, *Le Pacte Scolaire Belge et son application éventuelle au Congo Belge.* Léopoldville: The League, June, 1959. 13 pp.

Le Manifeste du P.S.C. [Le Parti Socialiste Chrétien] sur le Congo. February 26, 1956. 4 pp.

Le Programme d'Action du P.S.B. [Le Parti Socialiste Belge]. July 1–2, 1956. 5 pp.

Rapport de la Seconde Conférence Scolaire. July 25–August 2, 1933. Kimpese: Le Conseil Protestant du Congo, 1933.

Slade, Ruth. *L'Attitude des Missions Protestantes vis-à-vis des Puissances Européennes au Congo avant 1885.* Extract from *Bulletin de l'Institut Royal Colonial Belge,* Vol. XXV, No. 2, pp. 684–721. Brussels, 1954.

VanWing, R. P. Objectivité *"Sur Mesure."* Bruxelles: E. Vandenbussche, 1955. 47 pp.

MIMEOGRAPHED DOCUMENTS

"Allocution du Ministre Michel Colin de l'education Nationale du Gouvernement Central, Léopoldville, le 17/7/63."

Commission Constitutionnelle Gouvernementele, "Avante-projet provisoire remanié, Texte sans commentaire, Régime unitaire décentralisé." Léopoldville, no date.

Groupe de Jurisconsultes Constitutionnels, "Avant-projet de Constitution Fédérale, Mémoire Explicatif." Léopoldville, 1963.

Letter circulaire, signée par le Ministre, Michel Colin, du Ministere de l'Education Nationale du 13/7/63. Objet: Réforme de l'Enseignement secondaire. Résolution XI de la Deuxième Conférence des Responsables de l'education.

République du Congo, Gouvernement Central, Ministère de l'Education Nationale, 5ème Direction, "L'Education Nationale en 1962, Conjoncture et Problème." Léopoldville, April 1, 1963.

"Résolutions finales de la deuxième conférence des résponsables de l'Education réunie à Léopoldville du 8 au 9 avril 1963."

CORRESPONDENCE

Letter from Emory Ross, General Secretary, to member missions of Congo Protestant Council, April 21, 1931.

Letter from Emory Ross, General Secretary, to member missions of Congo Protestant Council, June 8, 1932.

Letter from H. Wakelin Coxhill, General Secretary of the Congo Protestant Council, to the Governor General of the Belgian Congo, July 6, 1935.

"Memorandum addressé à Son Excellence le Ministre des Colonies par le Conseil Protestant du Congo au Sujet de la Politique du Gouvernement Belge envers les Missions," February 14, 1933.

IV

CONGO—BRAZZAVILLE

GERARD LUCAS

Gerard Lucas is assistant professor at the Southern Illinois University School of Education and textbook advisor on the SIU/AID contract team attached to the Ministry of National Education, Republic of Mali. He was formerly an Associate of the Institute for Education in Africa, Teachers College, Columbia University. During nine years in Ethiopia he held successive posts as an elementary and secondary school teacher in a public school of Addis Ababa and as Administrative Assistant in charge of Foreign Personnel at the Ethiopian Ministry of Education and Fine Arts. As Research Assistant at Stanford University he spent the academic year 1961–62 doing field research in Paris and in Brazzaville, Republic of Congo, on which this chapter is based. He received his B.A. from the University of Ottawa, Canada, and his M.A. and doctorate from Stanford University.

All the Powers exercising rights of sovereignty or an influence over the said territories undertake to look after the preservation of the indigenous populations and the improvement of their moral and material ways of life and to contribute to the suppression of slavery and above all of the Slave Trade; they shall protect and assist regardless of nationality or cult all the religious, scientific, or charitable institutions and undertakings created or organized for those purposes or designed to educate the natives and to make them understand and appreciate the advantages of civilization.

The Christian missionaries, the scientists, the explorers, their escorts, belongings and collections shall also enjoy special protection.

Freedom of conscience and religious tolerance are expressly guaranteed to the natives as well as to the nationals and the foreigners. The free and public exercise of any cults, the right to erect religious buildings and to organize missions belonging to any cult shall be subject to no restriction nor hindrance.[1]

This declaration, signed in Paris on June 19, 1922, was a confirmation by the newly formed League of Nations of similar provisions already included in the General Act of the Berlin West African Conference of 1885 which resulted in the internationalization of the Congo Basin. It has significantly altered the religious missions in the territory concerned and considerably affected the quantity and the quality of the formal (European) education offered to the native inhabitants of the Congo Basin since 1885. Although historians may correctly claim that the provisions of these

<hr>

[1] *Congo Conference—Report of the Secretary of State* (Washington, D.C.: Government Printing Office, 1886). General Act of the Berlin West African Conference, Chapter I, Article 6, p. 394, entitled "Arrangements Concerning the Protection of Native Missionaries, and Travellers, as well as Religious Freedom." Translations throughout the chapter by the author.

two treaties have proved generally ineffectual, as far as the former French Congo is concerned, these international agreements constitute the basis for a claim to originality in church-state relations in colonial African education.

In 1883, the French Ministry of Navy and Colonies issued a decree concerning education in Gabon, formulating the cardinal rule of French educative action in Africa: "In the primary schools of Gabon, instruction must be given exclusively in the French language." [2] Soon after the signature of the General Act of Berlin, American Protestant missionaries established in Gabon protested that the French government's attempt to enforce this decree constituted a violation of the Berlin agreement. However, since Gabon lay outside the area defined as the "Congo Basin," the American missionaries' claim was rejected and their Protestant mission survived only because French Protestant missionaries of the "Mission Evangélique de Paris" were able to take the place of the Americans. The Roman Catholic missions in the same area did not suffer from any language handicap because they were run and mostly staffed by French missionaries from the start, and they flourished in competition with the "Mission Evangélique," sometimes encouraged and sometimes hampered by the French colonial administrators.

It was more than a quarter of a century before Protestant missionaries belonging to the Swedish Evangelical mission crossed the Congo River and moved from the Belgian to the French part of the Basin. But the Catholic missions, under the leadership of Bishop Carrie and of Father (later Bishop) Augouard, were established at the same time as French colonial rule. Indeed, they sometimes preceded effective French occupation. In 1883, for instance, Father Augouard, at the verbal request of Savorgnan de Brazza (a French Navy lieutenant in charge of an exploration mission in the Congo basin), traveled on foot from Loango[3] to the Stanley Pool, where Senegalese Sargent Malamine had been left by de Brazza in charge of guarding the French flag—and French "rights"—while de Brazza was rushing to Paris in order to obtain the ratification by the French Government of the treaty he had just signed with a Bateke chief, the Makoko. Upon arrival on the future site of Brazza-

---

[2] Decree No. 144, April 9, 1883, Article I.

[3] Loango is still a small village situated a few kilometers from Pointe-Noire, Republic of Congo.

ville, Father Augouard met with the hostile attitude of the local tribes who felt free to disregard the Makoko's instructions. Father Augouard prudently retreated some fifteen kilometers down the Congo River and established his first mission—and his first school —at Linzolo, among one of the friendlier Kongo tribes. This early example of church-state cooperation was repeated on numerous occasions whenever the two parties, for different reasons, had compatible aims. In most cases it will be very difficult to establish the historical facts, since discretion and even secrecy surrounded a relationship which neither party had any advantage to publicize. In the context of the fierce church-state struggle, which was intensified in France with the creation of the Third Republic and which culminated with the formal separation of church and state in 1905, no French politician or colonial administrator could afford the political risks involved in open cooperation with church missions.

In spite of such great risks, however, there can be no doubt that the French government and the Catholic Church did cooperate in many ways in the Congo. Jules Ferry, one of the most influential politicians in both the anticlerical and the pro-colonial actions of the Third French Republic, gave Father Augouard a ten-thousand-franc grant—out of secret state funds—for the purpose of establishing mission schools in the Congo. Savorgnan de Brazza, although not a fanatical anticlerical, was not a practicing Catholic. Yet, as mentioned above, he did not hesitate to request the help of the French Catholic missionaries in the interest of France. Later, as Commissioner General of the French Congo, de Brazza made an annual grant of between two thousand and four thousand francs out of his colonial budget to the Catholic missions. The following letter written by de Brazza to Bishop Carrie and dated January 11, 1888, is an example of such grants:

> . . . I am granting you for the year 1888 a subsidy of 2000 francs in favor of your establishment of Saint-Joseph of Lonzolo. Similar action will be taken in favor of any new foundations of this type where your efforts will be aimed at educating native children.[4]

At the same time, an additional grant was made to Father Augouard in support of his efforts to establish mission schools in

[4] This letter is part of a collection of "Documents and Testimonies" made available to the writer by His Excellency the Bishop of Pointe-Noire, Msgr. Fauret.

the area north of Brazzaville. The French government also contributed in various other ways to the development of French Catholic missions in the Congo. Free passage on French ships was on some occasions given to French priests and nuns; the parts of a river steamboat belonging to the Catholic missions were transported from France to the Stanley Pool with French government help. But when Bishop Augouard requested de Brazza's help in connection with the transport of a second steamboat, de Brazza refused and explained his decision in a letter to the Minister of Colonies. Mission boats, he contended, were being used by the missionaries for trips up the Congo and its tributaries during which numbers of young boy and girl slaves were purchased and brought back to mission stations. Although this was done with good intentions, de Brazza admitted, he feared that it was interpreted by the natives as a condonement of slave trading and he did not want the French flag to be associated with the practice in any way.

A few years later the steamboat, which the missionaries assembled and put in service anyway, proved very useful to the French government. The ill-fated Mission Marchand, in its mad rush toward the Nile River, was stranded at Bangui in desperate need of foods which the government lines could not supply. Bishop Augouard delayed a mission-founding trip to the interior and brought the necessary supplies at the request of the government. He bitterly complained later that his patriotic action was "repaid" by the local administration's withdrawal of promise of a land concession on the site of the very same mission which he planned to establish before coming to the rescue of the Marchand Expedition.

During the first twenty-five years of the Congo colony, numerous other instances of both clashes and cooperative actions could be cited. Only two others will be discussed because of their political implications as well as their relevance to education.

De Brazza, the great pacifist and humanitarian, intensely disliked the use of force[5] and preferred the art of persuasion—at which he was a master. When French penetration in Equatorial Africa met with the fierce resistance of Islamized populations, he conceived the plan of winning these populations over to the cause of France through diplomacy and education. In applying his policy,

[5] His tombstone bears the inscription: "Sa mémoire est pure de sang humain" (His memory is free of human blood).

he brought to the Congo four Algerian Moslem teachers trained in French "Madersas"[6] and tried to use them in the Upper Sangha area. For many reasons, this attempt was a fiasco: two of the teachers returned home, a third was drowned in a river accident, and the fate of the fourth is still undetermined. But mainly, during the late 1890's, de Brazza had been overtaken by events. The political and military requirements of the "Scramble for Africa" made de Brazza's time-consuming solutions seem quite inadequate. Hence the various French military expeditions that converged onto Lake Tchad, which they all reached in 1900. De Brazza's policy of conquest through education was criticized by Bishop Augouard on both political and religious grounds: it was a great mistake, he thought, to believe that Moslem teachers could serve the interests of France; and as a Catholic priest, he could not conceive of his country's official support of the Moslem faith. Besides, he remarked bitterly, this adventure cost the Treasury some 40,000 francs; that is, more than the subsidies the Catholic missions received toward the support of over six thousand Congolese pupils during the same period.

A few years later, when the Swedish Evangelical mission approached the French colonial authorities with a request for permission to establish a mission on French-ruled territory, a French official in Brazzaville informed the Catholic Bishop of Loango of the Swedes' intention and suggested that French Catholic missionaries establish a mission at once on the very site where the Swedes intended to move. Coming soon after the French government had closed down the religious orders' training centers in France, this request seemed more than ironical, as the Bishop of Loango pointedly remarked. Nevertheless, the bishop promised to do his patriotic duty and asked for financial support from the colony. The colonial administration did not actively pursue this line of action, and by 1909 the Swedish Evangelical mission had gained a solid foothold in the French Congo.

As stated above, the French authorities in the Congo Basin could not systematically prevent the missionaries from pursuing religious activities in the territory defined as the Conventional

---

[6] Named after the Arabic word for "school" and created by the French in North and West Africa for the purpose of gradually assimilating the Moslem populations.

Basin by the General Act of the Berlin West African Conference.
It is well known, however, that most French politicians in power
under the Third Republic were staunch secularists and wary of
organized religion. It follows that they considered highly desirable
the reduction of the missionaries' role to the minimum in French-
ruled territory. In the case of the Congo, international agreements
were added to political pressures from various sources to allow
missionary activities. Influenced by such diametrically opposed
forces, the French authorities could hardly adhere to a strict line
of action.

Given the necessity of admitting missionaries in the Congo,
however, the French authorities were not indifferent about what
groups of missionaries were involved and the exact nature of their
activities. And at all levels of administration there were many
opportunities for state intervention. It is obvious that the colonial
authorities were more tolerant toward French than toward "foreign" missionaries, who, at best, could only be indifferent to French
aims and objectives in the Congo. Missionaries coming from any
of the other major powers, such as Germany, Britain, or the United
States, would have been greatly handicapped if they had attempted
to move into the Congo. Even the Swedes were under suspicion; although no one could claim that they were furthering the political
aims of Sweden, it was repeatedly suggested that their Lutheran
connections linked them closely to Germany.[7]

It was one thing to allow religious missionary activity in the
French Congo; it was another to let French Catholics exercise a
virtual twenty-year monopoly over the education of the Congolese
Africans, and it was even more unlikely to let "foreign" missionaries engage in the same sensitive field of activity. For a nation that
took its *mission civilisatrice* so seriously, and for a government that
proclaimed the state's supreme rights and responsibilities in education, this situation can only be interpreted as an abdication—an
abdication which can be explained, if not excused, by two objectives which took priority over education during the twenty-five
years of French presence in the Congo.

Until the turn of the century, French efforts were focused on

[7] For example, see Bishop Augouard's letter to the French Minister of
Colonies (dated September 16, 1919). (Carbon copy in the archives of the Arch-
bishopric of Brazzaville.)

the military and political control of as extensive an area as possible in central Africa. At the same time, each new African colony was expected to contribute in large measure to the military and civil expenses its creation and maintenance entailed. Obviously, then much more than now, the Congo lacked the financial resources required to set up an adequate administrative machinery or to build up an economic "infrastructure," let alone to provide "social" services such as education and public health. Hence, the French government's tolerance and even halfhearted support of missionary educative action in the Congo.

Nevertheless, influential voices were raised in the early 1900's in favor of the active involvement of the French government in African education. Inspector General of Education Foncin urged the government to develop public school systems in all colonies.[8] True, Foncin was primarily concerned with providing public education to the children of the French colonists, but he did outline the role of the state in the education of the indigenous populations. It is significant, however, that he saw the state's role mainly as that of a model and a regulator of private (that is, mission) education. Foncin's scheme certainly influenced the creation of a public (that is, state) school system in French West Africa in 1903. Equatorial Africa, however, was farther removed from French preoccupations. But soon the "Congo scandal," originating in the Belgian Congo and also involving the French side of the river, shook French public opinion.

Savorgnan de Brazza, the popular humanitarian swept aside earlier but still highly respected by the French public, was asked to conduct a full investigation of the situation in equatorial Africa. It was also rumored that one of his specific assignments was to advise the government on the matter of public education in the Congo. De Brazza died during his trip back to France, before making a full personal report of his findings. But one of his assistants who was especially concerned with educational matters, Félicien Challaye, had a chance to express his views on the subject: "The State has done nothing to improve the intellectual and moral life of the natives. The only schools where the Blacks receive any sort of education and instruction in the French language belong

[8] See "De l'Enseignement aux Colonies" in *L'Année Coloniale* (Second year) (Paris: Librairie Charles Tallandier, 1900) .

to the Catholic and the Protestant (in Gabon) missions."[9] Mindful of the church-state controversy, Challaye hastened to add: "Missionary action does not present the same dangers in the Congo as in countries of ancient civilization (such as our Indo-China): here, the natives have no religion of their own, and they are too intellectually inferior ever to develop any fanaticism." Challaye did not, however, fail to point out that the mission schools, because of the very nature of their major objectives, lacked the means and the strong desire to pursue through formal education a more comprehensive range of political, social, and economic goals. In other words, he considered the missions to be valuable auxiliaries of the state whose educational functions the missions could not entirely fulfill.

The Catholic mission authorities did not agree with this last point. One of Bishop Augouard's assistants, Father Rémy, claimed that the state could most efficiently act at this time through the established mission school system, which, as he described it, closely followed the scheme outlined by Inspector General Foncin and recommended by Minister Clémentel. He emphasized one of the main features of the system, the *écoles de civilization*[10] or *écoles de premier contact,* which were in fact similar to mission outposts. Although not quite formal schools, these could, if spread widely in the colony with the moral and financial support of the civil authorities, establish European contact with the native population and prepare the ground for future systematic action. It should be noted that Father Rémy shrewdly refrained from flatly rejecting the state's claim to the direct provision and control of education. He tried instead to "buy time," pointing out that for the time being the state could do more at a lower cost by supporting an established system. On strictly monetary grounds, his position was impregnable. The dispute was, of course, a philosophical one: what the missions "could do" with state support did not correspond to the civil authorities' concept of the aims of public education. And so the Catholic missionaries' bid for preserving their monopoly over Congo education did not succeed.

[9] Félicien Challaye, *Le Congo français* (Paris: Cahiers de la Quinzaine [12ième cashier de la 7ième année], 1906), p. 93.

[10] See "Considérations générales sur l'établissement et la réglementation de l'instruction publique dans de Congo français," a typewritten report by Father Rémy, kept in the archives of the Archdiocese of Brazzaville.

French authorities, at last, paid attention to the school needs of the "Cinderella of French Colonies," as the Congo had come to be known. Following the administrative reorganization of the French colonial territories in central Africa and the creation of the federation of French Equatorial Africa (1910), a formal public school system was created by decree in 1911. The system consisted of primary, higher primary, and vocational schools. Since the system did not come into being physically for almost a decade, it is more important at this point to note the decree's omissions: 1) "secondary" education was not considered; [11] 2) private education was ignored; 3) no school inspection system was set up. One can legitimately claim that this 1911 decree *did not* mark the beginning of public education in the Congo; it merely laid down the legal framework without which no public school system could be built. Furthermore, the decree had a temporarily negative effect on the development of formal education in the Congo, since it failed to recognize the existence of the mission school system and thus prevented the local authorities from granting moral and financial support to the missionaries' efforts.

The tragic events of World War I may partly account for France's failure to implement the educational schemes planned for equatorial Africa: funds and personnel were obviously in shorter supply than ever. But the same events also brought about a re-examination of French intentions and policies regarding the Congolese. There appeared first a new determination to carry out development plans, and second, a recognition that the missionaries were a rich source of much-needed assistance which blind anticlericalism had up to now rejected or tolerated with reluctance. Now, two important decrees issued in 1917 and in 1921 showed that the French authorities had finally recognized that the missions were in the Congo to stay, and decided to channel their efforts in directions compatible with state goals. The first decree was aimed at insuring that missionary action would be French and Congolese: it ordered that all instructional materials used in Congo schools be printed either in French or in a dialect spoken in French Equatorial Africa; and that all school *moniteurs* be French subjects and speak French or one of the dialects spoken in French Equatorial

---

[11] The Catholic missions had provided this type of "classical" education from the beginning as a part of their course of training for African priests.

Africa. This first step was therefore intended to make sure that no educative action in the Congo would exert an anti-French, nor even a "non-French," influence. It was primarily directed at the Swedish Evangelical missionaries who were currently using in their schools textbooks written in dialects spoken in the Belgian Congo and *moniteurs* born and trained in that same territory, where their missions were concentrated. Thus the 1917 decree deprived the Swedish missionaries at once of their teaching tools and of their trained assistants. It would be almost ten years before the Swedish Evangelical mission regained its place in Congolese education.

The French authorities and the French Catholic missionaries benefited by regulations which forced the Swedish missionaries to undertake French-oriented action. Bishop Augouard seems to have had some influence in shaping the policy which led to the second decree, published on January 1, 1921. His 1919 letter to the French Minister of Colonies, as indicated above, helped attract the authorities' attention to the danger of letting "foreign" missionaries operate in the Congo. The decree, however, affected the Catholic missions as well as the Protestant, although the latter, because they were not French, were more seriously affected. Private education was at last officially recognized but subjected to specific regulations: 1) no schools for Africans could be opened in French Equatorial Africa without the authorization of the Governor General; 2) appointments and transfers of staff had to be reported to and approved by the administrative authorities; 3) the teaching of any language other than French was prohibited; and 4) all school textbooks had to be approved by the Administration. Two important distinctions were made between French and "foreign" applicants. The latter had to submit their applications *in person*, signing their request in the presence of the representative of a lieutenant governor. More important, whereas French applicants were not required to hold a certificate more advanced than the *Brevet Elémentaire* (approximately 10th grade), "foreign" applicants were required to hold a university degree whose equivalence to a French degree was to be assessed by the Governor General, and to demonstrate their knowledge of the French language. Such differential treatment was carried further by a decree published on January 15, 1921, which authorized subsidies to private schools *opened in the name of a Frenchman.*

It is probable that if the Swedish missionaries had chosen to protest strongly against these measures, the terms of the General Act of the Berlin West African Conference and those of the Treaty of Saint-Germain-en-Laye would have provided them with powerful arguments. But, as Bishop Augouard remarked, diplomats are adept at interpreting texts in their advantage.[12] In fact, the Swedish Evangelical mission decided to follow the new regulations, and in 1926, a first teaching certificate was granted to a Protestant Congolese. Ten years later, the Protestant school system had developed slowly but steadily to a point where it gained the acceptance and admiration of the French authorities.

Another consequence of the 1921 regulations must be mentioned here. From the time the missionaries engaged in Congolese education, no clear-cut distinction had been made between "catechism" schools and the more formal types of European schools. Some academic subjects—at a very elementary level—were taught in "catechism" schools, while religion studies often occupied an important place in the curriculum of the formal schools. Likewise in the area of language: elementary French was taught in "catechism" schools, while native languages were sometimes used in formal instruction. The 1921 regulations, in theory, forced the missionaries to establish a clear distinction between these two types of schools. For both Protestant and Catholic missionaries, such a distinction was a prerequisite to the State's recognition of their formal schools, and for the French Catholic missionaries, it meant small but welcome subsidies for state-recognized schools. In fact, few of these regulations were strictly enforced because school inspection was still left in the hands of colonial administrators who had neither the competence nor the time to exercise adequate inspection or supervision. Most of the period between the two world wars was occupied by the building of the Congo-Océan railroad, which absorbed most of the financial as well as the personnel resources of French Equatorial Africa. While the federal administration took the initial steps toward establishing the *Ecole Edouard-Renard,* a replica of the *Ecole William Ponty* of French West Africa, the main source of students for this school remained

[12] See above, Bishop Augouard's letter to the Minister of Colonies in which he attracts the government's attention to the threat to French aims that "foreign" Protestant missions constituted.

the slowly growing network of Catholic and Protestant primary schools.

1937 might have marked the "take-off" of public education in French Equatorial Africa. The federal administration, relieved of the burden which the building of the Congo-Océan had imposed upon it, turned to education in a real effort to build the public educational system, which up to that time had existed mainly on paper. The Governor General first appointed a young, energetic and competent director of education, then set up a new legal framework for education (which remained largely intact until 1961) and substantially increased budgetary expenditures earmarked for education. But once again, this burst of official activity in the field of public education was accompanied by a stiffening of the government's attitude toward mission schools. Although the new education decree[13] officially recognized private education, it spelled out in greater detail the content of education, made more explicit the rules and regulations governing both public and private school organizations, and made provisions for more thorough professional supervision and inspection of schools. It is at a rather informal level that the public versus private education struggle took place.

The struggle centered on the personality of the new director of education, whose anti-missions attitude had been developed during his years of training and experience within the public school system of France. He was convinced that Catholic education was miseducation and he gave little weight to the argument that French Catholic missionaries were making a contribution to the cause of France in Equatorial Africa. Indeed, on professional grounds, he was much more favorably impressed by the work of the Swedish Evangelical mission. He repeatedly commended the Protestant school authorities for their emphasis on quality rather than quantity. Even the effects of the Protestant mission's spending in the Congo were pointed out by the director of education as a contribution to the development of the colony's economy. At any rate, this new phase in church-state relations in the Congo might for the first time have resulted in the government's taking fuller responsibility in the field of education, with the missions relegated to a

---

[13] Decree No. 6 of January 2, 1937, *Journal Official de l'A.E.F.*, p. 134.

relatively unimportant role. But World War II soon upset all plans by completely altering the political, economic, and administrative position of the French colonies.

The early defeat of France and the establishment of the Vichy regime posed a serious dilemma to the French Catholic missionaries. One of Marshal Pétain's first actions under the Vichy regime was to close down the *Ecoles Normales Primaires*, the primary teacher-training schools which the Catholic Church considered fertile breeding grounds for anticlericals. If the Catholic missionaries throughout the French Empire had remained loyal to Vichy, the Church might have reaped important immediate benefits. But when the French African territories, following the lead of Governor Félix Eboué, rallied around the Free French flag of General De Gaulle, there is no evidence that the French Catholic missionaries in the Congo did not also transfer their loyalty to Free France. This proved to be a very wise choice. Félix Eboué was soon appointed by De Gaulle as Governor General of French Equatorial Africa and he made the development of education—in full partnership with the missionaries—the cornerstone of his "New Native Policy."

The task Governor Eboué assigned to education in the modernization of the Congo was as huge as it was urgent. He was not the first to recognize the size of the task, but he obviously felt a new sense of urgency and he realized that in the circumstances the state alone could not reach his educational goals. Although not a religious man himself, he nonetheless saw in the religious missions "the instrument in our hands: *all* the French schools in the colony."[14] By "French schools" Eboué apparently also meant Protestant Swedish schools, since it was during his term as Governor General of A.E.F. that Protestants began receiving subsidies from the colonial government. This new development reflected the success of the Swedish missionaries in their attempt to operate effectively in the Congo in spite of their delicate political position. It also served to demonstrate the sincerity of Eboué's desire to enlist the full cooperation of all existing agencies engaged in the educational enterprise.

Another practical step taken by the Eboué Administration had

[14] Félix Eboué, *La Nouvelle Politique Indigène* (Brazzaville: Imprimerie Officielle, 1945), p. 45.

far-reaching consequences for the development of mission schools in the Congo. Under the pressure of wartime conditions, Eboué relaxed an old regulation which insisted on the professional training of all *moniteurs* employed in mission schools: Eboué allowed untrained *moniteurs* to be used provided they did not constitute more than 10 per cent of a school's staff. For the missionaries this meant that a large number of classes officially unrecognized before —because they were taught by catechists untrained as regular teachers—became regular classes subsidized by the government. It opened a large source of inexpensive teacher supply while providing an increase in mission school subsidies. In practice, these advantages were compounded by the laxity of government inspection which allowed many mission schools to employ substantially more than 10 per cent untrained teachers. These developments enabled the missions to lay the foundations of the spectacular postwar expansion of their school systems. With embryonic schools already established in the remotest areas of the Congo, the missions needed only one more element to set off their large scale expansion, and this element F.I.D.E.S.[15] soon supplied: a relatively massive financial investment.

F.I.D.E.S. contributions in the early 1950's supported only half the cost of selected school building projects, and thus, theoretically, enabled the state to control the use of aid funds and to orient the development of private education along government-approved lines. In practice, F.I.D.E.S. funds freed equal amounts of mission funds for use in whatever way the missions chose. And the missions took full advantage of this opportunity to compete with one another and with the state in establishing primary schools in places which did not have them before. Another government regulation discouraged the establishment of a school where less than sixty school-age children could be found in a radius of five kilometers. In a sparsely populated country such as the Congo, the first agency to establish a school in a district was virtually assured of an educational monopoly. This built-in incentive for school expansion goes far to explain the rapid increase in school population which char-

[15] Under the terms of the *Fonds d'Investissement pour le Développement Economique et Social* (F.I.D.E.S.), France supplied funds from her budget, in the form of subsidies, for the development of French dependencies. Territories were also expected to make a contribution toward their development.

acterized educational development in the postwar period. But this incentive "rewarded" quantitative rather than qualitative development. It soon led to what the French authorities termed an "abnormal school situation" and set the stage for the last church-state controversy in the former French Congo.

The situation was considered abnormal mainly on two counts: 1) a disproportionately large percentage of the Congolese schoolchildren were enrolled in the lower grades and a very small number of pupils remained in school long enough to truly benefit from formal education—the few who completed their primary school and went on to some form of secondary education did not satisfy the trained manpower needs of the politically and economically developing Congo; 2) private education had been able to maintain and even to increase its quantitative lead over public education. Concern on the first count was widely shared among French and Congolese leaders; the partisans of public education were generally resigned to the idea of church-state coexistence in education, but they could not tolerate being in a minority position. The recognized need to "normalize" the Congolese school situation gave the opponents of private education the weapons they needed to carry out an effective anti-mission campaign.

The main factors which enabled the missions to increase their school enrollment after World War II have already been suggested. Briefly, they included: 1) a broad network of "religious schools" where some formal instruction was also provided; 2) the highly competitive situation in which the missionary groups and the states were placed partly as a result of official regulations; 3) some financial relief granted to missionaries through state subsidies; and 4) a temporary relaxation in the requirements for teacher qualifications. It is probable that these factors alone would not have made possible such a rapid expansion of the mission school systems. French officials were convinced that the missionaries were not following the school regulations issued by the government since 1919 and that there lay the key to their extraordinary rate of expansion.

In 1953, the colonial administration set up a three-man investigation committee whose real mission was to gather evidence in support of this contention. It was an easy assignment. The committee, led by an expert colonial administrator from Paris, included a French primary school inspector who had just earned an anti-mission reputation in Ubanghi-Shari.[16] As far as the Catholic missionaries were concerned, the mere presence of this gentleman on the committee precluded all chances of a fair and objective treatment of private education. In addition, the committee conducted its investigation during the long vacation, while the schools were closed, the staff was dispersed, and the school administrators were away on their holidays. Still, there is no doubt that the committee was able to collect more evidence than was needed.

The committee report[17] barely mentioned the public school system: indeed, the mission schools alone were under scrutiny. It started out by quoting various official regulations as they applied to the control and inspection of private schools in the Congo and went on to produce a long list of instances where the said regulations were being violated by the missionaries. The violations were presented under the following headings: Establishment of New Schools, Pupil Recruitment, Teacher Preparation, School Management and Inspection, Teaching Methods, and Curriculum. It was repeatedly suggested that these violations were at the root of the mission schools' "unexpected" rate of growth and explained why the public school system, hampered by its presumed adherence to regulations and standards, had been unable to keep up with the growth of private education. In conclusion, the committee report advanced a simple reasoning: the current "abnormal" school situation is caused by the anarchical growth of private education; this growth is made possible by the missionaries' almost complete disregard for existing official regulations which the government has the power and duty to enforce. Finally, the same regulations clearly prescribe adequate sanctions in case of violations. Therefore, let the sanctions be applied, let the regulations be respected, and solve the problem.

The missionaries, particularly those of the French Catholic missions, strongly protested against this treatment. Except in details, the missionaries did not challenge the validity of the committee's data. That so many regulations were being ignored was, in-

[16] Unofficial reports suggested somewhat illogically that this gentleman was a Free-Mason and a far-leftist, or a communist.

[17] "Coordination de l'Enseignement du premier degré au Moyen-Congo—Aperçu des conclusions de la mission d'inspection," a typewritten document dated 11/4/53/RB/DW. (Copy obtained by courtesy of Bishop Fauret of Pointe-Noire, Republic of Congo.)

deed, a matter of common knowledge. But, the missionaries claimed, the public school authorities were just as guilty in this respect as the private school authorities. One point, for example, concerned the fact that a high percentage of private school pupils were over-aged. True, said the missionaries, but the same conditions prevailed in the public schools, with the difference that the age of the mission school pupils was verified by certificates of baptism, while in the public schools pupils could conceal their true age by obtaining an official *jugement supplétif*.[81] Furthermore, the missionaries contended, the fundamental reason why the regulations were commonly violated and their sanctions not applied was that the regulations themselves were outdated and generally ill-adapted to the current conditions. The need for reforms, for more rational coordination of public and private efforts in Congolese education, was fully recognized by the missions, who were quite willing to cooperate with the government—as long as cooperation allowed the missions to continue to develop along lines generally acceptable to them.

"Cooperation" was also the policy adopted by the administration. New regulations tending to "normalize" the school situation were issued, but at the same time the Governor General, in a confidential letter to the territorial authorities, insisted that the regulations were to be applied in a spirit of cooperation. It is clear that the highest civil authorities did not subscribe to the idea that sound educational development in the Congo required confining the missions to a minor role under the strict control and without the help of the government. On the contrary, a sense of urgency prevailed and called for the coordination of all possible efforts toward the goals of universal literacy and adequate manpower training which the French government had finally adopted. This determination to abandon petty quarrels and to unite for the sake of a common task had its source in the French decision to speed up the political, social, and economic development of colonies within the framework of the postwar French Union. But high-level policies could easily have been thwarted by the inertia and even the active resistance of colonial administrators and settlers. Instead, the French-drafted timetable for ever greater measures of self-

---

[18] A "jugement supplétif," literally a suppletive decision regarding a date of birth, was obtained in a lower court on the basis of two witnesses' declaration.

government and eventual independence was considerably speeded up.

In the Congo, the emerging political élite was mainly responsible for this development. After 1946, these Congolese spokesmen, the majority of whom were mission-educated, used their purely deliberative powers fully and effectively to press for massive school development. They steadfastly refused to be involved in this *querelle d'importation,* as they called the church-state controversy. Their position was stated in succinct, simplified terms by Stéphane Tchichelle, a Grand Councilor who subsequently became Vice-President and Minister of Foreign Affairs of the Republic of Congo: ". . . the people of French Equatorial Africa favor the multiplicity of schools, whether denominational or public; in their view, education is education, whether private or public." [19] Thus was realized Félicien Challaye's 1905 prediction that Congolese would not become religious fanatics. Challaye based his prediction on the assumption that the Congolese were intellectually incapable of holding the strong convictions which presumably sustain fanaticism. In the 1950's the Congolese leaders indeed held strong convictions, but these rather concerned the belief that modern education was the key to the successful pursuit of the people's aspirations. [20]

The few French anticlericals in the Congo were probably resigned to the active presence of the missions in the field of formal education, but they strongly resented the leading position which the missions managed to maintain in relations with public education in spite of the fact that the latter received a much larger share of the public expenditures on education. The missions, of course, enjoyed independent revenues in addition to public subsidies, and their operating costs were also much lower than those of the public school system in most areas. European missionaries received no salary beyond subsistence expenses, enjoyed fewer home leaves, were satisfied with simpler quarters, etc. But the missions made even more substantial savings on the salaries they paid to their Congolese teachers, and at the same time created a most difficult

[19] Débats du Grand Conseil de l'Afrique Equatoriale Française, Session Originaire, 24 Avril 1950" (Brazzaville: Imprimerie Officielle, 1950), p. 114.

[20] This attitude has its drawbacks. It encourages the naïve belief that formal education, regardless of content, leads to desired goals.

problem for themselves. Low salaries complicated the missions' recruitment problem and made it hard for them to retain their competent and experienced Congolese teachers. The teachers who could qualify tended to transfer to the public schools; those who remained were less qualified and very dissatisfied.

The missions had a ready answer to their Congolese teachers' demands: "Government subsidies allocated to the missions are too meager to allow salary increases." This was a clear invitation to mission school teachers to lobby in favor of larger missions subsidies. The mission school teachers constituted one of the largest and most politically conscious group of Congolese *évolués*. Individually and through their professional organizations they were in a position to exert constant and heavy pressure on the Territorial Representatives and the Grand Councillors, who, in turn, pressed the administration to grant ever larger sums to the mission schools. Parents' associations also joined the campaign and achieved some degree of success which always fell far short of the private school teachers' demands. The administration, however, had a strong argument against this barrage of demands: the laws were such that the government had little or no control over the use which the missions made of government grants. The administration used complex formulae to arrive at the amount the various missions would receive annually for school construction, salary of personnel, school supplies, scholarships, etc., but once the lump sum was granted, the missions were only obligated to report on how and to what purposes the funds had been used. Thus, government subsidies increased in response to mission teachers' demands for higher salaries could be—and were—used to finance a further expansion of the private school system. This situation was improved to some degree in 1955 when the administration, following the expressed wish of the Territorial Representatives, obtained from mission authorities the written promise that a small additional grant would be applied to increases in Congolese teachers' pay. These measures were helpful but not completely satisfactory.

Pressures began building from all sides toward a "take-over" of the private school system by the government. Influential voices on opposite sides found it impossible to agree on this solution only because their interpretations of "take-over" differed radically. The missions, particularly the Catholic missions, understood that the government would take over all the costs of building and operating the private schools, but would leave the mission authorities in complete control of the same schools within some loosely defined educational policy lines. Their opponents rather favored what amounted to the "nationalization" of the mission school system. The former interpretation was in line with the centuries-old position of the Roman Catholic Church, a position which even the clergy admits is unacceptable to most modern states. The Salvation Army, third in importance among the missionary groups in the Congo, having very little to lose and much to gain, preferred the second interpretation. Indeed, the Salvation Army had less to fear from a nationalized, "neutral" school system than from a militant, largely Catholic mission school system. The Swedish Evangelical mission occupied a position somewhere in between: it was justly proud of its educational accomplishments in the Congo and interested in preserving them, but did not share the Catholic Church's basic opposition to the *école neutre*. Nationalization of the mission schools in the Congo, on the other hand, was virtually impossible to accomplish as long as the French government presided over the destinies of the Congo. It is probable that the solution adopted in France by the De Gaulle government, in 1959, would also have been applied to the Congo.[21] Indeed, a similar solution was adopted in the newly independent Congo under the leadership of the Congolese themselves.

The *Loi-cadre* of 1956 transferred the executive powers to a Congolese cabinet selected from among Territorial Assembly members. The Congo became an autonomous republic in August, 1958, and acceded to full independence in November, 1960, under the name of Republic of Congo (Brazzaville). While these great constitutional changes were taking place in rapid succession, no fundamental modifications were made in the educational system the French had brought to the Congo. Only changes in details had

---

[21] The law adopted by the French Assembly on December 31, 1959, offers three options to private schools: 1) *assimilation*—acceptance of total state control, in return for full financial support; 2) *association*—state control in some areas, in return for partial support, in accordance with the terms of a negotiated contract; 3) *simple contract*—conformance to limited state regulations, but little or no state support. Ministère de l'Education Nationale, Institut Pedagagique National, "Le mouvement éducatif en France pendant l'année scolaire 1959-1960." XXIIIe Conférence internationale sur l'Instruction publique.

been added through the years to the legal framework set up in 1937. A first attempt at adaptation was made in May, 1961, by the introduction of a new curriculum for primary grades. This was followed in September of the same year by the adoption of a new law organizing education in the Republic of Congo.[22]

As indicated above, the independent Congo adopted a school system very similar to the one the French had developed for themselves. Even modifications which the French brought to their own system after the Congo became autonomous were incorporated in the 1961 Congo education law. This remark is best illustrated by Title III of the law, which dealt with the status of private education. The private schools—formally recognized as part of the Congolese school system—were to be classified into one of three categories: 1) Assimilated Schools (*Etablissements assimilés*), 2) Subsidized Schools, and 3) "Free" Schools. Most of the mission schools existing in the Congo in 1961 were classified in the first category. This meant that for all practical purposes private schools became public schools staffed by missionaries or by teachers selected by missionaries, although the missions retained ownership and management of the physical plants. The schools of the second category enjoyed a little more freedom, but more limited financial support from the government; those of the third category were only subjected to a minimum of regulations, but enjoyed no financial support. Purely theological institutions belonged to this last category. It must be noted that the mission authorities themselves decided in what category each of their schools was to be classified and requested that the government approve their decision. Thus the missions voluntarily gave up some of their privileges in exchange for government financial support. Finally, the government made "assimilation" irresistibly attractive by offering to pay the full salary of all qualified private school teachers on the basis of the salary scale currently applied to public school teachers.

Congolese government spokesmen hailed this solution to the public versus private schools problem as the most just and reasonable one that any newly independent African country has adopted. They claimed that the mission school would be allowed to retain

---

[22] Cf. Law 44/61 published in the "Journal de l'Assemblée Nationale du Congo," Report of the September 28, 1961, Session (Brazzaville: Imprimerie Officielle, 1961).

its own personality. In the circumstances, the mission authorities generally agreed. It can be argued, however, that the Congolese "assimilation" of private schools amounts to outright nationalization, a solution adopted, for instance, by the neighboring Central African Republic. Indeed, "assimilated" private schools are subject to the same general regulations as the public schools, teach the same programs, and follow the same schedules. Private school authorities, however, still retain two opportunities to influence educational policy and practice in the Congo. Title II of the 1961 law created a Higher Council on Education and a number of School Boards in every *department*. But both types of bodies are purely advisory, and mission representatives are minority members of both. Also, Article 12 of Title III provided for the creation of private and public school "disciplinary commissions" designed to administer discipline and recommend promotions for teachers. This provision might have given the missions powerful means of controlling their Congolese staff and of greatly influencing the actual content of education through careful selection and direction of teachers. Now, a subsequent decree (issued May 16, 1962) set up a *single* disciplinary commission with authority over all teachers, public and private. Private education is represented on this commission by two members out of nine. Consequently, even a polygamous mission school teacher may continue to teach in a mission school if a majority of the disciplinary commission members approve of polygamy.

Private education in the Congo therefore enjoys a largely illusory freedom. The existence of private schools is formally recognized, but in substance the Congolese government exercises almost complete control over them. However, it appears that the Congolese government may have acted wisely in refraining from nationalizing the private school system. As long as the latter is not expected to move in radically new social and political directions, it may serve as an obedient and efficient instrument of national policy. At the same time, since the missions retained ownership of their schools, they are likely to continue contributing heavily to the construction and maintenance costs of the schools left under their direction. For the present, at least, the Congolese government would have little to gain and much to lose by depriving the private schools of their "own personality."

In conclusion, one can claim that the religious missions have played a major role in the development of formal education in the Congo. During the first fifty years of French presence in the area, the French government did not effectively fulfill its educative responsibilities, at time barely tolerating and at other times half-heartedly supporting missionary action, while insisting that this action be oriented in the directions of French cultural and political interests. The missionaries' willingness to cooperate with the French authorities—a willingness which came naturally to the French Catholic missionaries, but which political realities imposed upon the Swedish Evangelical missionaries—is the basic factor which made possible their educative action in the Congo beyond religious conversion. It must be recognized that, in spite of extremely difficult circumstances, the missions have provided directly more than half the educational opportunities of the Congolese, and indirectly enabled the civil authorities to develop in recent years a public school system second to none in Africa.

These accomplishments alone would entitle the Christian churches and their private school system to an important place in the present and future education schemes of the Congo. But, in the present political and cultural climate of emerging African nations, the church authorities are well-advised to look for other bases to justify their continued involvement of the education of African youth. Private education will have to be molded to suit the purposes of the emerging African nations. Judging from past performance, it is likely that the Christian churches will make the necessary adaptations—if given sufficient time.

Already, church hierarchies have been Africanized to a large degree. The Swedish Evangelical mission became the independent Evangelical Church of the Congo in July 1960, a few months before the Congo acceded to independence. A Congolese Catholic bishop, assistant to the French Archbishop of Brazzaville, was appointed about a year later. Congolese directors of education have also been appointed for Catholic and for Protestant mission schools. But these are merely superficial, structural changes. In most cases, the new Congolese appointees belong to the pre-independence generation. It is difficult to predict what their attitude will be under the pressures of the new generations who will wish to make profound changes in the actual content of education.

Since the adoption of the September, 1961, education law, the churches' influence in their own schools is entirely dependent on the work of the teachers which they prepared for their roles. A detailed study of these teachers' performances during the last few years could hardly lead to optimistic conclusions. Private education, in the immediate future, will provide the severest test of the quality of Christian missionary action in the Congo.

V

UGANDA

ROLAND HINDMARSH

Roland Hindmarsh is Director of Studies at the Bell School of Languages, Cambridge, and has been a staff writer with the Cambridge University Press, preparing English textbooks for secondary schools in Africa. From 1954 to 1960 he was Education Officer in Uganda and from 1961 to 1963 was an Inspector of Schools at the Central Inspectorate in Kampala. He is the author of UNDERSTAND AND WRITE *(a text for secondary entrance level in African schools), and his articles have appeared in* TRANSITION, MODERNA SPRÅK, USE OF ENGLISH, *and* UGANDA TEACHERS JOURNAL. *He received his B.A.Hon. and M.A.Hon. from Cambridge University,*

Introduction

There are four main phases in the contributions made by churches and the state to education in Uganda:

From 1875 to 1900 the churches provided religious instruction with some basic primary and technical education where possible. There was no secondary education, and teaching was irregularly given because of the disturbed state of the country. Some parts of Uganda did not go through this initial educational phase until after 1900.

Settled conditions were established in 1900 for most of the areas of Uganda. From then to 1925 the churches established regular primary education and founded some secondary schools for boys and girls.

Civil administration had grown slowly since its real beginnings at the turn of the century. In 1925 a Department of Education was set up. Its function was to coordinate the activities of the churches and to support them with what funds it possessed. Initiative still lay largely with the churches.

In the postwar years Uganda's economy improved greatly, and there was a large expansion in administration to provide improved services. The Department of Education began to found schools of its own at the secondary level, both grammar and technical. It became responsible for examinations and took control of most overseas recruitment. The churches have now lost most of the power and initiative they had earlier. Since independence in 1962, the feeling has grown among Ugandans that the schools are a national asset and that the churches should restrict themselves to matters of religion.

This essay attempts three things: first, to set out the historical background more fully; second, to describe the present educational situation in Uganda; third, to look some way into the future and assess probable trends.

Before beginning any of these, however, it is essential to give a brief factual orientation, by means of a brief discussion of some prominent features of the country today.

SOME PROMINENT FEATURES OF MODERN UGANDA

Uganda lies between and across two of the three main water courses that flow north to form the Nile. With so much water about, and with high mountains in the east, west, and southwest to catch the rain, few parts of Uganda are inadequately watered. The structure of the country is mostly that of an eroded plateau, with many swamps and some rivers in the valleys, formed long ago by erosion. The appearance of the country is green: a strong vegetation of tall grass with scattered bushes and trees covers the hill slopes, and becomes rather thinner toward the tops of the hills; in the valleys, strips of dense forest line the swamps, which are generally thickly set with clumps of papyrus.

The overall altitude is about four thousand feet, which keeps the average temperature within a range of from 85°F. (afternoon) to 60°F. (nights or cloudy days). The atmosphere tends to be humid, and strong winds blow only before and during a storm. Rainy and dry seasons are not sharply distinct; even at the height of the rainy season, it is unusual not to have several hours of bright sunshine, since most rainfall comes in heavy and very frequent thundershowers. The central area of Uganda, around Kampala, averages about 180 thunderstorms a year.

Cultivation is usually on the hill slopes, and the farms consist of small holdings of a very few acres, sometimes less than one, around or near a set of huts. The main food crops are plantains (bananas that do not turn sweet) in the southern half of the country and millet or other tropical grains in the northern half. The principal cash crops are coffee and cotton grown by the smallholder, with some sugarcane and tea on estates and tobacco in a few areas. Agriculture is the main occupation for well over 90 per cent of the working population.

Industry is still relatively undeveloped. Copper is mined in the west and smelted at Jinja; in this town textiles are also milled from Uganda cotton, and other industries have been set up. The industries draw their power from the nearby hydroelectric dam across the Nile, which supplies most of Uganda and some of Kenya with electricity. Rocks are crushed for cement at Tororo in the east and there are small mines in the southwest for wolfram, tin, beryl, and columbite.

Some seven million people live in Uganda, nearly all of them African. About eighty thousand are of Asian origin and about ten thousand are Europeans. The African population is made up of many tribes, only twenty of which each make up 1 per cent or more of the total. The twelve main tribes are the Baganda (16.2 per cent), Banyankore (8.1 per cent), Iteso (8.1 per cent), Basoga (7.8 per cent), Bakiga (7.1 per cent), Banyarwanda (5.9 per cent), Lango (5.6 per cent), Bagisu (5.1 per cent), Acholi (4.4 per cent), Lugbara (3.7 per cent), Batoro (3.3 per cent), and Banyoro (2.9 per cent).

Kampala (pop. *c.*172,000) is the capital and seat of the central government, which consists of a single elected house with a cabinet and ministerial system modeled on Westminster. This system is echoed to varying degrees in the governments of the four kingdoms within Uganda (Buganda, Bunyoro, Toro, and Ankole), and may be copied in other districts that aspire to the federal status that Buganda enjoys with the central government, or to the semi-federal status enjoyed by the other three kingdoms.

Central government revenue over the past ten years has varied between £20 million and £30 million, with expenditure usually making a deficit of a few million pounds. (Revenue and expenditure for local governments—kingdoms and districts—is very much lower; Buganda has rather less than £3 million and others considerably less.) About a quarter of the central government expenditure is on education and an eighth on medical services.

Ethnic groupings in Africa are often made principally on a linguistic basis, supported to some extent by anthropological and ethnological findings. Uganda has an exceptionally varied set of ethnic groups within her boundaries. The largest group speak Bantu languages and inhabit Buganda, Western Region, and much of the Eastern Region. In Teso and Karamoja live speakers of Nilo-Hamitic languages. In the north live Nilotic speakers, and in the northwest two Sudanic languages are spoken. These four groups seem to have no more in common with each other than have, say, French, Turkish, Polish, and Finnish. There is no *lingua franca* for Uganda, since Swahili has never won general acceptance as it has in Tanganyika and in some parts of Kenya. The national language of government and large-scale commerce is English. Local government is carried out in the dominant vernacular of the area, with some English where needed. Local trade is usually conducted in the various vernaculars, sometimes in a pidgin Swahili, and, among Asians, in Gujarati.

The Historical Background

It is incorrect to think of pre-European Uganda as an area without education. A system of education for boys and girls functioned within the structure of tribe, clan, and family and provided for spiritual, moral, mental, and practical needs. A good idea of what this was like, in another setting, may be obtained by reading Chinua Achebe's *Things Fall Apart,* a novel set in pre-European Nigeria.[1] In Uganda there would have been less emphasis on ritual and spirit worship than in Achebe's book, and the social code would, in the kingdoms, have reflected the hierarchical structure centered on the king, which appears to derive from the Egypt of the Pharaohs through the Meroitic kingdoms of the Sudan.

A fairly stable social structure existed in parts of Uganda for several centuries before the Europeans arrived. In the main this was due to the kingdoms set up by Hamitic invaders from the north between the thirteenth and seventeenth centuries in central and western Uganda and extending into what is now Rwanda, Burundi, and northwestern Tanganyika. In some cases the Hamites and the earlier inhabitants remained distinct as nomadic masters and agriculturalist serfs, as for example in Rwanda and Ankole; in others the distinction became blurred and virtually disappeared, as in Buganda. In the north and east, where Hamitic influence was slight or preceded the arrival of the tribes now there, the social structure is based on smaller units; tribes are often loose confederations of clans, some of which still tend to regard themselves

---

[1] New York: Ivan Obolensky, 1959.

as tribes in their own right. Authority rests in councils rather than individuals and hereditary rule is almost unknown.

Immigrants during these centuries appear to have reached Uganda principally from the north up the Nile, dividing at Lake Albert to follow the watercourse of the Victoria Nile by way of Lake Kyoga, or to carry on south along the edge of the Western Rift Valley toward Lakes Edward and George. Some immigrants also came from the northeast and possibly from the southwest. Archaeology so far suggests that few came from the Indian Ocean coast, although it is now considered likely that there was considerable contact between the coast and inland Kenya and Tanganyika, as well as north and south along the upland plateau.

In the middle of the nineteenth century, the situation in Uganda was broadly one of established kingdoms and societies in the south and west, with Bunyoro and Buganda the most powerful, and an increasing pressure of tribes moving into the northern parts. Arab traders from Zanzibar reached Buganda about this time and remained for eight years under Kabaka (King) Suna, who died in 1856. His successor, Mutesa I, received Speke and Burton in 1862 and Stanley thirteen years later. Egypt was by then extending her authority southward and had built forts on the Nile less than two hundred miles from Lake Victoria. It was mainly to obtain foreign support against this threat that Mutesa encouraged Stanley to write the letter appealing for missionaries to come to Buganda.

Stanley's letter of 1875 marks the beginning of modern education in Uganda. Two years later the first missionaries, sent by the Church Missionary Society in Britain, arrived, followed in 1879 by the White Fathers, a French Catholic missionary society. Instruction in religion, reading, writing, arithmetic, and simple handicrafts was given, but the missionaries' efforts were irregular. This was because Mutesa had misunderstood their intentions; he wanted them for political ends, and when he found they were unwilling to serve these, he periodically curtailed the freedom to teach which he originally appeared to have granted them. Things became much worse under his successor, Mwanga, who mounted the throne in 1884. Differences, too, among Catholics, Protestants, and Muslims led to open hostilities between these religious groups, and there followed a confused period of civil war, depositions, and factional fighting which made consistent teaching impossible.

In 1890 a combined group of Catholic and Protestants succeeded in reestablishing Mwanga, but with much reduced powers and with the real authority left in their own hands. During the following decade the Christian position was consolidated by the British under Lugard. Finally the Buganda Agreement of 1900, negotiated by Sir Harry Johnston, set the scene for the development of an established civil administration.

In the closing years of the nineteenth century the two main missions, Protestant and Catholic, had succeeded in establishing a regular system of religious and limited primary instruction in Buganda and in parts of the west, making wide use of Bâganda (natives of Buganda) who had been trained as catechists. The accent in this period lay on instruction in the faith and, especially with the Protestants, on literacy.

The period from 1900 to 1925 saw a very rapid expansion of education under the missions. In the closing years of the nineteenth century the Church Missionary Society (Anglican) had sent out three lady missionaries to establish the first schools, and had appointed a Mr. Hattersley to be an educational missionary. In 1901 Fr. Gaudibert was given responsibility for the development of education by the White Fathers, and in 1902 the first school intended to give limited secondary education was founded at Namilyango, near Kampala, by the Mill Hill Mission. In 1905 the C.M.S. established two secondary schools, one for boys (for the sons of chiefs) at Budo and one for girls at Gayaza. In the following year a second Catholic secondary school was begun at Rubaga, near the Cathedral; it was later moved out to Kisubi. All these schools were near Kampala. The following decade, 1911–1920, saw the spread of secondary schools to more outlying areas of Buganda, to Busoga, and elsewhere, though in the north and west of Uganda progress was much slower.

The curriculum followed in the early years at these schools should not be thought of in terms of a fixed academic discipline of modern content. Staffing was uncertain and pupil attendance often irregular. Equipment of all kinds was lamentably short. Without a talent for improvisation and a flexibility of program, no school could expect to function. But the hunger for education was enormous and pupils were devoted and grateful, even though family obligations and clan or tribal occasions might interrupt their attendance at the school. By 1903 the C.M.S. had 22,000 children at schools of all types. The rapid rise in numbers demanded an organization to handle them, and a C.M.S. Board of Education was set up in 1904, twenty years before any such body was contemplated by the civil administration of Uganda. Until 1925, education rested almost completely in the hands of the C.M.S. and Catholic missions, both administratively and professionally.

In 1925 the missions were providing education at various levels for about 157,000 children in Uganda. The size and importance of this undertaking forced the government to pay attention to it, and a report was drawn up on education in the Protectorate of Uganda under the auspices of the Phelps-Stokes Fund in 1925. It described its findings as follows:

> An educational system which branches out into the whole Protectorate has been brought into being by the missions in co-operation with the native chiefs, but without any supervision from the colonial government and, until recently, without any financial support.

In the same year, a Department of Education was set up and a director appointed. The total expenditure on education, which in 1923 had been less than £15,000, rose to £150,000 in 1939. (In 1962 it was over £5 million.) Also in 1925, a Central Advisory Council for African Education was constituted and district boards of education were set up. The beginnings of civil administration were laid, but for many years the staff of the Department of Education could not hope to be effective without relying heavily on the cooperation of the missions, with whom the main power really continued to lie until after the end of World War II.

During the twenties, the government had begun to take small initiatives; it set up a technical school on Makerere Hill in 1921, and a training college for teachers in 1927. (The first of these gradually shifted its emphasis until by 1938 it was concentrating on post-secondary academic courses, and moved out of government control in order to be able to serve as a higher college for other East African territories as well as Uganda.) The main interest of the civil administration, however, lay in keeping a smooth but effective working relationship between government and missions. This formed the principal term of reference of the Hilton-Young Commission in 1928 and, in a more practical sense, the aim of the Thomas Education Committee in 1940. The work of the latter resulted in six secondary schools and two teacher-training colleges becoming self-governing, with properly constituted boards of governors, in 1942. In the same year an Education Ordinance was promulgated, setting up Local Education Authorities to replace the district boards.

From the end of World War II to the present day, the main power in the field of education has moved away from the missions and into the hands of the civil administration. There has been a swift increase in government vision and planning; much bigger initiatives were taken than had been even considered earlier, and greatly enlarged funds were available to finance, and hence steer, educational development.

In 1946 the Worthington Development Plan based its scheme for future expansion on the number of teachers being produced by the training colleges and on an annual quota of extra teachers. In 1950 the experiment was introduced (to stay) of paying block grants to self-governing schools to cover the salaries of teaching and nonteaching staff, plus a sum to cover the annual cost of boarding each pupil in the school. In 1951, £572,000 was set aside for the improvement of buildings at post-primary schools and training colleges, many of which were in poor condition. The style and scope of this kind of government thinking contrast with the more modest aims of the Department of Education in the thirties, when the economic depression had made major forward planning impossible.

Following visits by Messrs. Weston and Ellis in 1947 and Dr. Harlow of the Colonial Office in 1951, an Advisory Council on Technical Education and Training was set up in 1952, and £2 million was set aside for the improvement of technical education. In 1952 the Binns report on the state of education in Uganda and the de Bunsen committee's recommendations for future organization and development were issued. The whole field of education was covered, and expansion and improvement were proposed for primary and secondary schools, for teacher-training colleges, and for the conditions of service of teachers at all levels. Almost all of the proposals were accepted in 1953, and £8 million were earmarked from the African Development Fund to effect the changes. This planning boom was helped by favorable world prices for cotton and coffee, Uganda's main cash crops, and by the dynamic attitude of the new governor, Sir Andrew Cohen.

The Department of Education was also taking specific initiatives in the educational field where missions were either not interested or had failed to find the resources to make a beginning. Kampala Technical Institute was expanded into an establishment of secondary and advanced level, giving instruction in over fifty different kinds of technical skills, with attendant academic courses required. Secondary grammar and technical schools were founded in districts inadequately provided for. A domestic science teacher-training college was set up; the training of teachers for junior secondary schools (years 7 and 8 in the educational ladder) was modernized and expanded. Secondary schools were begun for Asian pupils in towns where local initiative had been too weak to do so. A teacher-training college was built to serve schools under the Uganda Muslim Education Association, which had been set up in 1948.

One of the recommendations of the de Bunsen Committee in 1952 had been that responsibility for primary education be wholly devolved on Local Education Authorities. This was carried out during the subsequent years and the next process, the decentralization of authority over junior secondary schools, was begun by passing responsibility for this educational level to Buganda first, and later to other local educational authorities, giving them thus complete control outside syllabi, examinations, and the provisions of the Education Ordnance in force for the whole of Uganda.

The Present Educational Situation in Uganda

STRUCTURE

The broad outlines of Uganda's present educational structure are simple enough. There are virtually no nursery schools or kindergartens. Primary schools provide the first six years of the child's education, and junior secondary schools give a further two; these two types of school are being amalgamated to form a single seven-year primary course. Secondary education follows. This may be in a secondary school for up to four years; in a technical school for four years; or in a senior secondary school for either four or six years. The University of East Africa and Kampala Technical Institute take selected students for advanced courses after six years at a senior secondary school. Other courses of training, appropriate to the educational level reached, are open to students with four years of secondary education. Some of these forms of training are in industry and others in institutions run by ministries, for example in Health or Agriculture. Entry to a four-year teacher-training course is after eight (or seven) years of schooling; to a two-year course, after four years at a senior secondary school.

NUMBERS

The educational structure in Uganda therefore looks reasonable enough; it has a recognizably orthodox pattern, with sufficient variety to allow for the country's professional and technical needs, within the limits imposed by a developing economy still largely dependent on only two cash crops, coffee and cotton. In fact, however, the proportions within the structure are severely out of balance. Approximate figures show that, of 1,000 potential pupils for intake into the first class of primary school (P.1), only about 650 will actually join school. This figure is higher in some parts of Uganda, and very much lower in others; but a broad average shows that about 350 will not attend at all, at any rate at a school recognized and classified as primary, though a good many of them may go to unrecognized schools of a very low caliber.

Why does one child in three not attend a recognized primary school? Various factors are involved: the distance from school of the child's home; parental unwillingness to dispense with such aid as the children can give to the homestead in herding for boys and domestic duties for girls; lack of sufficient money to pay school fees. For the first two years of primary school, fees are usually ten shillings a year (about $1.40); they rise to twenty for the third and fourth years and to forty or more for the fifth and sixth years. Parents nowadays have a lively appreciation of the value of education for their children, although in the past parental indifference kept many children from school; in the more outlying areas it may still do so for girls, but in rapidly shrinking measure.

Of the 650 children that begin attending primary school, only about 350 reach the end of the six-year course. The causes for this alarmingly large dropout may again be distance (some children may have to walk ten miles to the nearest primary school); or money (the family may increase to the point where children have to attend school alternate years only, or leave halfway through to make way for a younger member); or disappointment with what the child is managing to learn (and in some primary schools progress is indeed slight). Children may also fail to complete six years simply because the school does not go beyond P.4 (though this is no longer common). The percentage of dropout is much higher among girls than among boys. This is because girls are increasingly useful in the home, especially in a country where aging sets in much earlier and where women not only look after the house but do most of the cultivation of the food crops; and also because children may sometimes not begin attending school until they are eight or nine, and are therefore, allowing for one or two years lost through non-attendance or repeating a class, fourteen or fifteen before the end of primary school—a nubile age for girls.

In the final term of P.6 every pupil sits the Primary Leaving Examination, but only 110 of the 350 qualify to enter junior secondary school. This proportion will increase with the amalgamation of junior secondary and primary schools to form a total of seven years of primary education, a trend which is already well developed in the Eastern Region of Uganda. A further, and even more drastic, selection at the end of junior secondary school cuts the 110 down to only about 30 students, who may then join senior secondary, technical, or modern courses; while a few more join primary teacher training colleges, a four-year course partly academic and partly professional.

Of the original 650, only 30 are therefore left to receive secondary education in the accepted sense of the term. Nearly all of these complete the course they have begun, but only about eight of them will be found suitable for the courses given during the last two years of the six-year senior secondary school, for which further selection takes place. Out of these eight, perhaps four go on to attend degree courses at universities.

The Government of Uganda is keenly aware of the narrowness

of the upper part of the educational pyramid. Following the Lewis recommendations,[2] the general development plan is to improve the quality of teaching but not greatly to increase the number of places available at the primary level; to integrate junior secondary schools into primary as fast as funds will permit, and to lay the principal emphasis on the expansion of secondary education until about four per cent of the intake potential at primary level gains entry into a secondary school of some kind. This may appear a humble enough aim, but its realization in a developing country makes very heavy demands on funds and on educated manpower.

AUTHORITY

Uganda is a unitary state with a semi-federal structure. The Kingdom of Buganda is in federal relationship with the central government of Uganda; the Kingdoms of Bunyoro, Toro, and Ankole are in semi-federal relationship; and the other districts are in relationships which in varying degrees and in a number of respects approach a semi-federal relationship. In the field of education the general policy is to decentralize control to district or kingdom level, and this has been done for all primary and junior secondary education. The control of secondary education has also, since 1963, been devolved on Buganda. As this process is currently going on, it is difficult to say how far the various spheres of educational administration are in fact being handled entirely by the kingdoms and districts; it is the practice of the central government to assist during the take-over period, first executively and later in an advisory capacity. In some cases, of course, this period is quite short, while in others it may be delayed by the lack of suitable personnel in a kingdom or district. The ultimate aim is the devolution of administration of all schools on the local authorities.

Overall control of the educational situation is retained by the central government through the Education Ordinances, the most recent of which was passed in 1959. These govern the responsibilities of kingdoms and districts and of all other bodies concerned with the administration of schools. Each secondary school is directly run by a board of governors, to whom the headmaster is

---

[2] W. Arthur Lewis, "Education and Economic Development." *Social and Economic Studies,* Vol 10. This paper was first read at the 1961 Washington Conference on *Economic Growth and Investment in Education.*

responsible for the general running of the school; the composition of the board is laid down in an ordinance drawing up rules for the boards of governors. The main ordinance also covers such matters as the recognition and classification of schools, which are the responsibility of the Central Inspectorate of the Ministry of Education at the secondary level, and of District Education Officers for primary and junior secondary schools.

A special feature of administrative control of education in Uganda is the part played by voluntary agencies. In Uganda, the main agencies are the Roman Catholic Church, the Church of Uganda (previously known as the Native Anglican Church and including the C.M.S.), and the Uganda Muslim Education Association. The first two of these are in fact responsible for having begun most primary schools, many junior secondary schools, and more than half of the senior secondary schools, as well as nearly all the primary teacher-training colleges in Uganda. It is therefore not surprising that the Government of Uganda in the past found it most convenient to exercise its authority through the agency of, and in collaboration with, the Christian and Muslim authorities. The Roman Catholic Church and the Church of Uganda each found it necessary to set up central and regional offices, and to appoint supervisors all over the country to ensure that teaching was being properly carried out and funds appropriately used. The functions and authority once exercised by these agencies are rapidly diminishing. In 1963 it was decided to abolish the post of mission school supervisor and to centralize development in Area Education Offices. Initiative, planning, and finance have passed almost completely into the hands of civil administration: the central government and the Local Education Authorities.

FINANCE

Almost the whole of capital development is financed by the central government, either directly or channeled through a Local Authority, a voluntary agency, or some other responsible body. The cost of providing new buildings and replacing old ones is very high indeed, even though less rigorous building standards may be adopted as a temporary measure in a country with such an equable climate as Uganda's. Help toward defraying the heavy expenditure has been obtained in the past from the African Development Fund and from Colonial Development and Welfare grants. Considerable support is now coming from AID for the secondary expansion program.

Recurrent expenditure falls under two main heads: salaries and maintenance. The central government pays the salaries of all teachers; this consumes more than half of the annual education budget of over £7.5 million recurrent expenditure, which with £1.6 million capital expenditure (1964 figures) makes the largest vote of any ministry in Uganda. Allowances for maintenance are calculated according to the number of pupils or students on each secondary school roll, and are given as capitation grants; for junior secondary schools and primary schools, block grants are given to each Local Authority in a proportion corresponding to the number of pupils it has under its charge. Block grants for *ad hoc* purposes are made from time to time to various responsible bodies.

Both the central government and the Local Education Authorities give scholarships and bursaries to deserving pupils; the central government restricts its aid to higher education, while the kingdoms and districts give help mainly at the junior secondary and senior secondary levels. Some junior secondary schools have boarding facilities, and a year's fees for boarding and tuition will amount to about 400 or 500 shillings (about $55 to $70), which is too much for very poor families to afford. Fees at secondary schools for boarding and tuition are between 600 and 750 shillings ($80 to $100). Most secondary schools are almost entirely boarding establishments, placed a few miles away from a nearby town; a small but increasing number of day schools exist, with correspondingly lower fees.

TYPES OF SCHOOL

There were in 1963 over 2,400 recognized and classified primary schools; over 400 junior secondary schools; 66 secondary schools; 5 secondary technical schools; 26 primary teacher-training colleges; 2 junior secondary teacher-training colleges; 1 technical institute giving courses at both secondary and post-secondary levels; and the University of East Africa with constituent colleges at Kampala, Nairobi, and Dar-es-Salaam. There are also 24 rural trade schools and 3 farm schools, none of which are as closely integrated in the general educational system as the preceding types.

Local Education Authorities are responsible administratively for all primary education, but nearly all primary schools are related to the voluntary agencies. In broad terms, about half of them are related to the Roman Catholic missions; some 40 per cent are related to the Church of Uganda; and the remaining 10 per cent are related to the Muslim Education Association or are under Local Education Authorities themselves. Most of the primary schools give the full six-year course, but in outlying areas a number still provide only the first four years of education. These schools are often situated near a church or chapel and come under the supervision of the parish priest or, increasingly, under a board of management.

In appearance, primary schools are usually one-story buildings with from two to four classrooms placed end to end. The walls are made of concrete, brick, or mud-and-wattle, with roofing in tiles, corrugated iron, or asbestos sheets. The doorways and window openings are sometimes fitted with doors and shutters, but these are often not provided, partly because they are expensive, but also because they can be stolen fairly easily. Wooden seats and writing benches are often fixed into the floor, which may be of concrete or merely beaten earth. Blackboards are usually walls treated with finer-textured concrete and painted over. Most classrooms do not possess a cupboard, since this is expensive and could also be stolen. Nearly every primary school has an office; this serves as a room for the headmaster, as a staff room, and as a school store. It is therefore equipped with a door that locks and with shutters and bolts. Many primary schools are without piped water, and very few can provide food of any kind. Proper playing grounds are seldom laid out, but most schools are set in sites spacious enough to allow for recreation, games, and physical education, though equipment for this is rudimentary.

The junior secondary schools are in general much better housed and equipped than the primary schools from which they draw their entrants. Brick and concrete are the usual building materials; doors and shutters are provided; the pupils sit on movable benches or at individual desks; classrooms usually have cupboards. Arrangements for boarding are sometimes made to accommodate pupils from greater distances, and dormitories, dining halls, and kitchens thus have to be provided, according to specifications laid down in the Education Ordinance. As the junior secondary classes form the avenue to secondary education, more money is available than in primary schools for their establishment and equipment, both through the LEA's and from the higher fees charged. This shows in the better all-round standard achieved during the two-year course and in the results of the examination at the end of the second year.

The senior secondary schools are in greatly varying stages of development. The longer-established schools have a two- or three-stream entry for the four-year course leading to School Certificate, followed in some cases by two-year courses in arts or science subjects up to the Higher School Certificate Exam, which marks University Entrance level. The student body at these schools may number three or four hundred boys or girls; schools are seldom mixed. There are laboratories and assembly halls; the dormitories are often arranged by houses on the English public school pattern; some 1,500 to 3,000 books are on the library shelves; playing fields are available; school societies are run. Recently founded senior secondary schools will be struggling to reach this condition, often under great difficulties. Funds may be short or their arrival delayed. Materials reach the school in fits and starts. Providing the range of subjects is often a severe strain on the resources of the staff of two, three, or four teachers that are appointed for the first year.

Technical schools, secondary modern schools, and teacher-training colleges vary even more than senior secondary schools in buildings and equipment. The technical schools have recently been reorganized and their resources concentrated; some older schools were closed down as uneconomic. Secondary modern education is holding its own, without much financial aid for capital development. Primary teacher-training colleges are in greatest need of modernization and re-equipment.

STAFFING

Primary schools are staffed mainly by two groups of teachers: those trained in the twenty-six primary teacher-training colleges (the usual method for the past eight or ten years), and those trained in the earlier vernacular teacher-training colleges, almost all of which have now disappeared. There is only a small percentage of untrained teachers in recognized primary schools in Uganda. The staffing ratio is one teacher per class (with average class size 34.7 pupils), plus the headmaster in some, but not most schools.   Staffing shortages are keenest in girls' schools. Another staffing difficulty is in providing enough teachers with a command of English sufficient to teach this language as a subject from P.3 to P.6.

Junior secondary schools are staffed either by teachers trained at junior secondary teacher-training colleges (the two main colleges are Kyambogo and Shimoni, both in Kampala) or by primary-trained teachers who have attended upgrading courses to fit them for junior secondary level teaching. The entry qualification for admission to the junior secondary teacher-training colleges is normally not lower than a School Certificate (twelve years of school); for the primary teacher-training colleges it is a fairly sound Junior Secondary Final Examination (eight years of school). Girls' junior secondary schools run by voluntary agencies sometimes have expatriate teachers on the staff because of the difficulty of keeping African women teachers on the staff. Single-stream junior secondary schools, having only two classes, find difficulty in covering the subjects adequately with only two teachers and a headmaster on the staff, especially when one of them may have to attend the meetings of an LEA committee held some distance away, or even be called to Kampala for in-service or refresher courses during term-time.

Senior secondary schools are mainly staffed by expatriates, often graduates sent under the Peace Corps or U.S.O. schemes. The training of African teachers for this level is carried out at the Faculty of Education in Makerere College, one of the constituent colleges of the University of East Africa. Two courses are given: a one-year course for graduates, and a two-year course for those who have completed the two final years of the six-year senior secondary school course but have not attended any part of a degree course. This latter type of training was temporarily taken over in 1963 by the Ministry. Applicants for these courses are still very few indeed, with a combined intake that varies from about fifteen to thirty a year; many of those who complete the course and take up teaching are soon offered wider prospects in administration, and are thus lost to teaching. It will be many years before senior secondary schools are mainly staffed by Africans, but some technical schools and many secondary modern schools have already reached this stage. Primary teacher-training colleges also have a majority of Africans on the staff, but not yet at the senior tutor level.

The principal examinations in the school system are at the end of each type of school course: the Primary Leaving Examination (after six years of school); the Junior Secondary Final Examination (after eight years). Both are set, administered, and marked by the Ministry of Education in Uganda, and will become one when primary education is extended to seven years. Further examinations are the London Chamber of Commerce examinations taken in secondary modern schools and in some senior secondary schools (after eleven or twelve years); the City and Guilds Examinations, taken in the technical schools (after twelve years); the School Certificate Examination (after twelve years); and the Higher School Certificate Examination (after fourteen years). All these examinations are set and marked in the United Kingdom, but administered by the local agent for the various examining bodies. The teacher-training college students take mainly practical examinations in the final year of their course; these are again internal to Uganda.

Curricula for primary and junior secondary schools are laid down by the Ministry of Education in printed looseleaf handbooks. The syllabi for each subject are at present under revision. At primary level the subjects taken are vernacular language, arithmetic, English, religious knowledge, geography, history, nature, singing, and physical education. In junior secondary schools the subjects are English, mathematics, geography, history, general science, religious knowledge, vernacular, music, art craft, and physical education. Junior secondary schools may also have organized out-of-class activities, especially soccer. The allocation of periods in junior secondary schools to the various subjects tends to reflect the subjects tested in the examination and the weighting given to them. English and mathematics are emphasized; geography, history, and general science, which have been combined in a new examination paper, will presumably be given more attention now than in the past.

The senior secondary schools themselves choose the subjects

that shall be studied, and no syllabi or curricula are laid down for them to follow; suggested syllabi are however drawn up for secondary modern schools in certain subjects—mainly maths and English—and for technical schools, while recommended (but not enforced) syllabi for certain subjects in primary teacher-training colleges are now under discussion. At senior secondary schools, English, mathematics, and science are always taught; the science may be general, or divided at some point in the student's school career into biology and physics-with-chemistry or physics and chemistry (taken separately); subjects nearly always taught are geography, history, religious knowledge or scripture; subjects sometimes taught are French, a vernacular language, art, music, physical education, craft, and health science. In the final two years of the six-year senior secondary school course, the subjects commonly taken are three of the following: English, history, geography, mathematics, physics, chemistry, and biology; some schools offer economics, applied maths, Bible knowledge, French, or art.

Present Issues and Future Trends

CHURCH AND STATE

The issue of church and state in the educational system of Uganda can only be understood in the wider social and political setting in which it belongs. The state of Uganda is a modern creation with boundaries drawn right through some tribes, bringing together other tribes which even now find it difficult to recognize any mutual affinity or even a community of interest. The Uganda government is therefore deeply concerned to give greater coherence to the state of Uganda by emphasizing the national character of all major assets and by eliminating factors of dissent within the nation as far as possible.

The inhabitants of Uganda are conscious of a continental sense of kinship with the peoples of other African countries; but this deeply felt sense of solidarity does not extend into the practical legislation of the individual state. There, separatist tendencies may still be strong, and the government must not insist on national unity so powerfully that regional or tribal loyalties feel trampled on. In Uganda, the Kingdom of Buganda has insisted on the continuation of its federal relationship with the central government which the British recognized. The other kingdoms have followed suit, and the districts, which a few years ago favored a strongly centralized government, are now more inclined to seek for themselves also semi-federal powers on the pattern of the lesser kingdoms. The political administration of Uganda may be described as increasingly federal, without having given up the claim to be a unitary state. The election in 1963 of the Kabaka (King) of Buganda as President of Uganda may mark the end of further federalizing tendencies for the present.

In the 1880's the central areas of Uganda were disorganized by a bitter and confused civil war among three factions: the Protestant, the Catholic, and the Muslim. Outbreaks of discord occurred well into the 1890's. Mutual suspicions were kept alive for many decades after that by dwelling on presumed past injustices and misinterpreting the background and motives of contemporary actions. When political parties were founded in the 1950's, groupings tended to follow a religious pattern, in that the Uganda People's Congress were mainly Church of Uganda (Protestant) while the Democratic Party were principally Catholic. Voting at local and national elections in some areas went strictly according to denominational allegiance. Both parties disclaimed the religious connection, and each had one or two leading members drawn from the other denomination. But the possibility of splitting the nation and risking civil disturbances between church groups remained.

In this danger, schools were indirectly involved. The Uganda People's Congress leaders came in a large part from leading Church of Uganda schools, especially King's College, Budo. Many Democratic Party leaders had gone to Kisubi and Namilyango, the corresponding Catholic senior secondary schools. Both political parties were, however, at one in wishing to strengthen the coherence of the whole country. The interests of the nation were paramount; religious differences must be minimized. An obvious way of doing this appeared to be to take schools out of the hands of the two main denominations. In advocating this measure, politicians were in fact only bringing towards its final stage a process which had begun in 1925, when district boards of education were set up under a Department of Education. Once civil administration had begun, it was always conceivable that the state would take increasing responsibility; and in the years since 1945, the trend had been strongly in the direction of more and more government control and initiative. Politicians have argued, not unreasonably, that schools in a newly independent, developing country are a national and not a denominational asset, whoever might have set them up in the first place. Furthermore, there were educational grounds for removing denominational bars; some children of Church of Uganda families living near a Catholic primary school might have to walk five or more miles to the nearest primary school of their denomination. On the way they might pass groups of Catholic children making the reverse journey. In other more outlying places, there might be a primary school for one denomination only; children of the other denomination would have to forego all their schooling, unless their parents moved to an area better served for them.

Interdenominationalism in schools has now been accepted as a principle in Uganda. In practice, however, tradition and parental desire tend to preserve denominational homogeneity in schools; the teaching of religion remains strictly denominational in schools still run by the churches. Pupils from the other church are few and have only come to that school for compelling reasons, and it will be a long time before real interdenominationalism is achieved in fact in the schools of Uganda. One of the main difficulties here is staffing. Every school staff should have something of a team spirit; one of the ways in which this can come about is through sharing common views and attitudes on spiritual and moral matters. This should not be so difficult among practising Christians, but enough antagonism and suspiciousness are still about to make cooperation in a denominational foundation uneasy. The ecumenical thinking of the last few years has had little effect on African Christendom. Even if an equal number of teachers from each denomination were appointed, the attempt to create nondenominationalism would have failed because the difference in religious allegiance would have been permanently underlined.

Nondenominationalism has always been one of the principles of schools founded by the central government or by Local Education Authorities. Here there is a better environment for breaking down interdenominational barriers. But it is ironic that, even here, suspicion has taken root. There are more Catholic secondary schools than Church of Uganda schools, even taken in proportion to the numbers in each denomination. Schools founded by the central government or LEA have therefore a higher proportion of Church of Uganda pupils, since they have been unable to find places in schools of their own denomination. This suggests to some suspicious minds that the schools were created out of national funds to favor the Protestants.

The secularization of education has been going on fairly gradually for some years; the machinery of educational administration used by the voluntary agencies was abolished in 1964, since its functions had progressively been taken over by the state. It is unlikely that any measures taken will be so radical as seriously to impair the educational efficiency of the schools. No one wants the system to collapse; no one wants to alienate the teachers, whose work is valued very highly. The schools must keep running, but they must not be so constituted or run that they perpetuate a division within the nation; they should on the contrary strengthen the unity of the country by means felt to be suitable, and without offending regional or district susceptibilities. To that degree, they will be forced to change.

In the churches, there is much recognition that this is a reasonable view. There even exists in the Church of Uganda, and to a lesser extent in the Catholic Church, a way of thinking that wishes to return to the purely evangelical function of Christianity in Africa. It suggests that the educational work undertaken by the missions was right in its context, but that modern conditions no longer require it. Much more important, it argues, is concentration on the Christianization of a society, which during nearly a century of missionary and Christian endeavour has become largely materialistic and is therefore still pagan, though changed.

THE HUNGER FOR EDUCATION

The three outstanding features of the educational situation in any African territory south of the Sahara are: the lack of money for capital development; the shortage and impermanence of staff; and the hunger for education. Western countries may also experience difficulties in financing and staffing institutions, but the shortages in Africa are very much more acute. The West has, moreover, nothing to compare with the intense drive toward educational achievement that is found in pupils and students throughout sub-Saharan Africa.

Most African countries have been able to provide primary school places for between one-third and two-thirds of any potential intake. School buildings may be poor, the classrooms ill-equipped, and a considerable proportion of the teachers untrained. Nevertheless, an African child stands a fairly reasonable chance of being able to get some primary education. Secondary education, on the other hand, is highly selective. In Uganda, only about thirty pupils from a potential intake of one thousand at primary entrance level reach secondary school proper. The pressure of pupils for admission to secondary courses is enormous, and it is well beyond the resources of any African country in money and personnel to provide buildings, equipment, and staff to satisfy this demand rapidly.

This situation led to the founding of a number of private secondary schools in Uganda. These claimed to offer secondary education up to School Certificate level, either with or without boarding facilities. A few did so reasonably satisfactorily, but almost all of these were associated with some wider organization, often a religious body. Some other private schools were making a genuine effort to substantiate their claims, under extremely difficult conditions. Yet other private schools were only ostensibly educational establishments; in fact they were businesses of a particularly objectional kind. They collected tuition fees of four or five hundred shillings from entrants and gave them intermittent tuition of very low caliber in overcrowded classrooms without proper equipment, seating, light, or ventilation. Boarding facilities, if they existed, were minimal: a roof, a bedframe, and a shelter for making food were probably all that the pupil received in return for an extra fee. Most of the fee money was pocketed by the school managers.

The government of Uganda was well aware of these schools and had already shut down some of the worst of them on hygienic or professional grounds before stricter legislation was introduced in 1963 to control private schools. In other countries in East and Central Africa much severer laws had been passed about private schools than in Uganda. The result was that Uganda had perhaps about one hundred of these schools, while the other countries in these regions had almost none. Young men, hungry for education, came from all over East Africa to try their luck at these private schools, about which they had heard—not read. They came up, too, from Zambia, Southern Rhodesia, Malawi, even as far away as Bechuanaland, a long journey by road and water. Even when they learned that the average success rate in the private schools in the School Certificate examination was forty-nine failures for every pass, they still came and paid. Even if the school did not improve its buildings, equipment or staffing, they still paid their fees—if they could find them—year after year. Even if the classes, in a smallish classroom, numbered from sixty to eighty pupils, even if only three out of every seven timetable lessons actually were taught, they still attended. The hope of success, however slender it might be, kept them there, intense, patient, dedicated.

AN AFRICAN ORIENTATION

Conferences on education in Africa (Addis Ababa, 1961; Tananarive, 1962) have emphasized the importance of reviewing syllabi at secondary, and more particularly at primary, levels and of recasting them where necessary to meet the child's needs in his physical and social situation. In Uganda panels were set up early in 1963 to do this.

It may appear peculiar that syllabi were not given an African orientation from the very outset. To some extent, of course, they were. The missions and, later, the government would indeed have preferred syllabi more closely tailored to the African environment. But under colonial rule, African leaders at all levels were deeply suspicious of government attempts at producing local variants. It was felt that the rulers might be trying to fob off some inferior version of the genuine European article on the African population, on the grounds that Africans were not fit for better. African insistence on getting the same treatment as was given to Englishmen or Frenchmen prevented syllabi from being realistic and effective. Now that African independence is largely accomplished, an African emphasis can be made without arousing any suspicions.

Drawing up new primary syllabi is of course only the first stage of a difficult operation. The materials for these new programs have to be planned and produced, and the money has to be found to furnish the schools with them. Planning the programs is in itself a pioneer operation in fields such as history, geography, and nature study. What, for example, would make an appropriate history

syllabus for a primary school child in Uganda? How far has historical research gone toward establishing facts of African history that
are of interest and relevance to the African student? In geography
and nature study the problem is mainly one of making an intelli-
gent selection, which helps the child onward into the world in that
kind of sequence that corresponds to his own growing areas of
awareness.

There is a great deal of exciting work to be done. But the
greatest problem of all in providing these programs has not yet
been mentioned. It is language.

THE LANGUAGE PROBLEM

In what language shall the new primary materials be written
up? Every African country faces problems here. The background
to the problem in Uganda is as follows:

There is no true *lingua franca*.

The African vernaculars belong to four major families, only
two of which are related in such a way that the average person can
recognize similar words here and there.

It would be impossible to foster any one of the African vernaculars as a *lingua franca* because of the privileged position the native
speakers of this vernacular would be put in, and because of the
consequent opposition of the other Africans in the country.

It is not possible to make a *lingua franca* of Swahili, as has
happened in Tanganyika, because antipathy to and contempt of
Swahili have been considerable in a large part of Uganda.

English serves as a *lingua franca* among educated adults and
to some extent adolescents at the secondary level. It is taught as a
subject in primary schools, usually from the third year, and does
not become the medium of instruction until the sixth year.

The choice of language for primary programs appears to be
between English and a number of African vernaculars. If English
is chosen, then the content of the programs is impoverished because the language learned at any given stage will not carry the
matter that would be relevant and interesting. If African vernaculars are chosen, a decision has to be made about which of the more
than thirty tribes shall have instructional material produced in its
own language. Uganda Radio broadcasts in about ten of the languages, and it is impossible to draw a line clearly and justly at any

point. Moreover the cost of producing school materials for small sections of the population will be very high. Many of the languages do not even have an agreed or consistent orthography, and the personnel to produce this would first have to be brought together and paid; most of them would in fact have to be trained before they could start work, and this would mean yet more expense and delay.

In Uganda, as in most other African countries, language is a national, political, and cultural issue. English is the official language. But African languages are, in a very living sense, the repositories and matrices of African culture. English is the language of power, of commerce, of educational achievement; but the African languages are the vehicles for immediacy, for deep feeling and conviction. At which values shall education aim: at the ability to grasp and handle the tool of intellectual and administrative power; or at the unfolding of the personality through an exploration of outer and inner experience? It is an agonizing choice. Already it is clear that the imagination of children begins to atrophy in primary schools because they are not given the tools of exploration in *either* their own language *or* English. It is a deadening that is tragic to watch.

THE EDUCATION COMMISSION 1963

A report was made in September, 1963, by a commission under the chairmanship of Professor Castle. It had very wide terms of reference, and as a result the main lines of educational planning may be described as: expansion of secondary education, involving the upgrading of many secondary modern schools into secondary schools; amalgamation of primary and junior secondary schools into a seven-year course; and improving the quality of primary education.

Bibliography

THE CHURCHES

Gale, H. P. *Uganda and the Mill Hill Fathers* (London: The Macmillan Co., 1959).
Matheson, Elizabeth. *An Enterprise so Perilous* (London: Mellifont, n.d.).

Oliver, Roland. *The Missionary Factor in East Africa* (London: Longmans, Green & Co., 1953).

Taylor, J. V. *Christianity and Politics in Africa* (London: Penguin Books, 1957).

HISTORY

Hollingsworth, L. W. *A Short History of the East Coast of Africa* (London: The Macmillan Co., 1949).

Ingham, K. *The Making of Modern Uganda* (London: Allen & Unwin, 1958).

Low, D. A. *Religion and Society in Buganda, 1875–1900* (Kampala: East African Institute of Social Research, 1956).

Oliver, R., and Mathew, G. *The History of East Africa,* I (London: Oxford University Press, 1963).

EDUCATION

Hunter, Guy. *Education for a Developing Region* (London: Allen & Unwin, 1963).

GENERAL

Colonial Office Reports, 1953, 1954, 1961.

VI

GHANA

NICHOLAS O. ANIM

Nicholas O. Anim has recently been appointed Head of the Department of Education and Assistant Dean in the University College at Cape Coast, Ghana, and was formerly Resident Tutor in charge of external examinations, Institute of Public Education, University of Ghana. He was educated in the Presbyterian Church of Ghana educational system. From 1948 to 1959 he taught in that system. In 1960 he joined the staff of the University of Ghana's Institute of Education, where he was executive secretary. He received his B.A. from the University of London and his M.A. from Claremont Graduate School. He is presently completing his doctorate at Teachers College, Columbia University.

Introduction

Harry Belshaw, in an article on "Religious Education in the Gold Coast" (Ghana), summarized the reasons which took men from Europe to this West African country in the crisp phrase "Gold, Government and God."[1] This may be in certain respects an oversimplification, but it expresses a triumvirate of interests without which much of colonial West African history becomes unintelligible. One takes for granted that missionary participation has been an essential ingredient in the whole colonial movement in Africa. One sees everywhere in colonial and former colonial Africa a strong stamp of the missionary effort not only on the churches, which are the logical outgrowth of such missionary activity, but on almost every aspect of essential social services. Today the people most actively involved in politics and in the day-to-day chores of nation-building are the first to acknowledge the part that the Christian churches have played in helping Ghana's drive toward independence. In a recorded address to the Philadelphia Fellowship Commission in 1952, Dr. Kwame Nkrumah, then President of Ghana, said:

I should like to take this opportunity to tell you that I am far from losing sight of the spiritual upheaval which exists in Africa today. So many changes are occurring in the lives of these communities, that we welcome the part which Christian Missions have played and are continuing to play in providing moral and ethical foundations for our new society.[2]

[1] Harry Belshaw, "Religious Education in the Gold Coast," *International Review of Missions*, XXXIV (July, 1945), 267.
[2] Christian Council, *Prelude to Ghana: The Churches' Part* (Edinburgh: Edinburgh House Press, 1957), p. 1.

The missions and the churches in their turn have received their share of criticism in various aspects of Ghanaian life; but the sheer weight of the history behind missionary activities in Ghana, as also in other new nations of Africa, does lend much strength to the words of Dr. Nkrumah quoted above.

A Brief Historical Survey of the Missionary Effort in Ghana

While the history of Ghana as a British colony dates from the middle of the nineteenth century, the country's contact with European powers goes much further back than that. The first European settlement on the coast of Ghana was established on January 20, 1482, by the Portuguese, although there is evidence that they must have first come to the area at least ten years earlier. This first European settlement is described as follows:

> They reached La Mina on the 19th January 1482. On the following morning they suspended the banner of Portugal from the bough of a lofty tree, at the foot of which they erected an altar, and the whole company assisted at the first mass that was celebrated in Guinea, and prayed for the conversion of the natives from idolatry, and the perpetual prosperity of the Church which they intended to erect on the spot.[3]

These Portuguese built the Fort Sao Jorge, which marked the beginning of a number of such forts and castles along the coast of Ghana that served as trading posts and centers of influence of their European owners. Each trading post—fort and castle—had a governor and a chaplain who seems to have been second in precedence only to the governor. These chaplains, as one would expect, established and officiated at the churches attached to the trading posts for the benefit of the European occupants; they also established schools for the children born to the European traders and their Ghanaian wives, but these schools were conducted only in the castles. Christian influence, which at first was meant only for the benefit of European traders in the castles, did spread somewhat, though only to such areas as were within the immediate influence and protection of the trading posts. Thus began a dialogue between the church and the government, at this time the government of the castles. This liaison continued to develop throughout the

---

[3] Quoted in *ibid.*, p. 3.

entire colonial era in Ghana; indeed, so close was the relationship in the early days that we find the following comment in the eighteenth century, written by a European employee in a castle:

We are very religious; we are obliged to go to Church every day, on forfeiture of twenty-five Styvers, except on Sundays and Thursdays, when the forfeiture for ommission is doubled: But I know you will reply, this is a forced service of God, and consequently not always accompanied with the most sincere intentions: And to confess the Truth it is not much better; for were not the restraint laid upon us, some would rather pay a visit elsewhere than to the Church.[4]

Under these conditions it is probably little wonder that the church did not flourish much in these early efforts on the coast outside the castles and forts.

The church in the older European settlements in the central coastal province of the country, around Elmina, fared no better than in the later settlements to the southeast. The Danes who built and settled at the Christiansborg Castle in the Accra area also had a church and school to take care of their castle community. Through the Governor's influence the Moravian Brethren sent the first Protestant missionaries to the country in 1737, but a very high mortality rate caused this venture to be abandoned in 1773.

Two missionary thrusts in Ghana in the early years of the nineteenth century had a more lasting influence on the country than earlier missionary attempts. They began with the sending of Thomas Thompson as missionary and chaplain by the Society for the Propagation of the Gospel to Cape Coast. Thompson came at the request of the Royal African Company of Merchants stationed at Cape Coast, and throughout his work "to make a trial with the Natives and see what Hopes there would be of introducing among them the Christian Religion"[5] he had ample support from the governor of the castle. His salary of £70 ($196) was made up to £120 ($366) in goods by the governor.

In the five years from 1752, when Thomas Thompson arrived, until his death, he established a school, and although he did not get any outstanding success in this venture, he managed to send three of his pupils to England for further training. Only one of

4 *Ibid.*
5 *Ibid.*

these survived; this one, Philip Quaque by name, was eventually ordained and became Thompson's successor in 1766. For fifty years after this date Philip Quaque was the missionary, school-teacher, and chaplain at Cape Coast. The school he built became the foundation for the strong educational complex that has been characteristic of Cape Coast through the years.

The second important Protestant thrust came in 1828, when the Basel Mission that had been invited through the Danish Governor of the Christiansborg Castle at Accra arrived to begin work along the eastern coasts of Ghana, taking the place of the Moravian Brethren mentioned earlier. The early Basel missionaries fared no better than the Moravians, but a change of base from the coast to the high and climatically more congenial mountains of the Akwapim ridge helped to arrest the trend toward a high mortality rate. The work of the Basel missionaries seems to have been more thorough than other attempts before them. In their educational work, for instance, they included industrial training as well as agricultural training. In order to facilitate the training of their converts, they created Christian villages alongside the original villages. Here the people erected their own churches, schools, and other community structures. This policy of segregating Christian from non-Christian has been one of the most criticized aspects of the Basel Mission venture.

In 1834 the Wesleyan Methodist Missionary Society began its missionary work in Cape Coast through Joseph Dunwell, sent to the Cape Coast Castle as chaplain, missionary, and teacher. But within six months he died. He was followed in 1838 by Thomas Birch Freeman, who became one of the best-known missionaries to West Africa. Freeman was, among other things, an ambassador of the British Wesleyan Methodists to the King of Ashanti; and his account of his first encounter with this king of the most powerful kingdom in the interior of Ghana has become a classic. The Methodist Church started in earnest in Ghana with the arrival of Freeman.

The Roman Catholic Church, whose chaplains accompanied the first European settlers in Ghana, is today the leading single church in size, with activities spread all over the country. Together with the Presbyterian Church of Ghana, the Methodist Church, and the Anglican Church—which had its early beginnings in the

Society for the Propagation of the Gospel—the Roman Catholic Church remains in the forefront of Ghanaian Christian life today.

Early Church and Education in Ghana
Before British Colonial Rule

The churches in Ghana, as in Europe, have had a long association with education in the country as has been hinted above. Contrary to the idea that the early European traders in the country paid no attention to schools—a view which was shared by the first Educationists Committee of 1920—the Portuguese did in fact have a school. King Joao III of Portugal, in his instructions to the governor of the fort of Sao Jorge and the city of Edina, said:

> Take special care to command that the sons of the Negroes living in the village learn how to read and write, how to sing and pray while ministering in church, and [how to carry out] all other duties connected with divine services. It is my wish that those priests who have the office of vicar and chaplains of the church there should take charge of these matters. Or, if they cannot, then some other person who may be better qualified for the task, one of those mentioned above, whom the captain should assign for the task.[6]

To insure that these instructions were in fact carried out, the king instructed that the master at the school should be paid two justos (a piece of gold weighing 121 grains) per pupil taught at the school, up to fifteen pupils. He also instructed that the captain or governor of Sao Jorge should be paid the same amount per pupil taught, and also one additional justo per convert. Thus the captain was made at one and the same time the custodian of the church and of the school.

Wiltgen also mentions that although this venture under King Joao's instructions did not last very long, the Portuguese seem to have sent some of the local children to Portugal for further studies to qualify as teachers.

These early efforts in education never had a lasting influence on the educational system of Ghana beyond pointing toward the close association between church and education. As pointed out

---

[6] Ralph M. Wiltgen, *Gold Coast Mission History: 1471–1880* (Techny, Ill.: Divine Word Publications, 1956), p. 16.

by Belshaw, the first school of the type we know today was established by "the Governor, his Council and the other Gentlemen on the Establishment"[7] of the Royal African Company of Merchants in Cape Coast Castle in 1788. The main object of this school, as has been pointed out elsewhere in this account, was "the welfare of the children belonging to the servants of the Committee"[8] of the Company of Merchants. The school was run by the chaplain of the castle and was financed by the Company of Merchants. A subsidiary source of income was a fine of seven shillings and sixpence per head levied on every officer in the company for "avoidable non-attendance at Divine Service."[9] This then was the pattern in the educational structure which remained very characteristic of the entire Ghanaian educational system: government sponsorship, church administration, joint finance of schools by the government and the church.

The Content of Education Under Early Missionary Influence

The one field in which the influence of the church became very outstanding was in the actual content of the education program. King Joao's instructions to the captain or Governor of the Fort in Edina in 1529, quoted above, included recommendations on the education of the sons of the local people. How much of this program was in fact put into effect has never been certain, especially as some of the pupils seem to have been sent later to Portugal to learn reading, writing, and, of all things, Portuguese etiquette. It is safe to assume, as Wiltgen does, that the textbooks used were those used in Portugal at the time, heavily geared towards religious teaching. The grammar of Joao Barros, published in 1539, is mentioned by Wiltgen as one such example of textbook series that must have been used in this period; it had for its reading lessons texts from the "commandments of God and the Church, a treatise on the Mass and also some prayers."[10]

Schools that followed in the wake of these early attempts had the same source—the church—to look to for textbook material.

---

[7] Belshaw, *op. cit.*, p. 267.
[8] *Ibid.*, p. 268.
[9] *Ibid.*
[10] Wiltgen, *op. cit.*, p. 16.

Even in the early merchant schools in which the chaplain played such an important role, each pupil who left the school was given a Bible, a fact which was to have a very vital influence on education in the early development of schools in the Cape Coast area. This town was then the center of European influence in the country, and for a considerable time Cape Coast was the capital city of Ghana. A letter written about 1841 gives the following account:

> Some of these lads prized the scriptures and diligently searched them. . . . From the scriptures they became thoroughly convinced of sin. . . . They resolved to make known the state of their minds to a serious Scotch merchant, William Topp. He advised them to meet once a week for the purpose of reading the Scriptures and prayer, and call themselves a "Society for Promoting Scripture Knowledge." They drew up for themselves a code of laws and they combined to meet together once a week. . . . This was the year 1831 and they continued these weekly meetings for 2 years. In the year 1833 the Barque Congo arrived at Cape Coast Castle from Bristol, commanded by Captain Potter, a member of the Wesleyan Society. The young men asked him if he had any Bibles for sale. The captain was much surprised at this request for Bibles. . . . He asked them if they would like to have a missionary to preach to them the Gospel of Christ. . . . They answered in the affirmative. . . . [11]

From this encounter began the work of the Wesleyan Methodist Missionary Society, which sent Joseph Dunwell to Cape Coast in 1834. He revived the school, which had had little help since the death of Philip Quaque in 1815, and the school he helped to establish became the basis for the Methodist Church's school system in the country.

This account dramatizes the part that religious training must have had in the early schools; the heavy religious bias in education was not just a reflection of the missionary influence alone, for the merchant governments and the colonial governments after them encouraged it as well. As has already been pointed out, the early merchants in the eighteenth century were fined for not attending church, and presumably they considered religious teaching in the school a vital affair. The British colonial government did indeed consider this so vital that religious teaching became part of the colonial educational policy in tropical Africa. A British Govern-

[11] *Ibid.*

ment White Paper on Education in Tropical Africa at the turn of
the century states:

> Since contact with civilization—and even education itself—must nec-
> essarily tend to weaken tribal authority and the sanctions of existing
> beliefs, and in the view of the all pervading belief in supernatural which
> affects the whole of the life of the African, it is essential that what is good
> in the old beliefs and sanctions should be strengthened and what is de-
> fective should be replaced. The greatest importance therefore must be
> attached to the religious teaching and moral instruction.[12]

This policy seems to have been taken seriously at least in
Ghana; for at about the same time as the policy was outlined, Governor Guggisberg had presented his "sixteen principles" of education in Ghana. Two of the principles stated that:

> Character training must take an important place in education.
> Religious teaching should form part of school life.[13]

It may be mentioned here that an educational commission financed
by the Phelps-Stokes Fund had a significant influence on educational planning for Ghana and other African countries at this
time. The commission also influenced the strong link between
education and moral and religious training. With all this background of strong religious education, it is not surprising that in
1942, almost twenty years after Guggisberg's sixteen principles
were outlined, a Ghana Government's Committee on Education
came out with the following statement:

> The Gold Coast people and Government have in the past recognized
> this truth [i.e., the relation between education and religion] by support-
> ing a Christian ideal and way of education. With all the more confidence
> therefore do we state our belief that the essential purpose of education
> is to open to all the citizens of a country a life which is rooted in the un-
> seen and eternal realities, from which all the potentialities of the chil-
> dren will draw the means of growth.[14]

[12] Secretary of State's Advisory Committee on Education, *Memorandum on
Education in British Tropical Africa,* quoted in Belshaw, *op. cit.,* p. 271.
 [13] Sir Gordon Guggisberg, *Sixteen Principles,* quoted in H. O. A. McWilliam, *The Development of Education in Ghana* (London: Longmans, 1959),
p. 53.
 [14] Gold Coast Government Committee on Education Policy, quoted in Belshaw, *op. cit.,* p. 271.

It is with this background that one must view the fact that the first lesson in many primary schools in Ghana is religious instruction.

The Church, the Government, and Education
Under British Colonial Rule

The emphasis on education which has characterized this discussion is merely an indication that nowhere else does the dialogue among the church, the government, and the people become more apparent than in the field of education. Such educational statistics as may be available show a bottleneck in institutions beyond the primary school level, particularly acute at the teacher-training level on which one would expect the entire educational program to be hinged. The following figures taken from the 1920's are representative of the educational climate of the times:

Government and Assisted Schools Enrollment and Grants[15]

YEAR	ENROLLMENT	GRANT-IN-AID
1925	29,573	£24,300 4s 6d.
1926	29,332	£32,225 2s 2d.
1927	29,640	£69,738 14s 6d.

The figures given above indicate the assistance the government was giving to the schools; it was more than doubled in 1927 because of a government change in policy. The number of pupils listed under "enrollment" does not in any way indicate the total number of children at school in the whole country. The schools represented in these figures are those that the government was aiding by direct grants. The missions also operated a number of schools which were not considered efficient enough to receive government grants.

The following table shows the number of schools on the government's assisted schools list. The list also shows the predomin-

15 Government of the Gold Coast, *Report on the Education Department for the period April 1927–March 1928* (Accra: Government Printing Office, 1928), pp. 8 and 9.

ance of the mission schools over the government schools; in fact, at this stage in the educational development of Ghana, there were three classes of schools: government schools, government-assisted schools, and other schools (often mission, occasionally private or native authority controlled).

Government and Assisted Schools in Ghana (Gold Coast)[16]

	1925	1926	1927
A.M.E. Zion	7	7	7
English Church	6	6	7
Ewe Presbyterian	22	31	36
Roman Catholic Mission	29	29	32
Presbyterian Mission	98	96	99
Wesleyan Mission	47	48	49
Undenominational	1	1	1
Secondary	2	2	2
Mohammedan	—	1	1
Total Assisted Schools	212	221	234
Government Schools	17	17	18
TOTAL	229	238	252

In the figures given above, the predominance of the mission educational institutions is impressive. It gives one the feeling that the government had relegated almost the entire problem of the education of the young to the care and direction of the missions. It must be remembered that there were a number of schools established by the missions that were not considered adequate to be included on this list. For all the schools listed above, and for the total enrollment of 29,640 in 1927, there were only three teacher-training colleges for men, and practically none as such for women. The Roman Catholics ran a teacher-training venture of sorts at the School of Our Lady of the Apostles at Cape Coast, where a meager band of twelve teachers were turned out each year. The three major teacher-training institutions and their annual intake are listed below:

16 *Ibid.,* p. 10.

Enrollment at Teacher-Training Colleges 1927[17]

	1ST YR.	2ND YR.	3RD YR.	4TH YR.	TOTAL
Akropong (Presby.)	50	45	53	47	195
Wesley College	32	32	29	24	117
Achimota	30	30	26	48	134

On the basis of the figures given above, an average of 36 teachers per college, or 112 for the whole country, were turned out each year. This was indeed a very poor reflection on the educational system of the time, considering the fact that there were many more children attending other schools not listed in the figures given for total enrollment shown above. One cannot lay the blame for this gap in the educational set-up to the management of the mission educational units alone; but since the missions were controlling the majority of educational institutions in the country, one would have thought that the problem of teacher training would receive greater attention under their direction than it appears to have done. The problem of finance was often the sore point with mission educational programs; but since the relationship between the missions and the government was extremely cordial at most times, and the missions were on most advisory councils in education, one finds it hard to exonerate them completely from blame in this situation.

Perhaps linked with the above is the general and greater problem of the missions' answers to the question of higher education. The problem of higher education took a decisive turn for the better at the insistence of Brig. General Sir Gordon Guggisberg, Governor of Ghana from 1919 to 1927. The missions were faced with a number of problems in this regard. First of all, the problem of finance was often very severe in higher education, as at other levels. It was fairly easy to get the local churches to build chapels and support an evangelist. Both chapel and evangelist were recruited into the educational organization on weekdays, and then turned over to the service of the church at the appropriate times. Thus a dual purpose was achieved on the single financial outlay.

[17] *Ibid.*, p. 12.

The same thing could not be done for higher institutions. There was also the problem of staffing higher institutions once they were set up; there were not enough African-trained personnel, and missionary teachers of the right type were not easy to come by.

The problem of higher education was at the same time further complicated by the fact that both the missions and the government were insisting on "character training"—a fact that tended to have a highly restrictive influence on educational planning. In his review of events following World War I, Governor Guggisberg gave the following reason why more was not being done for education in Ghana at the time:

> Delay is not due to financial stringency. The stumbling-block to greater education is the lack of sufficient African teachers with the necessary educational attainments and qualities of character that are necessary for the efficient training of both the youth and the young manhood of this country.[18]

Without discussing the very obvious questions in this type of argument, one may rightly take issue with the implementation of the "character training aspect" of the entire educational program under Guggisberg. All higher institutions beyond the primary school were to be residential. The financial burden that this places on the education budget is tremendous. Furthermore, under this residential system, only a comparatively small number of students could be taken care of at any one time. In many instances, there were no facilities for part-time students or students who could arrange their own accommodation. The figures given above for the enrollment of the three teacher-training institutions reflects the small capacity of these residential institutions.

In spite of these problems, it does not seem that in the problem of teacher training the missions should have had much of a financial problem. Apparently the government was very ready to give assistance. But the shortage of teachers was the greatest educational set-back of this period, and the paucity of operations at this level of higher education is the tragic hallmark of the educational activities then.

[18] Sir Gordon Guggisberg, "The Post-War Gold Coast: A review of events of 1923, with a statement showing the policy adopted by the Government for the progress of the people and the situation with regard to trade and finance," in *Report on the Education Department . . .*, p. 62.

As pointed out before, the most important figure in higher education in the 1920's was Governor Guggisberg. The development projects he initiated were based primarily on the improvement of education, which he called the keystone of the nation's development. In a Founder's Day address in 1945, the headmaster of Achimota School made the following statement:

> On the Gold Coast there stand three perennial—one might almost say imperishable—monuments to the memory of Sir Gordon Guggisberg; the African Hospital at Korle Bu, the deep-water harbour at Takoradi and the Prince of Wales College, at Achimota.[19]

One might point out here that although Guggisberg emphasized health, transportation, and agriculture, he considered progress in these and in all other fields of development to be dependent on education. In his review of the events of 1923, the governor pointed out that education was the keystone of the "edifice forming Government's main policy." He warned the legislature that he would be asking for increased appropriations to the value of £10-£15 thousand per year. In 1923 therefore he budgeted £120,000 for education alone, exclusive of buildings in the school program. This amount represented an increase of £14,000 over the previous year's budget for education. In this review he stressed that all other projects that he had proposed—in health, transportation, and agriculture—depended on education. His immediate proposal was the founding of Achimota College—an institution which, he said, was destined to be the "greatest institution for the higher education of the native races of Africa."[20]

Perhaps Guggisberg's success in the field of education is due to his clear and undistorted idea of the problems facing education of the time. On the immediate educational needs of the country he had this to say in his review of the year's events:

> It is obvious that the first step to be taken is to raise the educational standard of the African teachers for the Primary schools. Our present supply comes from Government Training College and similar seminaries conducted by the Scottish and Wesleyan Missions. All of these have one serious defect; the students are chiefly drawn from the primary schools;

---

[19] H. C. Neil, "Brigadier General Sir Gordon Guggisberg K.C.M.G. Founder of Achimota College" (Achimota, 1945), p. 1.

[20] *Report on the Education Department* . . . , p. 61.

they are taught to be teachers without having the necessary foundation
of education. . . . The system is rotten at the core.[21]

Continuing in this vein he suggested that what the educational
system really needed was an institution at which the future teachers
could obtain a higher education themselves before actually learning to teach; he pointed out that there could be no doubt that the
university was the eventual solution, but at the same time he acknowledged and worked on the principle that one would have to
start at the secondary school level.

Sir Gordon Guggisberg was a civil servant committed to seeing
the job well done by attacking it at the root. It is important to
note that he was by profession a surveyor and had, prior to becoming the Governor of Ghana (Gold Coast), been in charge of the
pioneer survey of the entire country. He therefore had adequate knowledge of the special problems which the country faced
in transport, health, and education. As he went through the for-
ests and savanna countryside in his preliminary survey work, he
encountered grave problems of transportation while at the same
time noticing the agricultural and other resources of the country
as a whole.

In the field of education, Guggisberg did not merely limit his
activities to building an educational system that was relevant to
the literacy needs of the time. His ideas about the type of educational system that he believed in were clearly spelled out in his
development program. In fact, one might almost say that it was
the type of education he believed in that made him trust education as the solution to the country's problems. On the nature of
education, he said:

> The Government does not consider that A-B-C is the beginning and
> end of education. While arranging for a progressive system of primary,
> secondary, and university literary education, the Government's pro-
> gramme includes first and foremost, the formation of character.[22]

Again, in referring to education as the keystone to the nation's
development, he said:

> We may dilate on the fact that the keystone of Progress is education;
> but all that will be idle rhetoric if we mix the materials of the keystone

21 *Ibid.,* p. 63.
22 *Ibid.,* p. 62.

badly. Leave character training out of our education system and the progress of the African races will inevitably become a series of stumbles and
falls that will leave a permanent mark on them, if it does not stop their
advance altogether.[23]

Guggisberg suggested no specific syllabus, but he contended that
the system adopted should graft the virtues of perseverance, thor-
oughness, order, cleanliness, punctuality, thrift, temperance, self-
control, obedience, honesty, respect for parents, and an appreciation of responsibility.

At the time Guggisberg was putting forward these ideas, education was primarily in the hands of two agencies: the missions
and the government, in that order of importance. Provisions for
higher education were meager in the extreme, and such educational facilities as existed succeeded in making the people barely
literate clerks. Guggisberg was outstanding in putting forward
far-reaching projects which were aimed not merely at making
people literate, but at training leadership among the Africans.

One factor which is very obvious in the church-government-
education triangle is the fact mentioned before that there existed
at most times a very close liaison working in this system. Even
where an important personality like Guggisberg seized the initiative from the missions in the field of higher education, his hold
was only temporary, and complementary to the ideals of the
church. At no point did he work in direct opposition to the missions, nor did he fail to stand by the Mission Educational Units
when government backing was needed. In the committees in
which plans on education were initiated and discussed, mission
and church representatives played a leading role. This role has
since diminished considerably in independent Ghana, as interest
in education has spread out to involve many more than purely
mission interests.

Guggisberg's achievement in education was a remarkable feat
in the context of a colonial government. It is an example of what
a strong personality working with the strong arm of the government was able to achieve in a colonial setting. But placed side by
side with the achievements of the present government of the new
nation of Ghana, Guggisberg's program in education seems rather

23 Neil, *op. cit.,* p. 3.

meager. All the development in education over a century of colonial rule, aided by missionary advice and philanthropic ventures, suffer considerably in comparison to the achievement in education in only a decade of self-rule in Ghana.

The suspended development plan of Ghana (1963–64 to 1969–70) recognizes education as the foundation on which industry and agriculture must be built. By development in these three areas the standard of living in the country can finally be raised. Indeed, spectacular progress has already been made. In 1952, free primary education came into being; since then education facilities in the country have so rapidly expanded that it has been possible for the government to introduce compulsory primary education.

With the change from colonial administration to self-government the person-to-person missionary approach on which educational opportunities were initiated, with its great emphasis on character-building, is giving way to a mass approach. In this mass approach the emphasis is on the development of manpower. Given this change in orientation, education now falls directly under the category of "economic development." Like all the other fields of rapid development, therefore, education is experiencing the heavy effect of the "bulldozer" approach: a massive development on all fronts at the same time. This situation is common to most of the new nations and areas of rapid development. No wonder, therefore, that a report on higher education in Nigeria is entitled "Investment in Education"; and it is not by accident that in the seven-year development plan of Ghana mentioned above, education is discussed under the general heading of "manpower development."

Under this seven-year development program, a total capital of £64 million was allocated for the development of educational services. It was hoped that through the expenditure of this sum and correspondingly heavier amounts on the recurrent costs of running the educational system, the country would be able to produce over 750,000 new workers with at least eight years of formal schooling, and another 110,000 with formal schooling beyond the elementary level. The present numbers are 35,000 and 5,930 respectively. Although this seven-year development plan is currently suspended for revision, there is every reason to believe that the demands on formal education will be substantially as indicated.

With the great increase in the pace of education, other concerns have developed in the field. The pattern of education itself has been undergoing considerable change: there is a definite effort being made to cut out wastage in school years. In the context of economic development, the government views education in two aspects: first, as a means of productivity, the people ought to be made receptive to new ideas; secondly, education should teach the population the specific skills needed to produce the goods and services required by the economy. The educational developments projected under the 1963-64 seven-year development plan aim at exactly these two phases—especially the teaching of the skills needed to run a modern economy. Thus while the mission educational schemes and those of the former colonial government aimed primarily at character training, any programs under the new government of necessity have to add attainment of skills that will fit the individual into the rapid development of the nation. A modern labor force is being built up for the rapid expansion in agriculture, industry, and other sectors of the economy in which revolutionary developments are envisaged.

It would appear from the above that in the field of education and allied concerns, the mission pattern has been seriously affected. Most people on the scene are willing to acknowledge the help that missions have given to a newly developing country such as Ghana. In an era in which unbridled exploitation was the order of the day, the missions were the only institutions that came with a primary concern for the African. Little though their contributions to the material progress of the African nations may seem in retrospect, it is evident that in some instances what the missions did contribute was the only educational foundation that some of the new nations have to build on today.

In the face of the present rate of development in Ghana, it must be emphasized that, in retrospect, the missionary effort in the field of education and essential services lose considerably in proportion and effectiveness. In a paper submitted for a seminar for Mission Board Executives,[24] David Apter has stated that the missions themselves are as monopolistic as is nationalism. Both demand total adherence of their followers. The ultimate goal of

[24] David E. Apter, "A Critique of Missions," in Federated Theological Faculty, University of Chicago, *Changing Africa and the Christian Dynamic* (Chicago: University of Chicago Press, 1960) , p. 3.

the missions is salvation, and perhaps at this stage in African development it would be expedient to turn over to African governments the nonreligious functions of the missions and transform the missions themselves into churches. This process has already taken place in many instances in Ghana and in other parts of Africa.

The Church and the Problem of African Culture

One of the most significant things that has happened to Africa within the past century has been the cultural penetration of the continent by the Western nations, in which Christianity was an active participant. Christianity never moves without a cultural cradle; and the Western cultural cradle in which it came to Africa was all the more closely associated with Christianity since the Western culture was distinctively different from the African culture. In fact, to many an African at the turn of this century, the vestments of Western culture became synonymous with Christianity. In a 1959 article in the *Christian Century,* the following statement appeared: "In its cultural wrappings Western 'packaged Christianity' has almost concealed the gospel of Jesus."[25]

The African convert came from a culture that had its own religious beliefs and customs; in accepting Christianity, therefore, there was a meeting of two religions and at the same time a meeting of two cultures. The African in becoming a convert was expected to break through the encrustation of his culture as well as that of the culture of the Western missionary in order to arrive at the core of the Christian faith. Often, however, he remained deeply rooted in his own culture and, in attempting to absorb the Christian faith, became entangled in the outer trappings of Western culture. He was therefore caught in two worlds; his own cultural and religious heritage and that of the Western missionaries. He did not quite leave the one and did not quite apprehend the other. The following quotation from the *Christian Century* is significant:

Many mission workers lack understanding of the African peoples— their clan relationships, their tribal organizations, their primitive cul-

25 Levinus K. Painter, "To Sit Where Kenyans Sit." *Christian Century,* LXXVI (November, 1959), 1336.

ture, their moral codes and their social restraints. Too frequently the first action of these well-meaning newcomers is figuratively to sweep clean the African hut of all primitive practices regardless of their worth to people living under long established cultures. As a result in many cases new and sometimes vicious customs take over before Christian moral standards can take root.[26]

The obvious problem here is: how does one make African Christians and not Western Christians of Africans? In an article on "African Culture and Christianity," Kwesi Dickson describes the Akan custom of pouring libation as a way of achieving a sacramental communion with the ancestors and thus a way of maintaining filial ties with the dead. Akan Christians do not find their participation in these rites a hindrance to their Christian faith; it is just part of their heritage, part of their life as Africans. They are in this rite realizing themselves by strengthening their ties with the dead of the tribe. To the Akan Christian, therefore, by thus clinging to what helps him to realize his identity as an African, he is giving of himself in fullness to the God he has come to accept in Christianity. The missionary has not of course been very sympathetic in these matters.

This clash of cultures, which the missionary came to realize was one of his most difficult fields of confrontation, was carried over into the educational system. In the content of education, therefore, one finds a predominance of subjects dealing with the western heritage and culture. It has been noted that the early Portuguese, who made the earliest efforts at imparting the Western type of education, included in their instructions "Portuguese Etiquette." One wonders what use this might have been in Ghana of the eighteenth century; but considered as a means of cultural penetration, it becomes understandable.

This may be an extreme example; but until very recently the history studied in Ghanaian schools was the history of the United Kingdom. Education as such was based mostly on the pattern that obtained in the metropolitan countries of the powers who governed the colonies in Africa. Since the missions were primarily responsible for education in the colonies, they became also indirectly responsible for advancing the culture of the metropolitan

[26] *Ibid.*, p. 1337.

powers. Their lack of understanding of the African culture caused them to give comparatively little attention to the subject in the education of the African youth. In many instances, matters concerning African culture were definitely discouraged in the school system. African music, for instance, received little encouragement in the churches, and for a considerable time the hymns sung at some African village churches were from English hymnals without even the veneer of translation into the local vernacular. Writing on this topic, John Wilson states:

> How powerful, all-embracing, and all-pervasive was the influence of the West in the cultural context was little realized either by the West European countries concerned or by Africa. Nor, despite much good intention, has it been thoroughly understood by the international organizations, and nations who, since the Second World War, have turned growing attention and effort toward African development.[27]

It is not by coincidence that the government gave particular encouragement to the establishment of an Institute of African Studies in the University of Ghana and took special interest in the progress of this institute. Since independence became a real factor in Africa, studies that have been made of education on the continent have all emphasized the need for special studies of African culture. A Commission on University Education appointed by the government of Ghana in 1960 stated the objectives of a university in Ghana to be among other things:

> To equip students with an understanding of the contemporary world and, within this framework, of African civilisations, their histories, institutions, and ideas.
>
> To undertake research in all fields with which the teaching staff is concerned, but with emphasis where possible on problems—historical, social, economic, scientific, technical, linguistic—which arise out of the needs and experience of the peoples of Ghana and other African states.[28]

A similar report on Nigerian higher education came out with an equally significant recognition of the need for African studies. On this issue the reports states that:

[27] John Wilson, *Education and Changing West African Culture* (New York: Teachers College Press, Teachers College, Columbia University, 1963), p. 2.
[28] Ghana Ministry of Education, *Report of the Commission on University Education, December 1960–January 1961* (Accra, 1961), p. 11.

The most obvious need for innovation in Nigerian universities is in the field of African studies. . . . The future of Nigeria is bound up with the future of Africa; and Nigeria's past lies in African history and folklore and language. It should be a first duty of Nigerian universities, therefore, to foster the study of African history and antiquities, its languages, its societies, its rocks and soils and vegetation and animal life.[29]

Perhaps the most significant emphasis in the development of African studies came from the UNESCO report on the development of higher education in Africa. In this report, special emphasis was centered on the adaptation of the curriculum to African needs and the African cultural inheritance.

In all the studies and reports that have appeared on the question of education in Africa, the need for a curriculum that is Africa-oriented has been of primary concern. There is a three-fold approach in this field. The recommendations center on, first, research into the African cultural past; secondly, study of the African scene and programs of the present; and finally, application of these studies to African aspirations and plans for a greater future.

Such preoccupation with African culture was certainly not a feature of the educational programs in the period of mission education. The objective was different; as has been mentioned before, the missions were concerned with salvation, and they were probably too ready to dismiss items in African culture as a great risk in their mission of salvation. This, however, has been one of the points of attack in the period of development of nationalism in the new nations. The criticism is that the missions used education and the Western culture in an attempt to deface the African personality; and the charge is often heard that the missions and the colonial powers were in fact complementary to each other—a charge which cannot be dismissed lightly. On the whole, however, the recent surge of nationalism has not tried to fight the missions as such; where necessary, nationalism has bypassed the missions and the church. Where the church has accepted the recent political change with grace and has operated in the context of the changes, there has so far been cooperation and mutual respect. The stand of the Ghana government is discussed below; one may only add here that the time will soon arrive when the

[29] Federal Ministry of Education, *Investment in Education* (Lagos, 1960), p. 23.

government will be called upon to assume total control of the entire educational fabric of the country.

The Church, Independence, and Education

With the achievement of independence in Ghana, one might expect that certain changes in the educational program would be effected to accord with the rapidly changing social situation. The government of independent Ghana has naturally taken a neutral stand in religion, since there are different religions represented in the country. This government cannot therefore in fairness come out strongly in support of any one religious persuasion as the colonial government before it had done. This neutral attitude is reflected in today's educational organization, although it is not so apparent at present in the southern part of the country, where church-related schools have been in the majority for a long time. With the increasing number of local council schools both in the south and in the northern part of the country, the government stand on religious education will become much more obvious.

The neutral stand on matters of religion taken by the new Ghana government does not, however, express itself against religious instruction of any sort in the schools. It is rather against the practice of compulsory religious instruction for pupils who attend church-related schools, and also against the admission of pupils into schools on the basis of their religious affiliation. Thus the new Education Act, 1961, provides that no pupil can, if the parents object, "be required to attend or abstain from attending any form of religious worship or observance."[30]

To further promote this neutral stand, and to ensure that institutions do not become top-heavy with church direction, the new act also requires that all higher institutions—secondary schools and training colleges—have their own boards of governors, established by the Minister of Education. The churches which sponsor particular institutions have their representatives on these boards and are therefore not cut off from the administration of the institutions concerned.

The church, in terms of the number of educational institu-

---

[30] Education Act, 1961, Section 22, *Freedom of Worship* (Accra, 1962).

tions, continues to play the significant role it has played in education since the beginning of the nineteenth century. In 1880–81 the government had only two schools in the country, while the Basel Mission, Wesleyan Mission, Bremen Mission, and Roman Catholic Mission together had 136 schools. The picture today is essentially the same in terms of the number of schools associated with the churches. According to the Ministry of Education's annual report for 1960–62, the churches control some 2,710 primary and middle schools and exercise temporary management over 1,478 Local Authority schools. It is interesting to note the significant increase in Local Authority schools; according to the report there are already 2,431 such schools. The churches have temporary management over some, pending such time as these Local Authorities will have adequate staff and organization to be able to handle all the schools themselves.

With the coming of independence, the government of Ghana has taken a greater responsibility in the educational expansion program of the country. By the end of 1962 the government had taken over responsibility for the salaries of all teachers in the country irrespective of where they might be teaching. Local authorities became responsible for school buildings, although in some parts of the country the government still gives grants-in-aid towards new buildings. Grants are also paid to schools towards the purchase of expendable equipment, although in some sections of the country local authorities are also responsible for this part of the school expenditure. The new seven-year development plan envisages that the government will ultimately provide the textbooks, exercise books, and writing materials for primary school pupils.

With all these developments going on, the strong grip which the church had on education is giving way; the schools may ultimately cease to possess the built-in device for increasing church membership which they had with nearly exclusive control of education in the days prior to independence of the country. The schools are becoming more and more an instrument for the manpower training program of an independent state; they are therefore subject to the meticulous planning that fits into overall economic planning of the country. Education is therefore not likely to be left at the mercy of the uncertainties of a philanthropic organization, however beneficent it might be. This is essentially a transition period, however, and the churches are called upon as before to play a significant role by putting their educational machinery and their experience at the disposal of the government and the nation. This they are doing with remarkable understanding.

The Church and the Changing Ghanaian Society

"At the root of every local disturbance lies the name of *a Christian.*" This was a view expressed in a government report in 1925, to which the church took exception, suggesting an amendment to read: "At the root of every local disturbance lies the name of an *educated man.*"[31] These two statements reflect both the total involvement of the church in every aspect of the life of the people and the contribution of the church to education which has been discussed above. The amendment suggested by the church also reveals a measure of reservation which the church has always had in involvement in the party politics that led Ghana eventually to its independence. The fact that in the minds of the people at a certain period in the history of the country an "educated man" was synonymous with a "Christian" also suggests that in an indirect way—by making education available to the people —the church had aided the cause of the nationalist struggle for independence.

Reluctant as the church might have appeared in involving itself in party politics, it is an unavoidable fact that it was inextricably involved in the entire political life of the people. In pre-independence Ghana, and before active party politics appeared on the scene, the church in its diverse forms was the greatest single countrywide organization which brought people of all tribes together. The church was also responsible in large part for the one greatest single contributing force towards independence—education. With these two very significant forces working within the church, it could not but be involved in all aspects of the life of the society.

[31] R. T. Parsons, *The Churches and Ghana Society: 1918–1955* (Leiden: E. J. Brill, 1963) , p. 182.

In many instances the church became the arbiter in very bitter tribal disputes; the church had often to protect its members against customary practices which it considered un-Christian and thereby again had to confront a local traditional authority. In many instances the church received active support from the chiefs in traditional authority; they helped build the church in return for the opening of schools by the church for their children. In many rural areas as well as urban centers, the way upward on the economic ladder lay through the church; one could scarcely avoid the mission schools if one wanted any education at all, and education led to social and economic self-betterment.

When some of the missions were transferred to the control of local churchmen, the latter gained experience in government and also proved to the colonial government that the people could handle their own affairs if given a chance. It is significant that some of the Protestant churches became self-governing long before political independence became a reality in the country. The criticism has often been made that when some leading Christians had the opportunity to serve in the country's legislature, they were too silent and therefore gave the impression of seeking compromises with the then colonial government. However justified or unjustified such criticisms might be, they cannot be taken as criticism of the Christian church in Ghana on the whole.

With the introduction of active party politics in the country, the church as a whole was under great pressure to declare its stand in the entire political struggle towards self-government. To the layman, the question was not one of principles or ideals; he wanted to be told in plain terms which party to support. This need for the church to express itself was even more vital as the pastor in a village church might well find his congregation bitterly split along party lines. Two tribes might be bitterly split in a similar way, with the church serving as a very tenuous link between them. The church was therefore drawn into the political struggle by its very existence and in spite of its natural and understandable reluctance to be involved in any very active way. The church reacted in several ways to this new field of expression. A minister nominated by the governor to the Legislative Council in 1952 made an appeal to "Christians to enter political life at levels, local, regional and central and to regard politics as a field of Christian service."[32]

The Methodist Church District Synod in 1956 is reported by Parsons as having passed the following resolutions:

1. That no Gold Coast [Ghana] minister "might in the future stand for election to the Legislative Assembly on a party ticket."[33]

2. That no minister should stand for election as Independent unless "special circumstances required the interests of the Church to be represented, or constitutional developments result in the formation of a second house where a few ministers of religion would have a place."[34]

It may be pointed out here that this decision of the Methodist Synod referred specifically to ministers and not to laymen, and the stand of the church on laymen's participation in political matters was not as rigid as may appear here. But one should also consider the fact that ministers tend to receive great respect and are treated with great deference by the communities among which they live and work. In some rural communities the minister may be the most enlightened person and possibly the most educated man available. When the people needed representation at a national level, therefore, it was only natural in the early days of political awareness to look up to the minister for such representation. Banning such a person from participation in the legislature of the country therefore cuts the ground from the feet of such rural communities, and leaves them with less than effective participation in their government.

The Presbyterian Church of Ghana seems to have taken a less rigid stand on the involvement of its members in the political struggle. The Synod of the church at its meeting in 1951 agreed that "Members of the Church should and must take upon themselves their political responsibilities, bearing always in mind that wherever they serve they must shine according to the light in which as Christians they had learned to walk."[35]

Whether the church as a whole liked it or not, it was now

[32] Parsons, *op. cit.,* p. 185.
[33] *Ibid.*
[34] *Ibid.*
[35] *Ibid.,* p. 184.

called upon to operate in and address itself to a new situation in the society. Any reluctance or ambivalence on the part of the church might be taken as open antagonism to and lack of sympathy for the new political struggle. It is here that the Ghana Christian Council, which had been formed in 1929 and which represented the only united voice the church as a whole has had, began to assume a leading rule. This organ was at least present at a vital moment to provide an avenue for joint consultation. In a statement issued in 1949 on "Christianity and Political Development," the leading churchmen who were also members of the Ghana Christian Council called upon "all men and women of good will" to direct their thinking to an eight-point program. Among these principles were: the right to self-government; the need for a good and representative government which finds out the real will of the people; government without regard to race or creed or any other discriminative principle; the realization that there can be no objection to affiliation with any party in so far as the object of the party is in accordance with Christian principles and the means employed to reach that end are honest and good.

The greatest weakness with the statement of the church members referred to above is that it was on such a controversial subject that it could not in fact be issued in the name of the Christian Council of Ghana, even though all the signators were members of this council. The statement began with "We the undersigned ... speaking for ourselves ...." This does not sound as if at this critical moment in the life of the country the church was bravely coming forward to help the people, who were equally overwhelmed by the rapidly changing events, to make up their minds. The rural layman could not but be completely awed by the statement, but might still be nowhere near the alleviation of his confusion. On other less momentous issues, however, the Christian Council had come out with unequivocal opinions and had aired its views in opposition to such issues as Sunday football matches, Municipal Lottery for Accra, and excessive imports of gin. Having started to be relevant in some issues, however, the Council has continued to gain the respect and deference that many Ghanaians have come to accord the church.

Resumé

While we cry ourselves hoarse after self-government and Africanisation, the Churches silently but surely are laying solid foundations for these; that is, while we labour and trouble ourselves, Africanisation and self-government come smoothly and naturally to the Churches. It is the gift of God.[36]

The above is an unsolicited testament for the church: a newspaper comment on the occasion of the installation of the first African chairman of the Methodist Church in Ghana. This is one more occasion in which the church has come out with a "first" in Ghanaian society. Few people would grudge the church its position when the achievements are considered. If in the future the church exercises less control over such essentials as education and medical services, it will not be because there is no more use for the services of the church, but rather because the church has helped to deliver the goods safely, and there is no more necessity to carry the load. From the very beginning the church has had close association with a colonial system; the fact that, with the overthrow of the colonial system, the church has not been thrown away with the hated system is indicative of the respect that the church has won over the years.

This does not imply that the church can now be self-satisfied for having helped to build up modern Ghana. It is left now to find other avenues of expression that will be germane to the problems of independent Ghana. In doing this, it cannot escape, as it did in earlier years, by building its separate community outside the old traditional environment, and thus avoid a direct confrontation with the environment it intends to influence. The church now has to exist in the middle of the community and face the most pressing needs of the community, and face also the embarrassing questions that will ultimately test the stamina of the church.

This need for the church to find new avenues of effective expression has been highlighted by events following the revolutionary changeover of government on February 24, 1966. Many Ghanaians could not look on the changeover of government as anything

---

[36] *Prelude to Ghana,* p. 14.

but an act of God; there has therefore been a general reappraisal of the role of the church in the education of the young. This is reflected in views expressed in various memoranda presented to an Education Review Committee appointed by Ghana's post-revolution government, the National Liberation Council, to review the entire structure of education in the country. One observer comments on education thus:

> It is the aim of our New Regime to make Ghana a God fearing Nation. The Regime has the hope that if our children are made to fear God "tyranny" despotism and nepotism which were beginning to gain roots in our society will die out quickly. Syllabuses of religious instructions therefore should be sent to schools and the Ministry should see that all schools in Ghana have religious instructions.[37]

The Christian Council of Ghana's own view expressed in its memorandum to the Education Review Committee states that "Our over-riding concern is that there should be built up in Ghana a national system of education in which sound spiritual and moral training is given in all institutions and at all levels."[38] The above are representative views being expressed by laymen and church officials alike, calling on the church to assume a new role in the education of a post-revolution Ghana. It would appear at this stage that while the government is still likely to retain its administrative role in education, the church will once again be called upon to play the role of a moral instructor. How the church will assume this role without the administrative machinery which it once virtually controlled is yet to be worked out. Judging from the records, however, it is obvious that the role of the church in education in Ghana is by no means over.

Bibliography

Accra, John, *et al. Christianity and Political Development.* Accra, 1959.
Baeta, C. G. *Prophetism in Ghana* (a study of some "Spiritual Churches"). London: SCM Press, 1962.
Belshaw, Harry. "Religious Education in the Gold Coast," *International Review of Missions,* XXXIV (July, 1945).

[37] Unpublished memorandum, Accra, 1966.
[38] Unpublished memorandum of the Christian Council of Ghana, Accra, 1966.

Birtwhistle, Allen. *Thomas Birch Freeman.* London: Cargate Press, 1950.

Christian Council. *Prelude to Ghana: The Churches' Part.* Edinburgh: Edinburgh House Press, 1957.

Cooksey, J. J., and McLeish, Alexander. *Religion and Civilization in West Africa.* London, 1931.

Federated Theological Faculty, University of Chicago. *Changing Africa and the Christian Dynamic.* Chicago: University of Chicago Press, 1960.

Ghana Education Act: 1961. Accra: Government Printer, 1962.

Ghana Ministry of Education. *Education Report 1960–62.* Accra: Government Printer, 1963.

Government of the Gold Coast. *Report on the Education Department for the Period April 1927–March 1928.* Accra: Government Printer, 1928.

McWilliam, H. O. A. *The Development of Education in Ghana.* London: Longmans, 1959.

Neil, H. C. "Brig.-General Sir Gordon Guggisberg, K.C.M.G. Founder of Achimota College." Achimota, 1945.

Parsons, Robert T. *The Churches and Ghana Society.* Leiden: E. J. Brill, 1963.

Wilson, John. *Education and Changing West African Culture.* New York: Teachers College Press, Teachers College, Columbia University, 1963.

Wiltgen, Ralph. *Gold Coast Mission History 1471–1880.* Techny, Ill.: Divine Word Publications, 1956.

VII

NIGERIA

DAVID B. ABERNETHY

David Abernethy is assistant professor of political science at Stanford University, specializing in African politics. He spent the summers of 1958 in Nigeria and 1960 in Guinea with Operations Crossroads Africa. Fifteen months during 1963-64 were spent in Nigeria on a grant from the Foreign Area Fellowship Program, where he studied the relationship between education and politics in Southern Nigeria. While there he was associated with the Nigerian Institute of Social and Economic Research; he has been a Fellow of Harvard's Center for Studies in Education and Development. He received a B.A. from Harvard, an M.A. in philosophy-politics-economics from Oxford, and the doctorate from Harvard.

Nigeria stands out in contrast to the other African states discussed in this volume, for within the confines of a single country not one but three quite distinct patterns of church-state relations have emerged. Prior to the military coup of January, 1966, each region of Nigeria was responsible under the federal constitution for primary and secondary education—the sphere in which church and state have common interests and in which they are most likely to interact—and the regions' use of their own powers in turn reflected differences in the pattern of missionary activity that existed long before the regions themselves were constituted. A discussion of church and state in Nigeria must therefore be more than a chronicle of major trends from pre-colonial times through independence; it must also describe and account for variations among the regions in their approach to mission education.[1]

By far the most important distinction to be drawn is between Northern and Southern Nigeria, the latter term embracing the Western, Mid-Western, and Eastern regions and the Federal Territory of Lagos.[2] In the South the Christian missions have been active since the 1840's, decades before the area was effectively occupied and administered by Great Britain. The first mission stations

[1] Significantly, the current military leadership has avoided reference to the "region," preferring instead the term "provinces." This implies that in the future the regional governments will be seriously weakened if not abolished altogether, their responsibilities devolving downward to the provinces and upward to the central government. This recent development does not of course diminish the utility of the word "region" in the present discussion, which is primarily historical in character.

[2] The Mid-West Region, consisting of two provinces in the Western Region, was created in August, 1963. All references prior to this date presume the inclusion of the Mid-West in the Western Region.

were naturally located in or near coastal ports such as Badagry, Lagos, Brass, Bonny, and Calabar, but in short order efforts were made to reach Africans living in the interior. West of the Niger River the mission strategy was essentially to advance from Lagos and Abeokuta to other important Yoruba towns toward the north and east, and by 1888 the largest and most enterprising of the early mission bodies, the Church Missionary Society (Anglican), had established itself in Ilesha, over 150 miles inland from Lagos. The Niger River proved an effective highway to the interior, the C.M.S. opening a station at the important river port of Onitsha in 1857 and the Roman Catholics following suit in 1885. To the east, the Cross River enabled what is now the Church of Scotland Mission, centered in Calabar, to plant its stations over fifty miles north of the coast by 1900. It goes almost without saying that the most significant proselytizing technique employed by all mission bodies was the opening of schools, where young people could acquire the rudiments of literacy and thus gain readier access to the printed Word of God. Most missions believed it in their interests to spread the benefits of schooling as widely as possible; for this reason they concentrated on staffing and equipping village primary schools, though secondary education was also offered in Lagos and Calabar by the turn of the century.

For their part, British officials were by no means so active as the missionaries in establishing an effective presence in Southern Nigeria during the nineteenth century. Apart from the annexation of Lagos in 1861, it was not until 1900 and the establishment of the Protectorate of Southern Nigeria that a genuine *Pax Britannica* was imposed on the area. In the field of education the lag between mission activity and official efforts at regulation was noticeable indeed. Not until 1882, or forty years after the pioneer Methodist missionary Thomas Birch Freeman had landed at Badagry, was the first important Education Ordinance passed, and in Nigeria this applied solely to Lagos and the immediately surrounding territory known as the Colony. An Education Department with jurisdiction over the remainder of Southern Nigeria was not established until 1903.

The mission preeminence in education, built up in Southern Nigeria during the nineteenth century, was not effectively challenged by the colonial regime during the early years of the twentieth. On only one occasion, in the 1890's, was it proposed by the Governor of Lagos that mission primary schools be placed under government supervision, but this plan was quickly dropped under heavy pressure from C.M.S. headquarters in London. Thereafter colonial officials readily acknowledged the leading role of the missions, viewing it as the government's function to provide nominal grants-in-aid to the so-called "voluntary agencies" and to establish government primary schools only in areas not previously penetrated by these agencies.[3]

There were several reasons for this official attitude. British policy-makers had no particular reason arising from their own background to oppose missionaries or organized religion as such, unlike the early French administrators in West Africa who carried with them to the colonies the bitter legacy of church-state controversy in France and who in many cases nurtured strong anti-clericalist sentiments. Moreover, the major interest of British officials in Southern Nigeria, prior to its amalgamation with the North in 1914, lay in creating an infrastructure of communications and transport facilities enabling the area to pay for its own future economic development.[4] Education was not a major concern of government, and to the extent that schools were needed—to produce clerks for burgeoning government offices—the most administratively convenient and inexpensive means of obtaining clerks was simply to permit the missions to get the job done. Little official concern was voiced over the potential conflict between the aims of church and state in education, or over the potential danger to the colonial regime of a swelling number of young Nigerians attending schools that were unsupervised and unassisted by government.

In the areas later to become the Western and Eastern regions, the pattern of church-state relations was identical; indeed, not until 1952, when Nigerians had gained a measure of autonomy at the regional level, did the West and East begin to follow divergent

---

[3] By 1908 over 50 government primary schools had been opened, the bulk of them in the educationally "deprived" non-Yoruba provinces. But after this date even this policy shifted, the government preferring to restrict the growth of its own institutions and to increase the number of mission schools receiving official assistance. See Colin Wise, *A History of Education in British West Africa* (London: Longmans, Green & Co., 1956), p. 51.

[4] See Margery Perham, *Native Administration in Nigeria* (London: Oxford University Press, 1937; reprinted 1962), pp. 61–62.

paths. The causes of this divergence are traceable, however, to a much earlier period, when the various mission bodies were planning their strategies of advance. To the west of the Niger, Protestant groups—Anglicans, Methodists, and Southern Baptists being the major ones in that order—assumed an early educational lead over the Catholics; in 1921, for example, 27,863 pupils were attending schools managed by the above Protestant missions as against 7,234 in Catholic institutions,[5] and this considerable lead has never been seriously challenged. Catholic activity in the West was directed by the Société des Missions Africaines, with headquarters in Lyon, France, and educational work was handicapped by the difficulty many of the early Fathers experienced in speaking English. East of the Niger, however, the Catholics fared much better in comparison with the Protestants. Under Bishop Joseph Shanahan, a dynamic figure who believed in mass schooling as the key to mass conversion, the predominantly Irish Holy Ghost Fathers began in the first decade of this century a dramatic effort to establish schools; by 1921 Catholic pupils numbered 31,778 in Eastern Nigeria as against 54,457 in the four leading Protestant missions' schools,[6] and by the early 1950's about half of the region's primary schools were in Catholic hands. Because of the intense drive of the Catholics in the East to convert through the classroom, Protestants there have felt particularly threatened, and Protestant-Catholic relations have been far more strained than in Western Nigeria. Precisely because of the success of the missions in proselytizing through the schools, interdenominational conflict has been internalized by Eastern Nigerians themselves, with the result that when in the 1950's they assumed control over the destiny of their region, what had begun as a conflict within the Christian Church came to affect the relations between church and state. Of this more will be said later.

In Northern Nigeria church-state relations took another course than that of the South because of differences in the timing of missionary advance, the nature of the society, and the outlook of

[5] P. Amaury Talbot, *The Peoples of Southern Nigeria* (London: Oxford University Press, 1926), IV, pp. 132–134.

[6] *Ibid.* The major bodies were the Anglicans (C.M.S. and Niger Delta Pastorate), United Free Church of Scotland, Primitive Methodists, and Qua Iboe Mission. Talbot's figures are adjusted to exclude Southern Cameroons.

the colonial government. Some of the earliest missionaries in the South had envisaged as their ultimate objective the opening of stations among the Muslims of the Northern emirates, but the pressing needs they observed in the South, combined with the enormous difficulties of converting Muslims as compared with so-called pagans, led them to abandon plans for substantial penetration north of the Niger or Benue Rivers. It was not until after Sir Frederick Lugard's first pacification campaigns in the 1890's against obdurate emirates that mission bodies—notably the C.M.S., Sudan Interior, and Sudan United Missions—began to view Northern Nigeria as a major field of operations. Thus in the North the Christian missions held none of the advantages of an educational head start over government that obtained in the South, and it was relatively easy for the government if it wished to control the activities of these newly arrived organizations.

It is by no means correct to view the population of Northern Nigeria as entirely Muslim and all the people of the South as traditionally pagan: the large though thinly populated area of the North known today as the Middle Belt consists primarily of pagan elements, while Islam has spread rapidly among the Yoruba people of the South since the early nineteenth century and today claims the allegiance of one-third of the Western Region's inhabitants. The important point is that in the North Islam has been intimately linked with the centers of traditional political power while in the South this has not been so. The famous *jihad* or holy war of Othman dan Fodio, launched in 1804, was a vehicle for spreading Islam as well as creating Fulani dynasties in the Hausa-speaking states of the Far North, and the emirates that emerged to dominate the Northern political scene provide striking examples of the close relationship between church—or rather mosque—and state. Given this situation, the mere presence of Christian missionaries could be deemed by colonial officials to have unsettling effects; even if the content of mission education benefited the people of a given emirate, the motive behind the teaching was still dangerous, because the implicit aim of instruction was conversion to the politically subversive creed of Christianity. In the eyes of colonial officials, it was one thing for missionaries to work among the pagans of the South or even the Middle Belt, because these officials held little respect for indigenous religious beliefs and practices and assumed they would not survive the advance of world religions. It was another thing where Islam, itself an advancing world religion, held sway.

The consequence of this way of thinking was a dual policy, first effected under Lugard's governorship of the North (1900–06). Christian missionaries were encouraged to open churches and schools in the pagan areas of the Middle Belt, while they were discouraged from operating in the emirates of the Far North. In the latter areas the emir's permission was needed before a Christian school might be opened, and for understandable reasons it was seldom forthcoming. Moreover, British officials, who had power to screen mission applications and to advise the Native Authorities on them, were well aware that peace in the North was conditional upon official non-interference with the Islamic faith. As one administrator wrote in 1911, "It has been deemed prudent by the authorities to restrict missionary enterprise in the Northern Mohammedan States until railway communication has rendered the military situation more secure."[7] So concerned was the administration with soliciting Muslim approval that when in 1910 it established a school in Kano for the sons of chiefs it paid for the construction of a mosque, and the Northern Director of Education, Hanns Vischer, personally donated the salary of the Liman or spiritual leader.[8]

It was not only the religious factor that impeded the progress of Christian missionaries in Northern Nigeria. The nature of the colonial regime likewise dictated a restrictionist policy. From the start British administration in the North was deeply influenced by the personality and philosophy of Sir (later Lord) Frederick Lugard. Far more than the administrators of the South, Lugard weighed policy alternatives in terms of their possible political effects, and his educational aims were intimately linked to his political objectives. Lugard's name is of course associated with the policy of Indirect Rule, whereby the colonial regime works through indigenous rulers, introducing new functions of government while conserving as far as possible traditional forms of author-

[7] C. W. J. Orr, *The Making of Northern Nigeria* (London: The Macmillan Co., 1911), p. 261.

[8] D. H. Williams, *A Short Survey of Education in Northern Nigeria* (Kaduna: Ministry of Education, Northern Region, 1959), p. 10.

ity. Essential to the success of Indirect Rule was an educational policy that provided high-quality instruction for the sons of the indigenous elite, on the one hand, and yet did not educate the common man out of his respect for this elite, on the other. The education system, in short, would have to be rather rigidly controlled by the government so that the "right people" entered the best schools and low-quality instruction among the peasantry was prohibited. Under the mission-dominated system of the South the exact opposite of these conditions applied, for the government there was unable directly to control recruitment policy and curricula in mission schools, and the missions wished for reasons of their own not to restrict education to the few but to extend it to the many. For these reasons it is quite probable that even had Islam not been strong in Northern Nigeria British officialdom would still have been unwilling, for political reasons, to allow voluntary agencies the free rein they had enjoyed in the South.

Several consequences flowed from the British approach to education in Northern Nigeria. First of all, to the extent that formal Western education was to be encouraged in the Muslim areas, initiative had to come from agencies of government—the colonial administration or the Native Authorities—rather than from mission bodies. As Director of Education from 1910 to 1919, Hanns Vischer actively encouraged the establishment of government schools in each province, and in 1921 the government opened the first and most influential secondary institution in the North, Katsina Training College. The state thus held considerably more leverage over the amount and type of education provided in the North than it did in the South. As for the Native Authorities, a number of them quite early decided to establish and independently finance their own schools— starting with Bida in 1912. By 1930, 116 N.A. schools were in operation, accounting for about 30 per cent of the North's primary school enrollment.[9]

Secondly, the dual policy on mission activity in Muslim and pagan areas created and then accentuated an educational gap between the Far North and the Middle Belt. As of 1932 an estimated 11,215 children attended 190 mission primary schools in the North, the vast bulk of these located in the Middle Belt, while only 4,570

[9] Williams, *op. cit.*, p. 33.

attended 129 government and Native Authority schools—and not all of these were located in the Far North.[10] It is true, of course, that in the Muslim areas an impressive number of children—estimated at 250,000 in 1900 and 390,000 thirty years later—attended Koranic schools, but the training provided there placed Muslim children at a distinct disadvantage compared with Middle Belt pagans educated in mission schools when it came to filling new, specialized positions within the colonial administration or foreign business enterprises.

Thirdly, just as an educational gap was created within the North, so the North fell far behind the South in its access to Western education. Primary school attendance figures for 1912, 1926, and 1937 were, for the North, 950, 5,200, and 20,250 respectively, while in the same years the silghtly less populous South had 35,700, 138,250, and 218,600 pupils.[11] This educational gap, due in large measure to different official policies towards missionary activity, was to have profound consequences for the course of Nigerian politics in the years ahead, as James Coleman amply documents in his classic study, *Nigeria: Background to Nationalism.*

The basic differences in church-state relations between North and South were already clearly demarcated by the time the two areas were amalgamated in 1914. One issue raised by amalgamation was whether an educational policy could be devised which applied to Nigeria as a whole and not simply to one of its component parts. Under Sir Frederick Lugard, who served as the colony's Governor-General from 1914 to 1919, and his successor, Sir Hugh Clifford (1919 to 1926), a formula was worked out that combined in an interesting way the early patterns of both South and North. On the one hand the mission bodies were given official recognition and approval for their educational endeavors and brought into closer contact with government—a situation paralleling that in postwar England, where the Colonial Office seriously considered the advice of mission leaders in formulating colonial educational policy. Lugard, whose view of religion was quite frankly pragmatic,

[10] Desmond Wright Bittinger, *An Educational Experiment in Northern Nigeria in its Cultural Setting* (Philadelphia: University of Pennsylvania Press, 1941), p. 229.

[11] Figures rounded off from Table 14 in James S. Coleman, *Nigeria: Background to Nationalism* (Berkeley and Los Angeles: University of California Press, 1958), p. 134.

favored Christian education in pagan areas as an effective means
of producing properly deferent Africans; his 1916 Code of Education had as its "primary object . . . the formation of character and
habits of discipline" and viewed the Christian religion as "an agent
for this purpose."[12] The effect of this Code was to double the number of assisted voluntary agency schools in the South in two years
(from 82 in 1915 to 167 in 1917)[13] and the result of the more far-
reaching Code of 1926 was a considerable increase in grants-in-aid
to the missions and a greater say by the voluntary agencies in a
revitalized central Board of Education. Official approval of missions in education did not radically alter the pattern in the Muslim
North, where even had the "indirect" rulers approved, the consent of the emirs was still needed before a Christian school could
be opened among their people. The government's policy did, however, make it easier for missions to expand their operations in the
Middle Belt, and in the South it virtually enthroned the missions
in their educational predominance.

But if the policy of Lugard and Clifford was "Southern" in the
sense that it underscored the vital role of the missions, their approach was "Northern" in its concern for the dangers inherent in
an educational system uncontrolled in the final analysis by the
state. Seen in one light, the provisions in the 1926 Code for ten
mission representatives on the Board of Education and the increased grants-in-aid merely indicated the dependence of government upon the voluntary agencies. From another perspective
these developments should be regarded as official efforts to discover
what the voluntary agencies were doing and to make them financially dependent upon the Nigerian exchequer. While favoring
Christian education in the abstract for instilling the proper "character" in the African, both Lugard and Clifford were profoundly
disturbed by the actual result of mission schooling in Southern Nigeria. For the sake of conversion the mission bodies—and the African churches that for various reasons had split off from European-
controlled denominations—were sponsoring hundreds of "bush"
or "hedge" schools in the rural areas; these schools, completely un-

---

[12] Great Britain, *Report by Sir F. D. Lugard on the Amalgamation of
Northern and Southern Nigeria, and Administration, 1912–19* (London: HMSO,
1920), p. 62.

[13] Southern Nigeria, *Blue Book Reports,* 1915 and 1917.

assisted by government, responded to a genuine popular desire
for any sort of education and up to the early 1940's probably accounted for over two-thirds of the South's primary school enrollment. From the government's point of view, the problem with
these unassisted schools was that they were not of sufficiently high
quality to produce clerks or others who could be of use to the administration, yet they did produce "detribalized" types who were
difficult for both colonial officials and Native Authorities to control. Lord Lugard clearly perceived the political liability of the

enormous number [of private venture schools], conducted for profit by
half-educated boys and others who cannot read or write properly themselves. They are lacking in discipline and in loyalty to any constituted
authority whatever, and the local chiefs find it very difficult to exercise
any control over them.[14]

If their growth were to remain unchecked, the unassisted schools
would quite literally undermine the system of Indirect Rule which,
following amalgamation, was being imposed by the government on
the South.

The Education Codes of 1916 and 1926 must, therefore, be seen
primarily as efforts of the state to limit the spread of low-quality education being carried out in the name of the church. The 1916
Code revised the criteria for grants-in-aid: instead of subsidizing
a school, as before, primarily on the basis of its pupils' performance
in examinations, the government viewed the school as a character-
building institution, and the decision to assist it was to be based
30 per cent on "tone, discipline, organization, and moral instruction." The 1926 Code insisted on the registration of all teachers to
insure higher quality in that profession, gave the Governor power
to close or refuse to open schools deemed inefficient or not beneficial
to the community, and provided funds for the missions to appoint
their own Education Supervisors to exercise more control over
their unassisted schools. It was assumed in both codes that by increasing grants-in-aid the government could exercise greater influence over the conduct of high-quality mission primary and secondary schools, spur those of somewhat lower caliber to improve their
standards in the hope of grants, and discourage marginal bush
schools from operating altogether.

[14] Great Britain, *Report by Sir F. D. Lugard . . .* , p. 59.

Once the Nigerian government had become deeply involved in subsidizing the missions for their educational work, the issue of church-state relations turned largely on the workings of the grant-in-aid system. Due primarily to the world Depression of the 1930's, annual expenditure by the Education Department remained stable at around £250,000 from 1928–29 to 1940–41, but of this amount grants-in-aid steadily increased, from £65,000 to £102,000 for the two years in question. Thereafter total education expenditure rose by about £100,000 annually until 1946–47, but grants-in-aid rose even faster and by the latter year accounted for £491,000 of a total of £746,000.[15] With each passing year, in other words, the government became increasingly committed to supporting a predominantly voluntary agency educational system, while the voluntary agencies grew increasingly dependent upon government for the maintenance of the system. A major explanation for this development was that the government was economy-minded—particularly during the Depression—and by operating through the voluntary agencies it saved itself the administrative costs of managing and inspecting a large body of schools. For their part the voluntary agencies were happy to accept government funds provided the administration did not imperil their religious activities within the schools.[16]

Generally speaking, then, church and state were on good terms from the time of Lugard and Clifford through the late 1940's. But any symbiotic relationship suffers from inner tensions which may not be apparent at first glance. The fundamental problem, at least in the South, was that the government's assumptions regarding the effect of increased grants-in-aid on the quality of education were not borne out by experience. The immediate effect of the 1926 Ordinance was to reduce the number of unassisted schools in the South from 3,578 in that year to 2,519 in the next,[17] mainly through

[15] See Sidney Phillipson, *Grants in Aid of Education in Nigeria. A Review, with Recommendations* (Lagos: Government Printer, 1948), Appendix G, p. 108.

[16] The Baptists' attitude towards grants-in-aid was particularly interesting. Missionaries from America tended to view acceptance of such grants as violating the cherished principle of separation of church and state, while Nigerian Baptists felt that the money enabled them to preach the Gospel more effectively in a pagan land. The latter view prevailed, and since 1924 the Nigerian Baptist Convention has accepted grants-in-aid for some of its schools.

[17] Nigeria, *Annual Report of the Education Department,* 1929 (Lagos: Government Printer, 1930), p. 44

consolidation of very small bush schools. But these figures rose again throughout the 1930's, and attendance in unassisted primary schools continued at about two-thirds of the primary total, doubling from 81,000 in 1929 to 164,000 a decade later.[18] Government was powerless to halt this expansion despite the provisions it had written into the books, and to the extent that it increased the grant-in-aid vote it probably only added fuel to the flames.

In a sense the voluntary agencies were also powerless to halt the trend, though interdenominational rivalry contributed greatly to unnecessary duplication of school facilities. The fact was that unassisted schools, with their untrained teachers and apparently irrelevant academic curricula, provided an outlet for the powerful and almost desperate aspirations of Southern Nigerians for modernity, and the missions found themselves under continuous African pressure to open new schools beyond the point that even the missionaries felt was wise. In this situation friction was bound to develop between the state and the church, for the former kept hoping that increased grants-in-aid would somehow improve the quality of the entire system, while the latter could never guarantee that the money was not in fact contributing to a further dilution of educational standards by encouraging ever more Nigerians to enter school.

Perhaps the most important consequence of the grant-in-aid system as it developed in expanded form following 1926 was that it forced Nigerians themselves to think about the larger issues involved when church and state are both active in education, the one as manager and the other as paymaster. Those most affected by the grants-in-aid were naturally the Nigerian teachers, for the bulk of the government subsidy to the voluntary agencies went to pay, or supplement, the salaries of properly qualified teachers. During the Depression the government felt obliged to impose a series of cuts in its grants to the missions, and these cuts were automatically passed on to the teachers in the form of reduced salary scales.

Faced with severe financial difficulties, and with a 1931 Education Code that raised the qualifications needed to obtain a given level of income, a group of teachers formed in 1931 the Nigeria Union of Teachers. The union, known by its rather unfortunate initials as the N.U.T., was composed almost exclusively of vol-

[18] Nigeria, *Annual Report of the Education Department*, 1949, p. 7.

untary agency teachers, and some of its complaints were leveled directly at these agencies, who legally speaking were the teachers' employers. But what is noteworthy is that from its inception the union functioned primarily as a pressure group on the Nigerian administration: N.U.T. leaders maintained close contact with the Director of Education, quickly won representation for the union on the Board of Education, and supplied Nigerian members of the Legislative Council with a steady stream of memoranda with which to question the government's educational policy. The union did not take the position that the state should replace voluntary agencies in the management of primary and secondary schools, but it did argue that the state could not evade ultimate responsibility for education and that teachers had a right to negotiate directly with government over their salaries and conditions of service. As the Union's first president, Rev. I. O. Ransome-Kuti, said in 1936,

It is the duty of the government to foster education and to look after the welfare of teachers, and no amount of whatever the missions can say or do can exonerate the government from final responsibility.[19]

The Nigeria Union of Teachers gave voice to this conviction in a number of ways. It vehemently opposed the official policy during the Depression of transferring some of the government primary schools to the voluntary agencies. The union intervened with government during the 1936 strike of Calabar teachers against the Church of Scotland mission, and through the Director of Education pressured the mission into restoring threatened salary cuts. More importantly, the N.U.T. leadership argued that voluntary agency and government teachers should be paid on the same scale according to their qualifications, which meant in effect that the salaries of the former should be raised to those of the latter.[20] And grants-in-aid, in the Union's view, should not only be greatly increased in quantity; they should be disbursed on the basis of so much for each

[19] N.U.T. Presidential Address, quoted in *Nigerian Daily Times* (Lagos), January 11, 1936.

[20] According to the 1937 scale, for example, Elementary Teachers working for missions started at £30 and advanced by £3 annually to £60. Government teachers with the same qualificaions started at £36 and advanced by £6 to £72. The usual justification for the difference was that the salaries of government teachers should be in line with those of other civil servants. Nigeria, *Ten-Year Educational Plan* (Lagos: Government Printer, 1944), Sessional Paper No. 6 of 1944, Appendix V, p. 20.

qualified teacher, regardless of whether the teacher worked in an assisted school. The cost to the government of adopting these proposals would have been considerable; officials estimated in 1936 that to pay mission and government teachers at the same rate would cost £100,000, which would virtually double grants-in-aid for that year.[21]

It will not be argued here that the Nigeria Union of Teachers was a highly effective pressure group during the colonial era, though it probably had as great an influence upon government policy as any body of Nigerians during the 1930's and early 1940's. The important point is that while the union's leadership accepted the important role of the church in education it insisted upon ultimate state control, to be realized through a massive increase and reorientation of the grants-in-aid system. The conclusion was Lugardian, though the reasons for it differed from those of the imperious Governor-General.

On the whole the missions were unhappy about the tendency of their teachers to compare themselves to government employees. European and American missionaries were in most instances individuals who had sacrificed a great deal to work in Africa, and they felt that Africans employed by the church should display a comparable spirit of dedication. A meeting of Catholic school managers in 1940 complained that

> the present outlook of our teachers, as shown by their repeated demands through the Federal Association of Catholic Teachers was that of Government officials or Civil Servants and it was strongly urged that a changed attitude was necessary if we were to get the best possible results from our missionary efforts.[22]

The government was also uneasy if only because of the financial implications of the teachers' demands, and the Governor of Nigeria, Sir Arthur Richards, referred in 1947 to the "mistaken notion" that voluntary agency teachers were virtually civil servants.[23]

But by the 1940's government resistance to the position adopted by the N.U.T. was in fact weakening. The view of education expenditure as an investment rather than a consumption item was

[21] Nigeria, *Annual Report of the Educational Department*, 1936, p. 16.

[22] From files of J. F. Odunjo, former Secretary, Federal Association of Catholic Teachers.

[23] Address to Legislative Council, August 28, 1947.

gaining acceptance in London, and the Nigerian government was embarrassed by the fact that in the 1930's it had spent less per capita on education than a number of other British African colonies. Pressures to increase the education vote were therefore felt within the administration as well as outside it. In order to halt the alarming exodus from mission teaching ranks of qualified Nigerians the government began during the war to allocate several *ad hoc* grants to the major or "approved" voluntary agencies to improve their teachers' salaries. In 1941, £26,000 was voted to pay certificated teachers in unassisted as well as assisted schools, and the following year even uncertificated teachers employed by the major missions shared the increase in grants-in-aid. In 1947, following N.U.T. threats of strike action, an "Interim Settlement" was reached which benefited all certificated teachers whether or not they were employed by approved agencies, and the government assumed half the additional cost of paying uncertificated and probationary teachers in unassisted schools at new, greatly increased rates.

By this time it was obvious that the old distinctions between assisted and unassisted schools or between approved and unapproved voluntary agencies had broken down, and that voluntary agency teachers were in practice, though still not in theory, being treated as quasi-civil servants. This fact, coupled with the administration's increasing concern over the burgeoning cost of subsidies to the private sector,[24] led to the appointment of Mr. (later Sir) Sidney Phillipson to reexamine the entire grant-in-aid system. The Phillipson Report, and the 1948 Education Code that embodied his recommendations, ran counter to the position adopted by the N.U.T. in one major respect: the notion that grants should be awarded in terms of teachers and their qualifications was rejected, and allocation on the basis of the "efficiency, educational necessity, and social usefulness" of individual schools was proposed instead. But if the principle behind grants-in-aid remained unchanged, the practical effect of Phillipson's recommendations was to give the teachers much of what their leaders had demanded. Phillipson believed that grants-in-aid should total at least the 1947–48 figure

[24] The "Interim Settlement" of 1947 raised the grant-in-aid bill from £529,000 in 1946–47 to £992,000 the following year. Grants-in-aid as a proportion of total educational expenditure rose steadily during the period of *ad hoc* concessions, from 39 per cent in 1940–41 to 80 per cent in 1947–48. See Nigeria, *Annual Report of the Education Department,* 1952, p. 20.

and that government should assume the burden of future salary increases. He advocated a four-year junior primary course for as many Nigerian children as possible, which implied that schools at this level would almost invariably be considered socially useful and hence that junior primary teachers would be eligible for grants-in-aid. As for the 1948 Education Code, it specified among other things that teachers be paid their proper salaries as a condition of grants-in-aid, and it forbade voluntary agencies to impose cuts or withhold increments without reference to the Department of Education.

As the state assumed increased responsibility for the salaries and service conditions of voluntary agency teachers, it thereby involved itself more closely in the educational activities of religious bodies. On the whole expatriate missionaries welcomed the Phillipson Report because it placed their own programs on a more secure financial footing, even though many missionaries continued to resent the "civil service mentality" of Nigerian teachers that had been so instrumental in prodding the government, through Phillipson, to reexamine church-state relations in education.

The immediate postwar years saw another development that had a significant bearing on the church-state issue: the devolution of authority from Lagos to regional and local governments. The 1946 Richards Constitution transformed Nigeria into a quasi-federal system; each region was to have its own legislative body with certain limited financial powers. Steps were taken to enlarge the functions and resources of the Native Authorities and, in the South at least, to render Native Authority Councils more responsive to the needs of local people. Political decentralization was a product of many factors; among the British, it reflected a genuine desire to grant Nigerians practical training in self-government, recognition of the great diversity of the country, and perhaps an interest in diverting the attention of a rising nationalist movement from affairs at the central level, while for a number of politically conscious Nigerians decentralization provided opportunities for creating a power base within their own ethnic groups.

The trend away from centralized government was naturally paralleled in the educational sphere. The 1948 Education Code provided for deputy directors and chief inspectors of education in each region and instituted Northern, Eastern, and Western boards of education. In 1949 the mode of financing education shifted markedly from Lagos to the regions, as part of a general reallocation of resources within what was rapidly emerging as a federal system.[25] The 1951 Macpherson Constitution was perhaps deliberately ambiguous in assigning legislative responsibility for education to both the central House of Representatives and the regional Houses of Assembly; but in practice it was the latter who made the important decisions, and the 1954 Lyttleton Constitution removed any doubt that in primary and secondary education each region was master in its own house.

Concurrent with the regionalization of education were several attempts by colonial officials to strengthen the hand of local authorities, particularly in primary education. Native Authorities were encouraged to establish more of their own schools, and beginning in 1943 Local Education Committees were set up in certain areas of the South to advise education officers on the suitability and siting of schools, recruitment of teachers, and so forth. These bodies, composed normally of representatives from the voluntary agencies, district officers, chiefs, teachers, and leaders of local progress unions, performed much useful work and were regarded by the British as the forerunners of Local Education Authorities on the English pattern. Then too, as the costs of education soared, British officials paid increased attention to the local community as a source of funds. The Phillipson Report proposed that the government assume in calculating grants-in-aid that the local community would contribute a certain amount, usually via school fees, towards the recognized expenses of its assisted schools; the government grant would then constitute recognized expenses minus the Assumed Local Contribution or ALC. In this way planning operations at the central and regional levels would be integrated with, and in fact based on, the efforts of the people themselves. Phillipson wished to stabilize ALC for a few years at about the level of nongovernment contributions in 1947–48, which placed the major financial burden of primary school expansion upon the

[25] The education estimates of the central government fell from 11.5 per cent of its total expenditure in 1948–49 to 2.06 per cent the following year, while in the same years the proportion of regional expenditure devoted to education rose from 8.4 per cent to 35.16 per cent in the West, 7.1 per cent to 31.1 per cent in the East, and 7.1 per cent to 20.5 per cent in the North. Nigeria, *Annual Report of the Education Department*, 1948, p. 14, and 1949, p. 39.

central and regional authorities. But the concept of ALC could be, and was, used to increase the financial responsibilities of local authorities, as when the central Council of Ministers agreed in 1952 that in the future 45 per cent of the total cost of primary education (rather than an estimated 30–35 per cent obtaining at the time) be borne locally. Phillipson's discussion of ALC also focused attention on means other than school fees of raising money. In 1950 the Native Authority Ordinance was amended to permit Native Authorities to impose "education rates." This amendment removed one of the most serious handicaps to the growth of local government in Nigeria and resulted, particularly in the East, in some significant experiments in local rating.

Decentralization in education affected church-state relations in several ways. First, it was clear after the end of the Second World War that "the state" was no longer synonymous with the central government in Lagos. Decisions affecting the education system were being taken at several levels, which meant that if the voluntary agencies wished to make their influence felt they had to be effectively represented not only in Lagos but also in regional boards of education and Local Education Committees. Secondly, regional differences in church-state relations were bound to become more apparent; this applies especially to Western and Eastern Nigeria, where different patterns of missionary activity that had not been relevant in a unitary state were reflected in policy decisions once the regions assumed control over educational matters. Thirdly, the increased role of local authorities in education meant that communal enthusiasm for schooling could now be channeled through secular as well as religious bodies. A Native Authority school became in many places a feasible alternative to one managed by a mission, and Local Education Committees encouraged mission representatives to think about the needs of each community as a whole rather than simply the desires of the "faithful" within the community. That the British envisaged eventual establishment of Local Education Authorities such as had evolved in their own country clearly showed that they were not averse to strengthening the secular hand in Nigerian education.

Along with decentralization in the political and educational spheres went a gradual transfer of power from the British colonial regime to a new Nigerian political class. The growth of the nationalist movement and the stages by which British rule was terminated have been described in detail elsewhere;[26] here it suffices to note that the watershed in Nigerian political history was the 1951 Macpherson Constitution, which provided for regional Houses of Assembly the great majority of whose members would be Nigerians selected through a multi-stage electoral college system, and which established regional Executive Councils or cabinets within which Nigerians constituted a majority. In addition, a central House of Representatives was created with a Council of Ministers; this legislature, most of whose members were selected from Nigerians already in the regional houses, had power to pass laws in all fields, including those of regional competence.

The prospect of regional elections elicited a burst of activity among politically conscious Nigerians, and 1951 saw the formation of two regionally based political parties, the Action Group in the West and the Northern People's Congress in the North, largely to counter the National Council of Nigeria and the Cameroons (NCNC), which was believed dominated by Ibos from the Eastern Region. Each of these three parties won control of the House of Assembly in the region of its greatest strength; at the national level no party was sufficiently powerful to control the House of Representatives, and a coalition Council of Ministers was established. The Macpherson Constitution molded the rough outlines of a political system that was to characterize Nigeria as it moved during the 1950's towards independence.

The assumption of power by Nigerians, particularly at the regional level where a single party effectively controlled each legislature, held important implications for church-state relations. Political leaders of all parties were well aware that education was a crucial determinant of desired social, economic, and political changes: the expansion of educational facilities was deemed necessary by Northern leaders if their region were ever to catch up to the South and by Southerners if their regions were to attain self-government and rapid economic growth without relying unduly on expatriate personnel. Because they placed a high priority on edu-

[26] See Coleman, *op. cit.*, and Kalu Ezera, *Constitutional Developments in Nigeria* (Cambridge: Cambridge University Press, 1960). On the concept of a rising political class, see Richard L. Sklar, *Nigerian Political Parties: Power in an Emergent African Nation* (Princeton, N.J.: Princeton University Press, 1963), pp. 480–494.

cational matters, politicians could not evade facing the closely related issue of the church's role in Nigeria's educational system.

This issue was less crucial in the North, however, than in the South. Though encouraging expansion at all levels, the Northern government placed special emphasis during the 1950's on adult education; enrollment in adult literacy classes soared from 78,000 in 1952–53 to 415,000 in 1955–56, a Northern Region Literacy Agency was established in 1954, and the officially controlled Gaskiya Corporation produced large quantities of posters and texts for use in literacy campaigns. Adult education was not a field to which the Christian missions had devoted much attention anywhere in Nigeria; hence there was no question in the North of the government usurping functions previously performed by the voluntary agencies.

In the South, on the other hand, politicians found it both necessary and expedient to concentrate their efforts on primary education, and the schemes of Free Universal Primary Education (U.P.E.) which were introduced in the West by 1955 and the East two years later were in many ways the most dramatic and far-reaching programs ever implemented in Nigeria.[27] Since the primary sector in the South was one in which voluntary agencies were overwhelmingly dominant, clearly the politicians could not plan U.P.E. without giving careful thought to the role that these agencies should play in the projected expansion of school facilities. Should the missions be permitted to expand at will? Should all new mission schools be subsidized by grants-in-aid? Should limits be placed on voluntary agency expansion, assuming that Local Authority schools were to be encouraged in the future? These basic questions had to be faced by a leadership committed to a crash program in primary education, and consequently the rather more peripheral issues of teachers' salaries and the mechanics of

[27] Between 1954 and 1955 the West raised primary enrollment from 457,000 to 811,000 (or from 35 per cent to 61 per cent of the 5–14 age group), upped the number of teachers from 17,000 to 27,000, and constructed 2,700 new schools. In the East between 1956 and 1957 enrollment rose from 775,000 to 1,209,000 (48 per cent to 73 per cent of the age group), the teaching force from 29,000 to 40,000, and 1,600 new schools were opened. Western Nigeria, Ministry of Economic Planning, Statistics Division, *Annual Abstract of Education Statistics, 1953–8.* Eastern Nigeria, Ministry of Education, *Annual Report,* 1956 and 1957. The 5–14 age group is estimated at 20 per cent of the census figures, with allowance for a 3 per cent annual growth rate.

grants-in-aid, which had occupied center stage in the 1930's and 1940's, were relegated to the background. In short, once Nigerians in the South came to power, the fundamental issue of the missions' right to monopolize formal education had to be dealt with explicitly.

The accession to regional power of Nigerians altered church-state relations in yet another way. The colonial administrator was the product of an alien culture, and his attitudes towards organized religion were only minimally affected by the behavior of individual missions in the colony where he served. But the Nigerian politician who replaced him was the product of a culture in which foreign missions had played a vital role, and his views could not escape the imprint of missionary activity, either because he had once attended a Christian school—as was the case with virtually all Southern leaders—or because as a Northern Muslim he was aware of the challenge which the Christian missionaries and their schools posed to religion and social structure. One might have expected as Muslim Northerners replaced predominantly Christian British officials that their policy towards Christian voluntary agencies would become noticeably less sympathetic, but at least until 1960 such was not the case. A major reason, of course, was that the British had been careful from the start to pursue an educational policy compatible with the interests of the Muslim power structure, so that Northern leaders simply inherited a policy designed not to alienate them. Another reason lay in the North-South educational gap: the 1952 census placed literacy in Roman script for those over seven years of age at 16 per cent in the East, 18 per cent in the West including Lagos, 3.3 per cent in the Middle Belt, and only 1.4 per cent in the Far North. A policy designed to bridge this gap would be ill-advised to alienate the Christian missions, whose schools accounted for over half the region's enrollment at the primary level and whose finances placed them in a favorable position to expand operations. The desire for regional advancement overcame potential Muslim-Christian rivalry, and the North's first Education Ordinance, in 1956, provided for generous awards to voluntary agencies (as well as to Native Authorities) wishing to expand.

A different situation obtained in the Southern regions, where the policy-makers were almost without exception the products of mission schooling. While some Southern leaders harbored strong feelings against the missions, many more not only favored Christian education but adopted the biases of their own particular denominations. Thus factors that might hitherto have been considered relevant only to the history of the missions—their strategies of advance, number of adherents, type of education offered, rivalry with other similar bodies, and rate of Africanization, for example —now came to affect official policy toward the missions themselves. The differences between Western and Eastern Nigeria in this regard are striking, and for this reason—as well as the fact that the church-state issue was not posed so sharply in the North during the 1950's—the experience of the two Southern regions will be recounted in some detail. Our attention will center on the Universal Primary Education schemes, in connection with which the most significant decisions regarding the church in education were made.

In the Western Region, the Action Group leadership was torn between conflicting impulses when considering the best means to expand the school system. Chief Obafemi Awolowo, leader of the party, Minister for Local Government in the 1952 Executive Council, and subsequently regional premier, was strongly in favor of reforming and strengthening local government, and among the first bills submitted to the House of Assembly was one establishing a three-tiered structure of divisional, district, and local councils. In order to make self-government meaningful at the local level these councils had to be assigned certain important functions, and it seemed only proper that in the field of education, enthusiasm for which clearly existed among the people, the councils be allowed to raise education rates, plan for future needs, construct their own schools, and perhaps even disburse grants-in-aid to local voluntary agency school managers on the pattern of the English Local Education Authority. From the standpoint of local government reform, then, it was desirable that special provisions be made under the U.P.E. scheme permitting Local Authority schools to expand. Another reason for not allowing the voluntary agencies a free rein in primary education lay in the desire of the regional government to encourage young Muslims to go to school. School attendance in the heavily Islamized provinces of Ibadan and Oyo had always been low, largely because Muslim parents there associated education with the Christian missionaries and did not wish to see their children converted to the new faith.[28] Local government schools would presumably be more acceptable to these parents, and regional support of such schools would refute the charge by Muslim leaders that "the whole [educational] grants have been, as it were, consecrated for Christianity."[29]

On the other hand, strong arguments were advanced within the Action Group favoring educational expansion through the voluntary agencies. An influential group within the party consisted of men who had risen within the hierarchy of the Anglican and Methodist churches before they had entered politics. These individuals—notably Canon E. O. Alayande, Rev. S. A. Banjo, and Rev. T. T. Solaru—argued that although the major voluntary agencies were European in origin they had struck deep roots in African soil, and in many respects they represented the true aspirations of African communities. With their wealth of educational experience, the mission bodies should not be ignored if U.P.E. were to succeed.

The Africanization policy of the major Protestant denominations bore fruit here, because it produced a pressure group of sorts *within* the ruling party that could ably defend the interests of all the Christian educational bodies. Another consideration, advanced by politicians who were not necessarily close to the churches, was purely financial: the voluntary agencies, it was argued, paid for their schools partly out of local contributions, the proceeds of Harvest Festivals, bazaars, and so forth, whereas Local Authorities must rely not on voluntary offerings but on compulsory rates or taxes. The greater the educational role of the Local Authorities the higher education rates were likely to be, and this prospect worried politicians. Better, they argued in effect, to work through agencies which operate their own tax system than to increase to unpopular heights the taxes owed directly by the people to their government.

[28] Such Muslim groups as the Ahmadiyya Movement, Ansar-ud-Deen, and Nawair-ud-Deen operated their own primary schools, but the number of these in the pre-U.P.E. period was very small.

[29] Y. P. O. Shodeinde, "Have Muslims Been Fairly Treated?" *Daily Service* (Lagos), March 15, 1952, pp. 2–3. The Muslim Welfare Association of Nigeria, formed in April 1952, threatened to wage an "education Jihad" against government for its alleged grant-in-aid discrimination. See *Daily Service*, April 24, 1952.

Since the proportion of school-age children actually attending school in the early 1950's was lower in the West than in the East,[30] and since intense regional competition bade the West catch up in this regard, the best means of expansion in the eyes of many Action Group leaders was that which was quickest and most efficient. From this pragmatic standpoint it seemed sensible to allow the missions, which knew how to build, finance, and staff new schools, to do so within certain limits. And if the Muslims complained, the solution was to grant special concessions to Muslim voluntary agencies rather than to penalize all such agencies because most of them were Christian.

Considerations such as these figured prominently in the evolution of the Western Region's policy towards the church in education. The terms of this policy, as they emerged during the planning for U.P.E., in the Education Law of 1954, and in subsequent legislation, could be summarized as follows: 1) voluntary agencies would not be asked to turn over their existing schools to the local authorities,[31] and schools previously unassisted by government would receive grants-in-aid; 2) of the new schools to be built under the Universal Primary Education Scheme, 60 per cent were to be under Local Authority proprietorship, 40 per cent under the voluntary agencies, the 40 per cent to be allocated in each district according the relative strength of the different missions there; whenever a dispute arose between religious bodies as to proprietorship of a new school, the Local Authority was to assume control of it; 3) in addition to their portions of the 40 per cent, the Muslim educational agencies might claim an additional 10 per cent of new schools, to be subtracted from the Local Authority quota; in this way the government recognized the Muslims' claims for special treatment as an educationally deprived group; 4) religious worship and instruction in a voluntary agency school would be in accord with the wishes of the proprietor, but if parents requested other forms of religious instruction these should be provided as well, and a child who did not wish religious instruction

30 In 1954 the percentage of the 5–14 age group in school was 35 per cent for the West and 43 per cent for the East.

31 A rumor to the contrary had circulated in 1953 and been hotly denied by the Minister of Education, Mr. S. O. Awokoya.

as offered in his school might be excused from such classes;[32] 5) voluntary agencies were free to expand at the post-primary level, including the secondary modern schools established at the same time as U.P.E.; 6) Local Education Authorities—in practice, district or divisional councils advised by Local Education Committees—were established in the mid-1950's to estimate future needs, manage Local Authorities' schools, sponsor teacher-training colleges, and disburse grants-in-aid to voluntary agency schools in the area.

These arrangements were accepted by the voluntary agencies with remarkable equanimity. One reason for this, of course, was that the terms were quite favorable to these bodies; not only could they construct new primary schools, but they could expand indefinitely at the secondary and teacher-training levels, which many missionaries believed held the keys to the future once primary education for all was assured. Another reason was that throughout the 1950's the Western Regional government made efforts to involve the voluntary agencies in educational planning, so the latter did not feel they were being excluded when major or even minor decisions were being made. The informal influence of preacher-politicians within the Action Group has already been mentioned. The regional board of education, which included an equal number of representatives from the voluntary agencies and the Local Authorities, was active through numerous subcommittees in planning for U.P.E.; in addition, the Protestant denominations in the Christian Council of Nigeria kept the government informed of their views through a Western Education Advisory Council. At the local level, voluntary agency representatives were included on the important district planning committees that chose U.P.E. school sites and supervised the registration of children for the scheme, and the 1954 Education Law specified that not fewer than one-third of the members of Local Education Committees were to represent voluntary agency interests. In general, the church placed its expertise at the disposal of the state, and educational expansion was thereby greatly facilitated.

[32] Western Nigeria, *Education Law, 1954* (W. R. No. 6 of 1955), cap. 23 and 24. These latter provisions, designed to insure religious freedom within schools whose aim was religious conversion, were rarely observed in practice.

By 1960, when Nigeria gained her independence, the education
system of the Western Region had shifted somewhat in the direction of secular control. Local Authority schools accounted for 27.6
per cent of the primary, 20.8 per cent of the secondary modern, and
25.1 per cent of the grammar schools, while C.M.S. figures for these
categories were 24.1 per cent, 23.6 per cent, and 23.9 per cent, and
Roman Catholic figures were 16.6 per cent, 24.0 per cent, and 19.8
per cent. No other mission body accounted individually for over
10 per cent in any category.[33] As anticipated, the Local Authority
schools absorbed a large number of Muslim children; still others
were enrolled in Muslim schools, which numbered 7.0 per cent of
the primary total in 1960.[34]

The most disquieting feature of the shift away from voluntary
agency predominance was the failure of the Local Education Authorities to perform their specified duties. During the planning for
U.P.E. it was assumed that district and divisional councils would
bear at least 15 per cent of the cost of teachers' salaries in their
areas, but due primarily to difficulties in tax collection at the local
level this percentage was reduced to 13 and then in 1959 altogether
eliminated, leaving the councils responsible only for "other expenses" such as school supplies. The experiment of disbursing
grants from the Treasury through the L.E.A.'s to the voluntary
agencies also failed in many places, as the councils used funds earmarked for education on other projects or simply squandered the
money. Direct disbursement of grants to the voluntary agencies
was eventually reintroduced, leaving the L.E.A.'s without the important functions assigned to them in England. Still, the existence
of Local Education Authorities was testimony to the government's
desire to plan educational development on the basis of community
need rather than sectarian rivalry.

[33] Western Nigeria, Ministry of Economic Planning and Community Development, Statistics Division. *Annual Abstract of Education Statistics, 1961,*
Table 4, page 5.

[34] A survey conducted by the author in June, 1964, of 1360 randomly selected primary, modern, and grammar school pupils in Southern Nigeria showed
that of 200 children attending Local Authority schools (90 per cent of them in
the Western Region) , 30 per cent were Muslim as against 24 per cent Anglican
and 20.5 per cent Catholic. The survey also indicated that of 210 Muslim children with Muslim parents (virtually all in the West) 42.4 per cent were attending Muslim and 27.6 per cent Local Authority schools, as against 15.2 per cent in
C.M.S. schools and 14.8 per cent in all other denominational schools combined.

In the Eastern Region the relations between church and state followed a different course. The contrast with the West was not traceable to a different evaluation of local government's role in education on the part of the regional leadership. Like the Action Group in the West, the NCNC in the East wished to strengthen local councils by assigning them educational responsibilities, and this meant both increasing the number of Local Authority schools and encouraging communities to finance their own educational expansion through increased education rates.[35] The difference lay rather in the government's view of the voluntary agencies and their use of schools for proselytizing purposes.

A few prominent Easterners opposed mission education on principle, as it allegedly turned the African against his own culture and perpetuated a subservient attitude towards the colonial rulers and white men in general. Many more individuals within the NCNC, while not doctrinaire in their opposition to Christian schools, were nevertheless deeply disturbed at the divisive effects of Protestant-Catholic rivalry upon their society. This rivalry had become very intense by the early 1950's; both groups were converting rapidly, there being no Muslim population to resist the inroads of Christianity. The Roman Catholics were by far the region's largest denomination and were in control of about half its primary schools. In addition, they were growing at a much faster rate than the Protestants, at not only the primary but also the secondary and teacher training levels,[36] and there was even talk at one time of opening a Catholic university. Catholic expansion was due in part to an enthusiastic reception by many Ibos—as the

[35] Local Authority schools accounted in 1956 for only 42 of the region's 5,076 primary schools. Eastern Nigeria, Ministry of Education, *Annual Report,* 1956, Table 1, p. 28. For education rate proposals, see Nigeria, *An Inquiry into the Proposal to Introduce Local Rating in Aid of Primary Education in the Eastern Region* (Enugu: Government Printer, 1952).

[36] The Roman Catholic Mission increased its primary schools in Ogoja Province, for example, for 200 to 560 in the 1950–1956 period, and school enrollment in the Onitsha-Owerri Archdiocese rose from 155,000 in 1950 to 287,000 in 1955. See Stephen Nweke Ezeanya, "The Method of Adaptation in the Evangelization of the Igbo-Speaking Peoples of the Southern Nigeria" (Unpublished dissertation, Pontifical Urban University "De Propaganada Fide," Rome, 1956), p. 7. Five of the seven secondary schools opened in 1956 were under Catholic auspices, as were 17 of the 29 Grade Two and Three teacher training colleges opened that year. Eastern Nigeria, Ministry of Education, *Annual Report,* 1956, pp. 17, 22.

popular saying went, "Ibos make good Catholics"—and in part to a policy whereby the Fathers received lower salaries than they were entitled to under grant-in-aid regulations, the amount saved being ploughed back into new schools. The Protestant bodies, fearful that in a few years they would be far outdistanced by the Catholics, expanded their own educational outreach accordingly. Not unreasonably, many Nigerians in the regional government believed that if a curb were not placed on voluntary agency expansion under the U.P.E. scheme, an unnecessary and expensive duplication of school facilities would occur and the rivalry between Protestants and Catholics would become more deeply entrenched than ever among the people of the Eastern Region.

The government's problem in dealing with the voluntary agencies was complicated by a legacy from the region's educational past. In addition to operating at the primary level the Protestant bodies had quite early established secondary schools, and through such institutions as Hope Waddell Training Institute (opened in 1895), Oron Training Institute (1905), Methodist College, Uzuakoli (1923), and Dennis Memorial Grammar School (1925) passed the bulk of the region's political and intellectual leaders. The Catholics, on the other hand, had concentrated on the primary school as the key to mass conversion. Not until 1933 did they open their first grammar school in the East, and only in 1948 did they begin seriously to challenge the Protestant lead in secondary education. The political consequence of these divergent policies was that the early leadership of the NCNC, and hence of the regional government, was overwhelmingly Protestant,[37] while the mass base of the party was to a large extent Catholic. This meant that the party leaders tended to view interdenominational rivalry from a Protestant—or at least a non-Catholic—perspective, one that did not oppose on principle the further extension of state authority into the educational realm but which did oppose in practice the ex-

[37] Only one member of the first Eastern Regional Executive Council was a Catholic. Another reason for the dearth of politically active Eastern Catholics was that up to the mid-1950's the mission discouraged its prominent men from entering political life, preferring that they engage instead in educational and other church-related activities. A similar pattern obtained in the West, but because Catholics there were in a decided minority among the populace, the small number of Catholic leaders within the Action Group had no important political implications.

tension of Catholic influence. A halt to all voluntary agency expansion would of course hurt the Protestants, but it would hurt the Catholics more because of their strength and the tempo of their educational advance, and since the Protestants were generally more afraid of Catholic domination than of secularized education under the state, they understood and to some extent welcomed a restrictionist policy.[38] The Catholics on the other hand lacked an effective pressure group within the top echelons of the NCNC, and their own hierarchy was still so predominantly European that rapport with the party was not easy. Not possessing informal channels to power, the Catholic Church resorted to other more public tactics in expressing its point of view. After the break with the government over U.P.E. policy, these included vigorous protests in the Catholic press, petitions, and demonstrations covertly organized by a lay organization, the Eastern Nigeria Catholic Council.

Given the attitude of the Cabinet and the lack of trust between the government and the region's major voluntary agency, U.P.E. policy was not made, as in the West, in consultation with the mission bodies. Since the government was seriously considering a policy that would be unpalatable to the Catholics, consultation with them or others was considered of little value since it would only stir up trouble prematurely. During the crucial years of 1956 and 1957 the Eastern Region board of education did not meet, and school managers from all voluntary agencies constantly complained that they were informed of policy changes only at the last minute and without prior indication of what these changes might be.

Although the regional government had announced a program of free primary education in 1953, it was unclear whether it could afford U.P.E. on the scale of the much wealthier Western Region. But the West's success in introducing the scheme in 1955, the breakdown of the East's education rating experiment in the same year, and political rivalry between the two regions virtually forced the East to announce in 1956 that in January, 1957, it would

[38] As J. H. Price observed of the Anglicans during 1956–57, "It seemed . . . that the Church Missionary Society had slipped into the position of non-conformists in England in the nineteenth century; they would sooner have secular education for all than allow the dominant church to run its own schools." J. H. Price, "The Eastern Region of Nigeria, March, 1957," in W. J. M. Mackenzie and Kenneth E. Robinson (eds.), *Five Elections in Africa* (Oxford: Clarendon Press, 1960), pp. 112–113.

abolish school fees throughout the eight-year primary course and provide places for all children eligible to attend school. The voluntary agencies, hopeful that they would be allowed to expand as in the West, greatly accelerated their primary school building program even though they were warned in May, 1956, that they should not construct unless the sites had been approved by December 31 of the previous year.

Not until after the registration of 482,000 children did the government announce its policy with regard to the voluntary agencies. A statement issued in August[39] outlined the following provisions: 1) proprietorship of existing voluntary agency schools would remain unchanged, and previously unassisted mission primary schools accepting children under the U.P.E. scheme would receive grants-in-aid; V.A. primary schools might expand their first-year intake to three streams; no restrictions were placed on mission activities in post-primary education; 2) unopened V.A. schools whose construction had begun before May 31, 1956, and which had applied by August 23 to open could be managed by the sponsoring agency, but proprietorship would be assumed by the Local Authority—normally a district council; 3) in the future all new primary schools would be under the control of Local Authorities, and henceforth only Local Authority schools would receive a building grant from government; 4) where a Local Authority did not wish to manage its schools the rights of management might be assumed for a specified length of time by a voluntary agency to be selected by a government education officer in consultation with the council and the voluntary agencies in the area; 5) religious instruction in Local Authority schools would be in accord with the wishes of the parents, and freedom to absent oneself from such instruction was recognized for all the region's primary schools; 6) trained teachers were to be posted only to schools that earned grants in 1956, while the new Local Authority schools were not to be staffed with trained teachers until a certain ratio of trained to untrained staff had been attained in the previously grant-earning schools (this policy was designed to prevent a dilution of standards in the

[39] Eastern Nigeria, "Universal Primary Education: Statement of Policy and Procedure for the Guidance of Education Officers, Local Government Councils, and Voluntary Agencies" (mimeographed).

existing V.A. schools); 7) children who had registered for U.P.E. but had been unable to gain admission to existing schools would be assigned to other schools by education officers in consultation with the local district planning committees; and 8) the hope was expressed that "in the near future" Local Education Authorities would be established, and that teachers might be bonded directly to government rather than to the V.A.'s.

Reaction to these proposals by the Protestant denominations was not exactly enthusiastic; some of their education secretaries complained about the building grant provisions, while others expressed doubts about the honesty and competence of the district councils. But criticism was muted by appreciation of what the government was trying to do and a recognition that the days of educational monopoly by the Christian bodies were over. In a press release of October, 1956, the Niger Diocese of the C.M.S. made its position clear.

We, in the past, in common with other churches have used our schools as one of the means of spreading that Christian Faith which we believe to be the true way of life for all. We shall naturally be sorry to see those particular opportunities restricted in future, but we recognize that when education is provided universally at public expense the churches cannot claim to continue to control nearly all the schools.[40]

The statement asked that unnecessary controversy over U.P.E. policy be avoided by all concerned.

The Catholic hierarchy, while careful to point out that it favored Universal Primary Education in the abstract, strongly objected to certain aspects of the government's policy. The ceiling on voluntary agency expansion and the power given district planning committees to allocate unassigned children to schools were deemed violations of the right of parents to choose where their children would be educated. As the bishops of the Eastern Region put it:

This right is entirely fundamental. Children belong to their parents by natural law, and the parents are responsible before God for their proper upbringing and education. They cannot fulfill this responsibility unless

---

[40] "Statement by the Education Authorities of the Niger Diocese on Educational Policy." Onitsha, October, 1956 (mimeographed).

they are free to choose the agency (or Mission) to which they give their children. Freedom to choose a school for one's children is an essential freedom. It should not be removed by any Government.[41]

Logically, this position implied that the state should never limit the expansion of mission schools, for whenever Catholic parents, for example, wished a Catholic school they should have it by right, and the state should presumably subsidize it. The church was further disturbed by the references to Local Education Authorities and government bonding of teachers, both of which suggested eventual state control of the educational system and a deemphasis of religion. In the words of the Catholic newspaper, *The Leader:*

if we accept this first step [establishment of Local Education Authorities] without protest, the second and third steps will provide a "full education service" which will exclude our Catholic religion from all grant-aided schools. The loss of Catholic education will be followed inevitably by the loss of faith.[42]

Catholic opposition to U.P.E. policy was expressed in many ways. Several Local Councils with a preponderance of Catholic members sent notices to provincial education officers that they did not wish to open schools and that the job could be done more cheaply and efficiently by the voluntary agencies. At a meeting of 5,000 Catholic members of the Parents Association of Port Harcourt, in September, a resolution was passed calling upon the government to amend its restrictive clauses. The chiefs and elders of Ndielo Nkporo, a village in Bende Division, wrote directly to the premier, Dr. Nnamdi Azikiwe, basing their appeal on party considerations.

The people of Nkporo as a whole have been supporters of NCNC (your party) and its leadership, because it is the party which caters for the welfare and development of every town and Division in Nigeria. In view of the above facts and our implicit confidence in the party, we have all hope that the Government which it leads will not a give deaf ear to our humble and immediate demand, i.e., the approval of the Catholic School in our town before December.[43]

----

[41] Bishops of the Eastern Region, "A Short Note from the Catholic Bishops on Universal Primary Education," issued May 22, 1956, printed in *The Leader* (Owerri), June 9, 1956. The dating of this statement suggests that the Catholic Church anticipated the government's policy well before it was announced.

[42] Editorial in *The Leader*, September 8, 1956.

[43] Eastern Nigeria, U.P.E. Files. D.E.E. 10532, Volume VI, p. 643.

Other similar "humble and immediate demands" were made through the activities of the Eastern Nigeria Catholic Council, a rather secretive organization of lay Nigerian Catholics who in many ways were more vehement in opposing the government than the Irish Fathers. At a higher level, some Catholics prominent in the NCNC, including the Government chief whip, came out publicly against the ceiling on voluntary agency schools. All the while, the Catholics continued to construct primary schools, hoping that government would change its policy or that at least such schools could be opened privately.

Vehement Catholic opposition to the government spurred Protestant Nigerians to come to the defense of Dr. Azikiwe and revived anti-Catholic sentiment in the region. Charges of "Irish imperialism" were levelled against the Catholic Church—an allusion to the continued dominance of Irish Fathers within the mission and its relatively cautious Africanization policy. A Convention of Protestant Citizens was formed in Onitsha to counteract the influence of the Catholic Council. One index of the polarizing effect of the U.P.E. issue was the change in political climate that occurred in late 1956 and 1957 at Onitsha, headquarters of both the Catholics and Anglicans.

> . . . a spectacular realignment of political groups occurred; overnight the formerly intense conflict between the Onitsha indigenes and the non-Onitsha Ibo settlers was eclipsed by an inter-denominational row between Catholic and Protestants that persisted well beyond the 1957 election.[44]

By late 1956 the Eastern Regional government found itself in a quandary. Its commitment to Local Authority expansion had already been made, its dislike of religious politics and its underlying fear of Catholic aggressiveness remained as strong as ever. Yet a regional election was in the offing,[45] and Universal Primary Education had obviously become not the monumental political asset it had been designed to be but quite possibly a liability. The

[44] Sklar, *op. cit.*, p. 188.

[45] See J. H. Price, *loc. cit.*, for an analysis of the election of March 15, 1957. This election was held under special circumstances. Dr. Azikiwe had been accused of depositing government funds in his own bank for personal gain, and he wished to clear himself before the electorate rather than continue as premier until the expiration date of the current House of Assembly. The bank issue and the personal character of the premier were thus the major issues in the campaign, but the U.P.E. issue unquestionably figured prominently as well.

strength and persistence of Catholic opposition brought home to the leadership that at the popular level the Catholic Church commanded a considerable following; the prospect that Catholic "Independents" would run against the NCNC was disquieting. Moreover, it was clear that Local Authority schools were being constructed too slowly and in insufficient numbers to absorb the thousands of pupils assigned to them, and once U.P.E. began in January, 1957, it was equally clear that these schools, with their inexperienced managers and untrained teachers, were unpopular because they were no match academically for the voluntary agency schools.[46]

The government tried to resolve the dilemma by defending the position it had taken, on the one hand, while offering a series of substantial concessions to the voluntary agencies on the other. Party and official statements insisted that the government, far from opposing the Catholic Church, had in the past greatly assisted it via grants-in-aid, and they defended the government's right to decide how schools supported by public funds should be controlled.[47] At the same time the voluntary agencies—which meant in effect the Catholics—were placated by revisions in U.P.E. policy. On December 28 the government announced that all voluntary agency schools completed by December 31 for which a request to open had been received by January 1, 1957, might operate under V.A. management; this legitimized the schools completed during the six months following the May 31 deadline. In February, 1957, after children had flooded into V.A. schools, it was announced that these schools might expand by an additional stream and that a certain number of children above the maximum permitted per stream might also be enrolled. This concession dropped virtually all barriers to voluntary agency expansion prior to U.P.E., though the government emphasized that a ceiling would be reimposed for the 1958 school year.

[46] Largely due to the government's own policy regarding trained teachers in new schools, only about 5 per cent of the teachers in Local Authority schools were trained in 1958, while the figure for previously aided schools was over 30 per cent. Eastern Nigeria, Ministry of Education, *Annual Report*, 1958, p. 30.

[47] See Nnamdi Azikiwe, *After Three Years of Stewardship* (Enugu, 1957). The Ministry of Education's viewpoint is elaborated in *Education in the Eastern Region with Special Reference to Universal Primary Education* (Enugu, 1957). 20,000 copies of this document were distributed to all parties concerned with education.

Thus appeased, the Catholics somewhat modified their protest campaign, but its effects were still felt in the election of March 15. A *Leader* editorial on election day put the Catholic position forcefully.

It is an incontestable fact that the main issue at stake in the election is that of education. The natural rights of Catholics have been violated, their protestations ignored. They and their Church have been the object of a lie-and-smear campaign. On March the 15th the religious future of their children is in their own hands. After March the 15th it is in somebody else's.[48]

The election was an NCNC sweep, and in only one instance did a Catholic Independent win a seat. But NCNC candidates who were also Catholics did particularly well in Dr. Azikiwe's home town of Onitsha, and in general "organized Catholic action appears to have made an impression on the NCNC leadership."[49] About half the ministers appointed to the post-election cabinet were Catholics; in 1958 the former chief whip who had opposed the government over U.P.E. was made Acting Minister of Education, and the following year another Catholic was assigned to head the same Ministry. These men were not able to change the basic policy of halting the growth of voluntary agency primary schools, but they did keep the government aware of the Catholic viewpoint and may have modified its stand on some issues. It is noteworthy, for example, that the 1956 proposals regarding Local Education Authorities and government bonding of teachers were never pressed thereafter by the government.

The Eastern Region's scheme of free and universal primary education collapsed after one year of operation, and the notion of Assumed Local Contribution was reintroduced, with the result that only the first two years of the course were free while fees for the last two years were about £6 per pupil. The cause of the breakdown was financial; U.P.E. simply cost too much for a poor region, the Acting Minister of Education himself estimating that if it were continued the cost of education by 1964 would absorb virtually the entire regional revenue.[50] It is not unreasonable to suppose,

[48] Editorial in *The Leader,* March 15, 1957.
[49] Sklar, *op. cit.,* p. 189.
[50] See the speech by Hon. B. C. Okwu in Eastern Nigeria, House of Assembly, *Debates,* February 13, 1958. The primary school bill alone was £4.45 million in 1957, about one-third of the region's total recurrent expenditure.

however, that the furor created over the role of the church in education contributed to the failure of the scheme. The government, mistrustful of the voluntary agencies, did not benefit during the planning period from their expertise and advice. The religious bodies in turn were unwilling fully to cooperate with a government which did not consult them, and they helped to prejudice the populace against the new Local Authority schools. Individuals on both sides of the controversy focused their attention on the religious rather than the academic aspect of education, and their doctrinaire arguments ignored until it was too late the underlying practical issue of how to pay for a very expensive scheme whose effects on productivity would not become apparent for many years, if ever.

By 1960 Local Authorities were proprietors of 25 per cent of the region's primary schools, while the Roman Catholic Mission accounted for 38 per cent, the C.M.S. for 19 per cent, and the other voluntary agencies for under 10 per cent each. Local authority primary schools were still regarded by the populace as academically inferior, but their standards were rising. Most of the schools opened privately by the Catholics in 1957 had closed, as parents could or would not pay the fees charged. At the secondary level government played a smaller role: of 80 grammar schools, Catholics were proprietors of 26 (an enormous gain from twenty years earlier), Independents of 18, the C.M.S. of 9, communities of 9, county councils and the regional government of 4 each; the remaining 10 were under smaller Protestant agencies.[51]

To summarize, church-state relations developed quite differently in Western and Eastern Nigeria during the crucial years of transition to self-rule. The West allowed the church to take part in the remarkable expansion of primary education which took place during the 1950's, while the East took the more "radical" course of trying to confine this expansion to secular local government bodies. It should not be forgotten, however, that it is the West that embarked on the potentially "radical" course of establishing Local Education Authorities, while the East was unwilling to press for such a reform out of fear that this would further

[51] Eastern Nigeria, Ministry of Education, *Annual Report*, 1960. Also, Ministry of Education, *Directory of Teachers' Colleges, Secondary Schools, Commercial Schools, Trade and Technical Schools, 1962*, Appendix A, pp. 40–41. Secondary modern schools were not established in the Eastern Region.

inflame the already tense relations between church and state.

Developments in the period following Nigerian independence and prior to the 1966 coup may most usefully be analyzed region by region, following which certain common features of church-state relations will be briefly discussed. In the Southern regions the legacy of U.P.E. was an enormous primary school sector which by the early 1960's badly needed consolidation. It was not simply that too many primary schools had been too hastily constructed during the 1950's, but also that enrollments in both regions, after reaching their peak about the time of independence, began slowly to decline thereafter.[52] Moreover, as both governments expanded their commitments in all fields, they grew increasingly concerned that their education budgets were regularly consuming over 40 per cent of recurrent expenditure, over two-thirds of this amount at the primary level alone. The problem facing cost-conscious politicians and Ministry of Education officials was thus no longer who would open new primary schools, but whose schools should be closed down. In order to avoid controversy, both regions pursued a policy of consolidating if at all possible along proprietary lines— that is, of urging each proprietor to merge those of its own schools which were economically unfeasible—and both tried to maintain each proprietor's portion of the primary school total throughout the consolidation phase. The voluntary agencies consequently had little cause to complain; indeed, if any proprietor was particularly hard hit by consolidation it was the Local Authorities, whose schools, far from eliminating duplication of V.A. facilities, in many instances simply "triplicated" them and hence were demonstrably uneconomic.[53] Though the Southern regions remained firmly committed to the Local Authority experiment in education, their

[52] The West's peak was 1,131,000 in 1961. Enrollment the next year declined by 22,000 and in 1963 by a further 10,000. In the East, compression of the primary syllabus from eight to six years was largely responsible for a drop from 1,430,000 in 1960 to 1,173,000 in 1964. Nigeria, Federal Ministry of Education, *Statistics of Education in Nigeria, 1963* (Series No. 1, Vol. III), p. 9; Eastern Region, Ministry of Education, *1964 Directory of Elementary Schools in Nigeria.* Parental disillusionment over the Primary School Leaving Certificate, which in the post-U.P.E. era was almost worthless as a passport to salaried employment, probably accounts for the decline in the West and a portion of it in the East.

[53] 203 of the 556 primary schools closed down between 1961 and 1964 in the East—that is, 36.5 per cent—were in county council hands. As already shown, county council schools accounted in 1960 for only 25 per cent of the total. Eastern Region, Ministry of Education, *1964 Directory.*

commitment to cutting costs in primary education conflicted somewhat with a policy of gradually secularizing the school system.

In the Western Region, official efforts were made to oversee
more closely the educational work of the voluntary agencies. The
so-called Banjo Commission Report of 1961 argued against the
supervision and inspection of V.A. schools by the agencies' own
staffs as wasteful of scarce resources, and it proposed that these
functions be performed by school managers accountable to all
schools within a given locality. This proposal was not implemented, but the responsibilities of V.A. supervisors were later
curtailed by the Ministry of Education without notable protest
from the missions. The latter were unhappy, however, that in its
drive for economy the regional government was placing an undue
strain on their own structures. Referring in March, 1964, to a
recent decision that new classrooms would no longer be financed
through grants-in-aid, the Anglican Bishop of Ibadan, Rev. Simeon
Odutola, complained:

When it is becoming clearer that education must primarily be the duty
of the State it seems that the State is trying, at least in Western Nigeria,
to ask the church to bear the cost to an extent which its revenue and
nature of its administration as a charitable and voluntary organization
cannot afford.[54]

In a sense, the complaint was the reverse of that which the Catholics had been making in the East.

The Eastern government, meanwhile, attempted with scant
success to minimize the religious tensions which had become so
manifest during the preparation of U.P.E. County council proprietorship of primary schools did not necessarily eliminate controversy; many councils simply became the local arena for the old
dispute between Protestants and Catholics, council members dividing sharply over whom to employ as headmaster and what religious syllabus to employ in their schools. In an effort to resolve
this latter issue for the region as a whole, the Minister of Education, Dr. Samuel Imoke, proposed in early 1964 that a common religious syllabus be adopted for all schools. But this announcement
merely exacerbated existing tensions. The Catholic hierarchy
denied the right of the state to interfere in that portion of the cur-

54 Quoted in *Daily Times* (Lagos), March 3, 1964.

riculum relating to religious knowledge; more privately, priests complained that Dr. Imoke, a Presbyterian, was trying to "Protestantize" the region. Shortly after the Minister's announcement, 500 women representing the Eastern Nigeria Association of Catholic Women staged a protest rally before the House of Assembly, until they were dispersed by the police,[55] and the Eastern Nigeria Catholic Council called for Imoke's removal from office. The various Protestant denominations, while willing in principle to accept a common syllabus provided time were permitted each voluntary agency to propound its own tenets, objected to the unilateral manner in which the announcement had been made. In the face of the furor, the Minister decided not to publish the outline of the proposed syllabus, and the whole issue was quietly dropped. In another controversy, over 1,000 Catholic mothers in Port Harcourt marched on the provincial commissioner's office protesting inadequate school facilities in that rapidly growing city and insisting that new Catholic schools be opened.[56] The government's response was to reinforce its own U.P.E. policy by releasing an additional £100,000 for construction of new county council schools throughout the region, one-quarter of this amount to be spent by the Port Harcourt Municipal Council. As these illustrations suggest, the struggle among denominations and between them and the state continued to make news in the Eastern Region following independence, with no single contestant emerging unambiguously as the victor.

The situation in Northern Nigeria was less well publicized, but there were signs that some highly significant developments in church-state relations were taking place. By 1960 primary school enrollment was beginning significantly to expand; the figure by 1963 had reached 411,000, double that of 1957 and 13.7 per cent of the school-age population.[57] So committed was the regional government to expansion at this level that it set 50 per cent enrollment as its 1970 target rather than the 25 per cent suggested in 1960 by the well-known Ashby Commission. Rapid expansion did

[55] *Daily Express* (Lagos), March 25, 1964.

[56] *Daily Express,* February 15, 1964.

[57] The statistics on Northern Nigerian education which follow are derived or taken directly from Northern Region, Ministry of Education, *School Statistics of Northern Nigeria,* 1961, 1962, and 1963, *The 1963 Directory of Primary Schools,* and *School Directory for Northern Nigeria,* 1964.

not pose a serious problem concerning the proprietorship of new schools as it had in the South; indeed, by 1962 the number of primary schools seems to have stabilized at about 2,600, increased enrollments being reflected in a 43 per cent rise in the number of pupils per school from 1960 to 1963. The real problem was rather a geographical one: the six provinces of the Middle Belt, historically already well ahead of the Far North in access to European schooling, were now experiencing an upsurge of popular interest in education which simply accentuated the gap between the two areas of the region. Thus, between 1961 and 1963 the proportion of Middle Belt children enrolled rose from 23 per cent to 28 per cent, in the Far North from 6 per cent to 8 per cent. This phenomenon was even more striking at the secondary level. The Middle Belt, with under 30 per cent of the regional population, accounted for over half the grammar schools in 1961 (24 of 47), and of 18 new schools opened in the 1961–64 period 15 were located in these six provinces. The Far North was beginning to stir, but not even such highly publicized schemes as free primary education in Kano City could bridge a gap with the Middle Belt which was in many respects more profound than that separating North from South.

As real power within the region shifted from British civil servants to Northerners, and as the "Northernization" of the bureaucracy became entrenched official policy, the educational gap within the North evidently became a source of concern to the political leaders, whose power base lay in the emirates of the Far North. Would their policy, designed to exclude Southerners from preempting the top administrative posts, lead to a monopoly of these posts by Nigerians from such "southern" provinces as Ilorin, Kabba, Niger, or Benue? That this question had its religious dimension could not be ignored: would effective political power remain in Muslim hands if the administration were increasingly entrusted to Christians, recent converts from paganism at that? One way to resolve the religious dilemma, of course, would be to give maximum official encouragement to educational expansion in the Muslim areas, and this seems to have been done at all levels, particularly in the vital teacher training field. Another approach would be to limit in some way the impact of the Christian missions on the Middle Belt, where they were strongest. Such a policy clearly posed short-range political problems, for if the missions were to complain too loudly about religious discrimination they could easily rouse popular support not only in the Middle Belt, where the people were desirous of more mission schools, but also in the South, where politicians were eager for evidence that the Northern government was guided by "reactionary" religious prejudices. A policy of limitation would therefore have to be discreetly implemented.

Official statistics suggest that this latter approach has been pursued, albeit without fanfare. At the secondary school level the missions have apparently been able to expand without hindrance, but at the primary level this was not so. Of new primary schools opened in the Middle Belt between 1961 and 1964, 184 of 227 or 81 per cent were in Native Authority hands; as N.A. schools constituted 26 per cent of the Middle Belt total in 1961, this suggests that a ceiling policy similar to the Eastern Region's had gone into effect. Even more noteworthy has been the assumption of proprietorship over voluntary agency primary schools by the Native Authorities in some areas. Thus in Ilorin Province between 1961 and 1964 the number of schools rose from 188 to 227; the V.A. figure *fell* from 158 to 123 while the N.A. figure rose from 30 to 104. It is highly probable that most of the 35 schools that left the V.A. list are still in operation, but under N.A. control. Interestingly enough, this development has not been publicized, even though it represents a more radical policy towards the church in education than either of the Southern regions ever adopted.

It would be unjust to infer that the Northern Nigerian government has set out on a course of persecuting and eventually ousting the Christian educational enterprise; officially the leadership is committed to religious toleration, and in any event the voluntary agencies' cooperation is vitally needed if the North as a whole is even to begin to match the educational output of the Southern regions. That certain new limits have been placed on the missions, however, seems undeniable. This is easily explained if one considers that in the North the basic policy decisions have been made by men who are Muslims, whose power base lies outside the area where Christian activity has been most concentrated, and who fear the consequences of increased educational differentiation between the northern and southern portions of the region.

As this essay has stressed throughout, the pattern of church-state relations in Nigeria has varied considerably from region to region, reflecting and in turn contributing to the remarkable diversity of Africa's most populous nation. Yet it must not be forgotten that these are variations on a common theme, and it is on this theme that we wish to conclude. In all three regions the transition from British to Nigerian control has been marked by a moderate increase in the educational activity of the state, representing a challenge to the predominant role played in the past by the Christian missions. Voluntary agency expansion at the primary level has been restricted, local government councils have become deeply involved in school proprietorship, and the Ministries of Education have increased their supervisory functions over all educational institutions. But at the same time the voluntary agencies have given evidence of their continuing vitality in an independent Nigeria. Except for a few instances in the North, their schools have not been taken over by secular authorities. The missions train the bulk of the country's teachers, are expanding rapidly in secondary education, are assured of regular financial support for major operating expenses through the grant-in-aid system, and in the South at least enter vigorously into public debate when they feel their interests are threatened. An equilibrium of sorts seems to have been established in Nigeria, church and state each recognizing somewhat warily the part the other plays, and neither willing radically to alter the existing relationship.

To the observer from Europe or the United States, such a situation may appear strange indeed. Surely an educational system under secular control is one of the marks of a modern or modernizing nation, and surely Nigerians must prefer such a system to one so closely associated with an imported religion and foreign domination. Why then is there no evidence that the voluntary agency sector in education is rapidly withering away? To this question several complementary answers can be hazarded. By and large Nigerian Local Authorities are poor, inefficient, and inexperienced in educational administration; as an alternative to the voluntary agencies they do not exactly inspire public confidence. The regional governments might have attempted directly to administer all schools receiving grants-in-aid, but such a course would heavily tax their own administrative structures and greatly increase the cost of education at a time when the regions were attempting to economize in this field. The basic dilemma is that the various Nigerian governments, like so many in the underdeveloped world, are trying to provide certain features of a welfare state—such as widespread, relatively inexpensive education—without the resources to finance welfare; consequently it has made sense to place part of the financial burden on private institutions that operate their own "parallel taxation system" based on levies and voluntary contributions. One expert on Nigerian education estimates that if control of the voluntary agency schools in the south were to be assumed by the regional or local authorities, running costs to government might rise by as much as a third.[58] This stark economic fact of life is probably the major deterrent to a rapid secular takeover of the mission school system.

Another set of explanations lies in the nature of the voluntary agencies themselves. Their commitment to conversion has given them extensive experience with Africans in the rural as well as urban areas, and while this commitment has led them to reject many indigenous practices and values, it has also made them quite responsive to the expressed needs of the communities they served. This responsiveness has been particularly evident in education. Many voluntary agency schools are really community schools, the initiative having been taken by the local people, who built and maintained them and simply called on the missions to provide teachers and overall supervision. Insofar as the voluntary agencies represent the interests of African communities, their position politically as well as educationally remains strong in the post-independence era. It is widely believed, moreover, that voluntary agencies are more efficient and honest in educational administration that secular authorities; hence if the agencies were displaced, a populace already concerned over what it regards as declining educational standards would very likely raise an outcry. Another factor is that as the voluntary agencies have Africanized they have become indigenous rather than expatriate interest groups, intimately involved in the political process precisely because they are *of* Africa as well as *in* it. The rate of Africanization varies widely, with the Catholics far behind most Protestant denominations, but in the 1960's it no longer makes sense to regard the Christian

[58] Personal communication from Father James O'Connell, Lecturer in Political Science, University of Ibadan.

Church as somehow inherently alien to the African scene. As expatriate missionaries lose their influence it becomes more difficult to charge the church with being a foreign, neocolonial influence, disqualified on these grounds alone from instructing the younger generation.

The strength of the voluntary agencies is also a function of the way they are organized. Partly, perhaps, because of their foreign origins, these agencies are oriented towards public policy issues, and towards no issue more than that of education. They are thus in a position to exert pressure on Ministries of Education and to focus public attention on matters of educational policy in a way that other interests with a less specific frame of reference, such as tribal unions, are unable to do. The missions, moreover, command support over a wide geographic area transcending tribal lines, and as Nigeria modernizes this could be a source of great strength. Denominationalism, for all its obvious evils, has at least the dual merit of introducing new cleavages within ethnic groups and new loyalties across ethnic lines, thereby creating the basis for a plural society in which one's tribal identity is not always the primary determinant of his political behavior.

That an equilibrium of sorts obtains between the Christian Church and the various regions is, then, a common feature of the post-independence period. Another development affecting the country as a whole has been a growing belief among many Nigerians that the federal government should play a more active educational role, approximating in some ways its position prior to 1946. In recent years the federal government has been concerned mainly with higher education, which absorbed over 60 per cent of its education expenditure in 1962–63. As the burden of paying for primary and secondary education has grown increasingly onerous for the regions, not unnaturally voices have been raised in certain quarters urging that part of the pre-university expenditure be financed by the federal authorities. Attention has also been focused on Lagos by the recent activities of the Nigeria Union of Teachers. The union called a nationwide strike in October, 1964, to pressure the federal government into establishing a commission charged with setting teachers' salaries and conditions of service on a national basis. The individual regions were represented on the commission that was eventually established, but it is significant that the teachers felt their problems required a truly national solution. This new emphasis on the responsibilities of the federal government has of course been given a substantial boost by the coup of January, 1966, which followed months of tension between Northern- and Southern-oriented political factions. Though it is too early to tell, there is a strong possibility that Nigeria's regions will be weakened relative to the central regime, if indeed the regions survive in any recognizable form. Hence many new responsibilities in the educational field may revert to Lagos, implying a more unified approach to church-state relations than was the case during the past two decades.

How the current military regime, or its duly elected successor, will respond to the dominant role of the church in education remains an open question. The replacement of the old political class by younger, more vigorous and self-disciplined men does raise the possibility of radical policy changes, most probably in the secularizing direction. The new regime may, however, regard other problems, such as unemployment and a flagging Six-Year-Plan, as top priority items and leave education alone for the time being. The military leaders seem particularly anxious, moreover, to devote the nation's financial resources to immediately productive ends. If anything, the amount they devote to primary and secondary education may decline, and under these circumstances the expropriation of voluntary agency schools, an action which as we have seen would raise expenses significantly, seems unlikely.

The future of voluntary agency educational work will clearly depend in part on the kind of political system Nigerians fashion for themselves. But it will also depend on the church's evaluation of its own priorities. It is not inconceivable that many, though not all, denominations will give serious thought to deemphasizing their current programs in primary and secondary education as the cost of these programs rises, as popular disenchantment sets in with an educational system no longer able to guarantee certificate holders salaried employment, and as other religious commitments appear more attractive. The need for a reappraisal along these lines has already been suggested by the General Secretary of the International Missionary Council, referring to Africa in general.

A decreasing involvement in education will enable the churches to recover a balance in their total work which they have almost lost. Pressure to expand school facilities has reduced many missionaries to frustration, as they find themselves no longer free to work creatively with people but merely administering a vast system for the government under increasingly strict regimentation . . . . Other means of Christian action—youth work, Sunday Schools, and the like—have too often remained undeveloped because education seemed to have a prior claim on the limited time and energy of the staff. Hence many church leaders will be relieved rather than dismayed if a larger share of general education is carried by government.[59]

At the present time such an attitude is held by only a few Nigerian religious leaders, and it is stronger among expatriates than among Nigerians themselves. But, for the reasons suggested, it may be more widely accepted in the future. If so, the future of church-state relations in Nigeria may well turn not on the struggle of these two institutions to control the educational system, as in the past, but on the efforts of both groups gradually to disengage themselves from heavy financial and administrative responsibilities that, in the light of their noneducational commitments, may no longer be unhesitatingly justified. The outcome of such a "disengagement struggle" could have profound consequences for the political as well as educational development of Africa's potentially most important state.

[59] George Wayland Carpenter, "African Education and the Christian Missions," *Phi Delta Kappan,* Vol. XLI, No. 4 (January, 1960), p. 195.

VIII

REPUBLIC OF
SOUTH AFRICA

A. P. HUNTER

with a commentary by J. J. Fourie

*A. P. Hunter is lecturer in education at the University of Basutoland,
Bechuanaland, and Swaziland. A South African citizen by birth, he has
taught in schools in England and South Africa and at the Natal Training College and Rhodes University. He received his doctorate from the
University of California, Los Angeles.*

When the Nationalist Government assumed office in South Africa in 1948, the local management of the African school system was mainly in the hands of Christian missions, and the control of this system was vested in the provincial councils. Today the local management is in secular hands, and the control of the system has been centralized under a national Department of Bantu Education. Before 1948, all university institutions were under semiautonomous councils, which had the power to decide whom they would admit as students. Today these institutions may admit only students of particular ethnic groups, and the colleges for nonwhites are under direct state control.

These examples illustrate the pattern of change in the roles of the state and the church (and other interested parties) in South Africa's education system. The central feature of this process has been the accruing to the state of radically increased power over the school system. Many powers formerly exercised by religious bodies, by the semiautonomous councils of educational institutions, and by individual persons have been taken over by the government. Furthermore, within the governmental structure there has been a diminution of provincial powers and a corresponding increase in the powers of the central government.

These changes, produced by legislation and administrative directive, have been associated with the implementation of the policy of separate development. The crucial role of the education system in carrying out this social policy has been recognized by the regime's supporters and critics alike. To the latter, the legislative changes affecting the control of education represent an exploitation of the school system's potentialities as an instrument of government propaganda. The adherents of the government, on the other hand, interpret the measures as a justified series of steps taken to insure the congruence of the education system with the overall social policy of the country. For, as will be indicated below, South Africa's education system, as inherited by the Nationalist Government in 1948, contained many elements inconsistent with apartheid.

Since state intervention is the dominant theme of recent educational development in South Africa, this essay on the roles of the state and the church in education will give far greater attention to the former.

Most South Africans are at least nominally Christians. The numerical strengths of the various religious groups in the country are indicated below.

Distribution (in thousands) of religious affiliation within ethnic groups[1]

	AFRICAN	WHITE	COLOURED	ASIATIC	TOTALS
"Dutch Reformed Churches"					
Nederduits Gereformeerde Kerk		1326	443		
Gereformeerde Kerk	557	101	7	(0.5)	2630
Nederduits Hervormde Kerk		190	4		
Anglican	748	390	269	5	1412
Presbyterian	205	111	8	(0.3)	323
Congregational	135	16	137	(0.2)	289
Methodist	1313	270	118	2	1703
Lutheran	539	34	73	—	646
Roman Catholic	761	193	120	10	1084
Apostolic	305	108	70	1	483
Bantu Christian Churches	2188	—	—	—	2188
Other Christian	508	166	132	15	802
Hindu	—	—	—	311	311
Islam	—	—	93	98	192
Jewish	—	116	—	—	116
Other and unspecified	3650	67	35	34	3785
	10908	3088	1509	477	15982

(The "total" figures are derived from the original full data, not from the summaries thereof in thousands. This has produced some minor inconsistencies in the summary totals.)

[1] Based upon South African Bureau of Statistics, *Report #6 of the Population Census, 1960;* tables 1.1, 2.1, 3.1, 4.1 (derived from a 10 per cent sample of the White, Coloured, and Asiatic population and a 5 per cent sample of the African population).

Of the inferences which may be drawn from the above table, the following seem to be the most significant for our purpose:

1. Of the republic's total population, about 72 per cent acknowledge a Christian affiliation. The country's non-Christian groups are relatively all very small: about 2 per cent of the people are Hindu, about 1 per cent are adherents of Islam, and 0.7 per cent are Jewish in religion. (These small groups will not be treated in this essay.)

2. Of the African majority, about two-thirds are Christian. Of this two-thirds, 30 per cent are members of various "Bantu Christian Churches." (This census category covers about 2,000 different "separatist" African sects.) [2]

3. Among the whites, about 94 per cent are Christian. The largest church is the Nederduits Gereformeerde Kerk (N.G.K.). The three Calvinist-oriented Dutch Reformed Churches together comprise about 52 per cent of the white population. As the strongest religious group within the dominant ethnic group, the D.R.C.'s occupy a crucial position in the country's power structure.

The recent power shifts in education—from church (and individual) to state and from province to center—have not affected the long-standing enshrinement of Christianity in ordinance and textbook, in syllabus and official circular. Not only is the Christian tradition reflected in the programs of many secular subjects; state schools are required to open each day with prayer and a reading from the Bible. Provision is also made for the study of Biblical history, but dogmatic interpretation is forbidden.

There is of course great variation in the spirit in which these regulations are carried out. An investigator who made a survey of religious education in the English-medium white state schools of the Transvaal in 1959 concluded that the provisions of the relevant ordinance were being but superficially implemented.

> In the primary schools principals and teachers alike accept the conditions laid down by the Ordinance but in a rather superficial way. The subject appears on the timetable in accordance with the times laid down; opening observances of a sort are held; Bible stories according to the syllabus are told when they do not get in the way of more important activities; the palest tinge of doctrine is avoided. . . . There is no suggestion of hypocrisy; only the neglect of indifference.
>
> In the high schools, the same remarks are generally applicable, but

[2] See B. G. M. Sundkler, *Bantu Prophets in South Africa*, 2nd ed. (London: Oxford University Press, 1961).

the neglect of the syllabus is infinitely more marked, and there is obviously little attempt made by scripture teachers to grapple with the religious problems of the adolescent of the day and generation.

The standard of religious knowledge is low and the methods of instruction restricted. . . . The children become bored and do not respond to the teacher who in turn becomes bored because he concludes that the pupils are not interested. . . .[3]

There are relatively few teachers formally qualified to give religious instruction at a level appropriate to the high school. Regulations permit a pupil to be withdrawn from the religious instruction at the request of his parent; and the requirements in connection with prayer and Bible study do not apply to those state schools which are (in the words of the Transvaal Education Ordinance of 1953) "established and maintained primarily for or attended mainly by children of non-Christian parents." It should be pointed out that such non-Christian parents are normally those of religious minorities such as the Hindu or Moslem.

Today, the republic's eleven million Africans (known officially as Bantu and formerly as Natives), three million whites, one-and-a-half million Coloureds, and half-million Asiatics (mainly Indians) live under laws designed to separate the ethnic groups as far as possible. In 1948, however, when the Nationalist Government assumed office, there were, amid the segregationist conventions and legislation, certain distinct trends towards integration —in the educational as well as the economic and social domains.

The social situation in the immediate pre-apartheid era was a relatively fluid one. With the mass of non-whites very poor and ill-educated by white standards, and with very few of them in jobs above the unskilled level, segregation in social relations remained the dominant convention. There were exceptions to this pattern, however; a small but significant amount of "social mixing" among educated Africans and whites showed some increase with the economic and educational advance of the non-whites. Likewise, there were exceptions to the general practice of residential segregation, and to the tradition of separate facilities in public utilities. Most whites and non-whites appeared to accept racial discrimination as the natural order of things, but a growing articulate minority

---

[3] Harold Holmes, *Religious Education in the State School: A South African Study* (Johannesburg and London: Nelson, 1962) , p. 251.

of non-whites was coming to press for the reduction or abolition of color bar restrictions, and some whites were expressing misgivings about the justice of the social order. Particularly after World War II, many features of South African society seemed to suggest the possibility of gradual development in the direction of a racially integrated society.

The educational system reflected the ambiguity of the social system. The nine university institutions followed independent policies on the criteria for the admission of students. Most of them accepted white students only; one operated separate white and non-white campuses with a common faculty; two admitted all races to the same classrooms, but its integration did not extend to social and athletic activities. There was also one small college primarily for Africans, attended also by members of other non-white groups. Finally, the examinations and courses of the University of South Africa at Pretoria, which taught only by correspondence, were open to all races.

Of the ten technical colleges, some provided instruction for non-whites at segregated branches; there was also, in Durban, a college especially for non-whites.

At the elementary and secondary levels, Africans and whites[4] were everywhere taught in separate schools, though in some areas Coloureds and Indians, and in others Coloureds and Africans, were at school together. (In earlier times white and non-white had attended the same schools in some parts of South Africa.)

Over 80 per cent of the white pupils in elementary and secondary schools were in public institutions. With some exceptions, secondary institutions with a vocational bias fell under the jurisdiction of the Union Department of Education. In some cases this was a direct control, but in most cases such secondary schools formed departments of semiautonomous technical colleges. Other schools in the public sector were controlled by the provinces. From its own sources of taxation, each provincial council met half the cost of its white school system; the other half was provided from subsidies by the Union government. Many private schools received partial subsidies from the provincial education departments, and

[4] For reasons of brevity, this study concentrates upon the two larger ethnic groups, the African and the white, though some illustrations are taken from the Coloured and Indian school systems.

such schools were subject to a certain amount of provincial supervision. Those private institutions which did not seek subsidies included some of the academically most successful (and socioeconomically most select) schools in South Africa. Some of the private schools were directly under the control of a particular denomination; in other church schools the religious tradition was less formally reflected.

Nearly all the private schools provided instruction through the medium of the English language only, but in state schools there were many patterns of school organization in connection with the medium of instruction, and there was some variation within as well as between the provinces. "Single-medium" schools provided all instruction in either Afrikaans or English. Usually this was the pupil's mother tongue, but in most cases parents were permitted to have a child instructed in the "second" medium if such facilities were available. (Mother-tongue medium was compulsory in elementary schools in the Orange Free State, then the only province under National Party control.) In small linguistically heterogeneous communities the usual pattern of organization was the "parallel-medium" school, in which the two media were used in parallel classes of Afrikaans- and English-speaking children. In order to promote bilingualism, some provinces provided "dual medium" education, in which pupils were taught some subjects in one language and some in the other. In the smaller communities the paucity in enrollments provided an economic reason for the adoption of the "dual" rather than the "parallel" structure. In the province of Natal, half an hour a day was devoted to "other medium" instruction in the primary school. The Transvaal was gradually increasing the proportion of "other medium" instruction with the intention of attaining an equal distribution between the two in 1951.

The implementation of such policies suffered from a shortage of bilingual teachers and met with increasing opposition from Afrikaner Nationalists, who were insistent upon the need for compulsory mother-tongue instruction in single-medium schools. In their view, it was an injustice to a child to allow his parents to have him taught in a tongue other than his own, for this handicapped his learning. Nationalists also made it clear that they feared the anglicization of Afrikaner children by English-medium instruction or by education in a school environment not purely Afrikaner.

Where the majority of white schools were state institutions, most schools for Africans were run by Christian missions under the supervision of the provincial education departments. In 1945, for instance, there were 5,360 schools of this type and only 230 state schools. The mission schools were heavily subsidized by grants from the provinces, which in turn received all their money for African education from the Union government. Many Africans and whites had suggested that the time had come for the ending of the management of African schools by the missions. Some African leaders sought a greater say in the schooling of their children, and sectarian rivalry was seen by many as a hindrance to the overall development of African education. Furthermore, the professional and private lives of African teachers were often subject to great influence from the missionaries who were their employers, though their salaries were paid from state funds.

Though education for whites was universal and compulsory to the age of fifteen, schooling for Africans was not compulsory. In the Cape Province in 1946, for instance, 41.9 per cent of the African children in the age group 7–16 were attending school. The corresponding percentages for the other provinces in that year were: Natal, 26.9; Orange Free State, 35.2; Transvaal, 30.0. In the period 1946–49, 49 per cent of the African children at school were in the lowest two grades, 42 per cent were in the next five grades, and only 6 per cent were in the secondary classes. The corresponding percentages for white children in that period were 21, 51, and 26.

African schools were much less generously financed than white schools. In the Natal Education Department report for 1948, for instance, it is recorded that in that year the public purse provided (in Natal) a total of £1,355,972 (£1=$2.80) for 32,726 white pupils and £570,487 for 139,791 African pupils. This meant a unit cost of £41.4 for the whites and £4.1 for the Africans.

One of the most serious results of this discrepancy in financial provision was the relatively low level of education of the African teacher as compared with his white counterpart. The minimum qualification for an African elementary teacher, for instance, was eight years of elementary school plus three years in a teachers' college, with no high school education intervening; for the white teacher of these grades, the minimum qualification required two years of teachers' college after twelve years of elementary and high school education.

The low relative level of expenditure upon African education thus produced a school system which was, in comparison with the white schools, ill-equipped, overcrowded, and understaffed. There were, however, a number of efficient institutions at the secondary level. At the elementary level, the programs for what was then officially called "Native education" differed somewhat from those of white schools, but in secondary institutions Africans were prepared for the same external examinations as were whites.

There were a number of features of his education which tended to sow in the young African the seeds of loyalty wider than his tribal group. African high schools—nearly all of them boarding schools—commonly drew their pupils from more than one tribal group. Those missionaries, many of them expatriate, who ran the African schools often did not share the racial views of the average white South African: the attitudes of most missionaries towards segregation ranged from outright rejection to an undogmatic acceptance for reasons of expediency. Furthermore, the close links which the mission teachers often felt with corresponding Christian groups overseas gave many of their pupils a vision of a worldwide community. (The segregation-oriented Dutch Reformed Churches at that time concentrated their African mission work in territories beyond South Africa's borders, and were consequently not strongly represented in the pre-apartheid system of African education. They were, however, by far the most important religious body in the education of Coloureds.)

The African education system was then correctly perceived by the Nationalist Government to be incompatible with its vision of the future South Africa.

The shifts in the roles of church and state in education since 1948 have resulted mainly from legislation at the national and provincial levels, and from a vast body of regulations arising from this legislation. (The principal legislative steps are set out in Appendix I, p. 300.) The most important law was the Bantu Education Act of 1953. This measure took from the provinces and from the Christian missions the functions they had long exercised in relation to the schooling of Africans. It gave to the central government the power to ensure that this enterprise was carried out in accordance with the national racial policy, and made provision for some participation by government-approved Africans in the local administration of their school systems. This was followed in 1955 by the Exchequer and Audit Amendment Act, which changed the basis for the financing of African schools. Hitherto paid for out of the country's general revenue, the Bantu school system was henceforth to be financed by a fixed amount of 6½ million pounds per annum from general revenue plus 80 per cent (later changed to 100 per cent) of the general taxes collected from Africans. In 1959 the Extension of University Education Act provided for the establishment of a group of non-white state-controlled colleges and the cancellation of the right of the existing universities to admit non-whites.

Regarding the education of whites, the Vocational Education Act of 1955 gave the Minister of Education the power to take over control of the technical colleges which had previously been under the authority of their own semiautonomous councils. Apart from this, schooling for whites has remained a provincial matter, but significant limitations upon provincial powers have resulted from the exercise of national governmental powers in the appointment of a senior provincial official (the Deputy-Director of Education, Natal, in 1959) and from the establishment of a National Advisory Council on Education in 1962.

Three of the four provinces have removed from white parents the right to decide which of the official languages—Afrikaans or English—shall be the medium of their children's instruction; and in these provinces it is now the policy that Afrikaans- and English-speaking children shall be educated in separate "single-medium" schools rather than together in "dual-medium" or "parallel-medium" institutions.

In 1963 the Coloured Persons Education Act transferred the control of Coloured schools from the provinces to the central government, and while permitting the continuance of state subsidies to Christian mission schools (unlike the case of African missions) the act gave the government the power to take over the management of such schools. All staff appointments in such schools have been made subject to government approval. A similar transfer of the control of Indian education was enacted in the Indians Education Act of 1965.

As a result of this legislation and its derivative administrative action, the following have emerged as the socially most significant features of the South African education system:

ethnic grouping of pupils and students;

differential allocation of resources among the major ethnic groups;

curricular reflection of racial policy;

insistence upon the use of the mother-tongue as the medium of schooling; and

centralization of control.

Under each of these five heads, the present policy will be described, the regime's rationale will be indicated, and an attempt will be made to assess the situation in the light of educational criteria and in terms of probable social consequences.

Ethnic Grouping

In the education system which the Afrikaner Nationalists inherited, white and non-white were at separate schools, but within each broad ethnic category a certain degree of "mixing" at school was possible between (say) Zulu and Sotho, or Afrikaner and English-speaking white. Under the present system, the segregation has been carried to a deeper level: the main African tribal groups have separate constellations of schools; and, although there are still many parallel-medium schools, English- and Afrikaans-speaking white children are in general separated from one another in different schools.

Furthermore, this policy has, in most of its aspects, been carried through to the university level. Though white students who are Afrikaans-speaking may still attend English-medium universities if they wish, and vice versa, non-white students must go to the colleges which have been especially established for them: one college each for the Zulus, the Xhosas, the Sothos (with the Vendas and Tsongas), the Coloureds, and the Indians. (With government approval, a non-white student may go to another institution if the program he wishes to study is not available at his "own" college, and if the government agrees that there is a need in his ethnic community for someone with the particular qualification he is seeking.)

What is behind this facet of the educational policy? Fundamentally, it would seem, the notion of "separate development." Because of the close link between racial policy and educational policy, the basic issues in the former will be briefly mentioned here as a foundation for further discussion of the educational picture. For the supporters of apartheid, the inhabitants of South Africa are not members of one nation but are from a number of different national communities. These national communities have been juxtaposed by history, with a great deal of abrasion, in one geographical area, and are at present under one political authority whose duty it has become to devise the best way of insuring the development and welfare of these various peoples, without permitting them to exploit one another.

Referring to the dispute between the segregationists and the integrationists, a prominent pro-Government political columnist, W. van Heerden, has written:

That the political order in Africa has changed, and that the change is coming to fruition is disputed as little by the one as by the other. That this affects our South African racial situation and that we shall have to keep pace with the changes that take place, is realized by the opponents of so-called "liberalism" as much as by its supporters. And that we must bring about a dispensation which is fair to the non-white and will open up to him such opportunities in all spheres of life as non-white peoples elsewhere in Africa intend to enjoy, is conceded with as little reservation by the one as by the other. In this, therefore, we do not differ. Where we differ is over the best way of seeing that the non-white gets his due, that there accrues to him that which we all know he must get, without sacrificing that which is the white man's due and which he must retain. We differ over how to ensure that we, as a white people, do not disappear in the political quicksand of a non-white majority, while still adapting ourselves to the current and coming political emancipation of the non-white populations of our part of the world.[5]

While no inherent inferiority of any of these groups to any other is necessarily implied by the advocates of apartheid, the cultural differences between the groups are seen to be so basic and

[5] W. van Heerden in *Dagbreek en Sondagnus,* November 15, 1964. Translation by A. P. H.

so enduring that the groups must not be allowed to mix. It is believed that social and political integration would lead either to the swamping of the white minority or, were the whites to monopolize political power indefinitely, to the denial of the non-whites' rights of self-determination. The distribution of land and resources need not be proportionate to the sizes of the various groups: in general that (majority) portion of the country which has come to be settled by whites is designated the "white area"; those relatively small regions long reserved for Africans become the Bantu homelands, even though most Africans live in the "white" area where it seems inevitable that for many decades yet they will outnumber the whites.

The development of African society must, in the regime's view, be in accordance with its tribal heritage; uncontrolled ac-culturation within white society inevitably produces "imitation whites" who are frustrated because they cannot be accorded full rights. In his separate "homeland," however, the African may develop to his full potential, preserved from competition with the more advanced whites and secure in the tribal structure in which he has his roots. Such separate areas should by stages be accorded self-government. The current friction arising from conflict of in-terests within the same geographical area will be replaced by the peaceful cooperation of contiguous states bound ultimately by economic and other agreements such as those of Western Europe.

It is conceded that the achievement of this separate develop-ment presents many formidable obstacles, and that for many dec-ades the economic needs of both white and non-white will require the presence in "white" areas of millions of non-whites. The latter are treated as visitors and have no political rights, except that for urban Africans a system of municipal self-government is being evolved within the segregated communities of workers. Under the government's plans, the rural "reserves" are to be developed into politically and economically viable homelands for the various Afri-can tribal groups. This is a formidable undertaking, widely re-garded as impracticable by those who are not committed to the social philosophy of apartheid. And under the government's scheme, these African homelands would constitute no more than about 13 per cent of South Africa's land surface, despite the fact that the Africans form 68 per cent of the total population. Furthermore, with the exception of the Transkei, these reserves do not constitute substantial blocks of territory: they are split up into small stretches of land scattered among "white" areas. Finally, the type of African self-government in existence and planned under the scheme leaves real control in the hands of the white cabinet at Pretoria.

One white South African wrote this in 1964:

Today we in South Africa are wont to justify all forms of discrimination against certain groups—like job reservation, etc., on the ground that it is not unfair because the coloured groups will ultimately enjoy all these privileges and rights in their own areas. As temporary sojourners in our midst they are not really part of white South Africa and cannot claim these rights. They are not citizens but are only allowed in to sell their labour outside the homelands. But—and this has become a serious matter of conscience to many in South Africa—*if we are convinced that millions of Africans, for instance, are among us to stay, and many were born here, the question arises: may we still condone blatant discriminatory measures like job reservation on the strength of a political philosophy that, in terms of actual results shows no possibility of being realised?* According to all present indications the non-whites will form a permanent majority in our midst, if there is not to be a radical redistribution of land—which the Government categorically rejects. May we, in the light of these facts continue to condone discriminatory legislation like job reservation? If we are once convinced on the strength of actual facts and trends that the non-whites will form a permanent majority of the population of socalled "white South Africa" *does it not become immoral to continue supporting certain steps or legislation based on a philosophy which clearly promises more than it can ever deliver?* For in terms of present population trends and realities and without any possibility of a redistribution of land it can only mean one thing: that the majority of the inhabitants of the Republic of South Africa (the non-white elements) can only face one future: *that of a landless proletariat.* Here the idealism and the "poetry" of separate development "granting every group in its own area what you claim for yourself" run into the doldrums. These millions *can never* and will never be able to own land where they work and live. Will the fact that they may be better paid, educated, fed and clothed than most people in the rest of Africa be accepted as compensation for the landless status? I am convinced that it is a dangerous illusion to believe that they will accept it in the long run. Even among these landless millions a certain percentage may, through trade or other services in the African townships, next to the white cities, reach middle class status. It seems to me that the present concept of separate development or apartheid as a total solution must break down on the realities mentioned above. That does *not* mean that separate development within limits cannot greatly contribute towards a solution for South Africa's race problem.[6]

The argument for an integrated society in South Africa is not an immediately obvious and compulsive one. The populace is heterogeneous to a degree exceptional among the citizenry of a modern state. The long-standing divisions and tensions among the various cultural groups lead one to give serious consideration to the possibility of some form of partition. Were it possible to effect an equitable division of land and resources, arrived at in consultation among elected representatives of all groups concerned, this line of development might realistically be pursued. But in separate development, be it noted, there is neither the equitable division nor the representative consultation: what emerges as the central feature of this dispensation is the entrenchment of privilege by the white group which is in control.

The present writer believes that a common society, without racial distinctions, is the only one in which justice can be done to all South Africans. That there are substantial obstacles to the achievement of a common and integrated society, and that it cannot be attained overnight, may readily be conceded. (The proponents of apartheid have conceded the same about the road upon which they have set out.) This belief will of course determine the criteria by which the present educational system is judged, and for this reason comments upon this chapter have been sought from an academic critic who supports separate development (see pp. 307–313).

Most white South Africans support racial segregation, though a substantial number, represented by the Parliamentary Opposition, object to the rigor and rigidity of the legislative and administrative measures designed to implement the program of separate development. As the national legislature effectively represents only the whites, it does not reflect the spectrum of public opinion in the country.

Since the assumption of office by the Nationalist Government in 1948, Parliament has approved a vast program of legislation

[6] Ben Marais, *The Two Faces of Africa* (Pietermaritzburg: Shuter and Shooter, 1964), pp. 66–67. Italics in original.

aimed at the reduction of interracial contact, at the entrenchment of racial discrimination in all significant social and economic facets of South African life, at the growth of a consciousness of separate ethnic identity among the various linguistic and racial groups, and at the suppression of effective extraparliamentary opposition to the policy of separate development.

Under these circumstances, most aspects of educational segregation can be seen as a safeguard against the possible effects of equal-status cooperation.[7] As Dr. Verwoerd said in 1958:

> We do not want [non-whites] in the same university as the young students of today, who are the leaders of tomorrow. We do not want the whites to become so accustomed to the Natives that they feel there is no difference between them and the Natives.[8]

And the previous year one of his fellow Nationalists had expressed this view of the proposed legislation regarding separate universities for non-whites:

> The real reason for this legislation is to ensure the maintenance in South Africa of that which is one of the greatest treasures of the white man, namely, abhorrence of miscegenation.[9]

So much for separation between white and non-white. But why separate the various African groups? According to the report of the Commission on the Separate University Education Bill (the

[7] A singular refinement in the application of the segregation principle is that whereby the councils and senates of the non-white colleges each comprise two separate bodies: a substantive board and an advisory one. In each case the former is white, and the members of the latter are of the ethnic group served by the institution. This innovation, to its supporters an ingeniously consistent solution to a unique problem, and to its opponents a grotesque *reductio ad absurdum,* was proposed by the Commission on the Separate University Education Bill (par. 62) on the grounds that a resolution passed by a mixed body was seldom if ever accepted by non-whites as the real decision of non-white members. Furthermore, maintained the commissioners, mixed bodies easily generated feelings of inferiority, frustration, and irresponsibility on the part of non-white members, since the whites on the one hand were tempted to keep all the power in their own hands, and on the other hand were inclined to give more attention in meetings to feelings than to facts and correct action. It envisaged that at an appropriate stage in the development of each institution, the white bodies would become advisory, and the non-white bodies would assume the powers hitherto exercised by the whites.

[8] *Cape Argus,* March 19, 1958.

[9] South Africa, *House of Assembly Debates,* 1957, col. 6982. Hereafter cited as Assembly.

De Wet Nel Commission, 1958), to put all the African groups together in one institution would be to overlook the profound differences between the various groups, to disregard the importance
of common cultural traditions and language in building up a
college, and to ignore the university's role in the general development of a particular group.

Similar considerations, of course, would apply to education
below the college level. For the development of distinct national
loyalties, it is necessary that children go to school only with members of their own nation. In other lands with firmly established
nationhoods foreign pupils may with impunity be admitted to a
school system, but in the special circumstances of South Africa,
the school must counter ambiguities in affiliation, must inhibit
loyalties inconsistent with state policy. And since the young (say)
Zulu is to be a citizen not of South Africa as a whole, nor yet of
the Bantu segment thereof—for there are to be a number of such
segments—but of a yet-to-be-established Zulu state, his socialization via the school system must be to a Zulu nationhood, and if he
be destined for higher education it is to the University College of
Zululand that he must go. Were he to study alongside a Sotho or
Xhosa, the focus of his loyalty might be blurred. And were he to
study at a "white" university, he and the white students would be
open to distorted ideas of one another (as the De Wet Nel Report
put it, in par. 43), and he would be exposed to undesirable and ir-
responsible opinions expressed by immature white students, which
he, the non-white, might take as authoritative. Nor could his
presence enrich the experience of white students: according to the
De Wet Nel Commission (par. 44) such a claim could be based only
upon "the misconception that such contacts in a completely artificial atmosphere could be of permanent value."

But if such "ethnic grouping" of African pupils and students
could find its rationale in the government's project of separate
nation-states for these tribal entities, that could hardly be the
reason for separating English- and Afrikaans-speaking pupils at
school. (At college level white students may choose freely among
a group of English- and Afrikaans-medium instiutions, and in
1964 the new bilingual University of Port Elizabeth appointed its
first academic staff.) For the Prime Minister has repeatedly emphasized the necessity for national unity among the members of

the two white groups. However, in view of long-standing cultural differences and tensions, it was more advisable, according to Nationalist spokesmen, that mutual respect and tolerance be fostered not by obscuring important cultural distinctions in the cause of assimilation, but by educating the children of the two groups in different schools which could then more faithfully reflect the distinct cultural traditions of the two components of the white nation.

The necessity for separate schools for Afrikaans- and English-speaking white children was stressed in a manifesto issued in 1948 under the auspices of a nationwide federation of Afrikaner cultural, political, and religious associations, the *Federasie van Afrikaanse Kultuurvereniginge*.[10] All white children, state the compilers of this document on "Christian National Education," should be educated according to the philosophy of life of their parents. As Article 1 of the statement puts it,

> By Christian instruction and education for Afrikaans-speaking children we mean instruction and education given in the light of God's revelation in the Bible as expressed in the articles of faith of the three Afrikaans churches. By national instruction and education we mean instruction and education in which adequate expression is given in the whole content of instruction and in all the activities of the school to the national principle of love for one's own, based on and within the framework of Christian principles, so that the child is introduced to the spiritual and cultural heritage of the nation [*volk*] and becomes a worthy bearer of that culture. [Translated from the Afrikaans by A. P. H.]

Since an education with this particular religious, cultural, and political focus would hardly be possible in a school serving a heterogeneous community, separate schools are a logical consequence.

At least two comments seem called for when one views this

[10] In the nineteenth and early twentieth centuries the British colonial governments had attempted to anglicize Afrikaner youth by means of the state school system. One of the fruits of Afrikaner reaction to such attempts was the growth of a body of prescriptive writing relating education to Afrikaner traditions and in particular to the tenets of the Dutch Reformed Churches. This 1948 manifesto indicates the structure proposed for an educational system intended to give each group a schooling in accordance with its particular heritage, and then makes a series of propositions about the education of the Afrikaner group. The significance of the statement lies in the fact that it articulates many of the basic notions underlying the educational changes discussed in this chapter, and in the fact that its compilers included a number of men of considerable eminence in the Afrikaner Nationalist political and academic world.

structure in the light of educational criteria. First, this pattern entails great inequalities in educational opportunity. Even if a per capita distribution of resources were to be made irrespective of ethnic or cultural affiliation (and, as will be indicated in the next section, this does not take place), the socially disadvantaged group would tend to have inferior teachers and a generally inferior educational experience. "Separate but equal" is meaningless in an educational context, and separation leads the school experience to have the effect of widening rather than bridging the gap between privileged and underprivileged.

Secondly, since so much that a pupil learns is the result of his association with his schoolmates, segregation represents an impoverishment of the educational experience. And since one of the generally accepted purposes of schooling is an understanding of the world in which one lives, to maintain segregation at school is to deprive children of important opportunities of learning at first hand about the people and traditions and problems of their country.

As far as universities are concerned, there could be no serious claim that the facilities available in the universities now reserved for whites could be equalled by any of the non-white institutions. The enrollments at the former are all in the thousands, while from parliamentary replies by the Minister of Bantu Education[11] the following facts emerge:

(a) The total number of students who were enrolled in the three Bantu university colleges at the end of the 1963 academic year was 597, and for the 1964 session 759.

(b) Non-matriculants, i.e. students unqualified for degree study but admitted to professional diploma programs, constituted 46 per cent of the 1963 enrollment and 32 per cent of the 1964 group.

In many departments at the non-white colleges, the staff-student ratio is far more favorable than at the white universities. In the writer's opinion, however, the consequent opportunities for tutorial work are more than offset by the effects of departmental (as well as institutional) smallness. Students at such colleges must necessarily have available to them an educational experience far less rich, varied, and stimulating than those at the larger insti-

[11] Assembly, 1964, col. 5027.

tutions, not only because of the paucity of academic personnel and the relative inferiority of material equipment, not only because of the restrictive regulations for students (which will be discussed in the section on control), but because of the "college climate" which results from a student body characterized by smallness, homogeneity, and a large minority unqualified for academic studies to the level of a bachelor's degree.

What long-term social consequences may be expected from such segregation at school? At one level the policy probably works as intended: the homogeneity of the pupil's peer group reinforces the other social influences leading him to regard South Africans who are not of his kind as members of so many out-groups. (And some groups are more "out" than others.) From the regime's point of view, this is an aid to its aspirations. But this narrowness in socialization may have effects less advantageous to the stability of South African society. National unity among the whites, in the regime's view a *sine qua non* in the country's long-term emergence, cannot but be hampered by the separation between the young Afrikaner and his English-speaking fellow white. And since the regime requires some degree of loyalty even from those whom it is grooming for separate Bantu nationhood, and some degree of social cohesion among those groups whose diversity it stresses, the growth of a strong anti-white sentiment among students at segregated African colleges (students many of whose predecessors would have been at the then "open" universities and so in close contact with at least some white equals) cannot but be a threat to the peaceful solution of South Africa's problems. It may be that the regime considers these dangers insignificant, or is willing to pay the price for the maintenance of its apartheid policy.

The people of each ethnic category continue to be served, as under the previous regime, by private (mainly church) schools as well as by the state schools, and in view of our overall theme it is appropriate to record here some recent proposals and practical developments in relation to these schools. In some sectors of the education system the division of the school population according to religion has been reduced, in others increased, and at least one group of people concerned with church schools has proposed the bridging of the primary gulf between white and non-white pupils.

As a result of the withdrawal of state funds from mission insti-

tutions, the number of private schools within the African sector
fell from over 4,000 in 1953 to fewer than 700 in 1961. (This
financial aspect of policy will be discussed in the next section.)
Most of the latter are Roman Catholic institutions. Since 1962
the government has forbidden Catholic schools to admit non-
Catholic pupils, on the grounds that non-Catholics are adequately
provided for by the state system.[12] Most other Christian schools for
Africans have been secularized since the mid-fifties, so that the
overall shift has been in the direction of greater religious heterogeneity in the non-Catholic African schools and a sharper segregation of Catholics arising from the exclusion of non-Catholics
from their schools.

Regarding church schools for whites, two recent developments
merit attention: one within the Anglican community, the other
within the Calvinist.

In 1964 the Church Schools Action Group, comprising a number of recent graduates of seven Anglican private schools, issued
a pamphlet which maintained that church schools in South Africa
were in danger of allowing their pupils to become socially conditioned, first by their failure to teach their pupils the social implications of Christian belief, and secondly by their racially exclusive
character.

The criticism of the Church schools goes much deeper than the question of integration. The basic query is whether the Church schools are in
fact producing committed Christians who are able to give reasons for the
faith that is in them, and who are determined to live out the social implications of Our Lord's commandment—to love our neighbours as ourselves,
and to do unto others as we would have them do unto us. In other words,
are the Church schools producing Christians, free from the taint of snob-
bishness or prejudice, equipped to play a positive, if humble, role in the
South Africa of today and, particularly, in the South Africa of tomorrow? [13]

Among its proposals the most radical was that non-whites be
admitted to the "white" church schools. The group had sought

[12] In 1961, 30 per cent of the 90,000 pupils in Catholic schools were non-
Catholic: *Race Relations News*, November, 1961; *Natal Mercury*, October 18,
1961.
[13] Church Schools Action Group, *The Challenge to Church Schools* (private circulation, [1964]) , p. 4.

formal legal opinion, and had been advised that no government permission was required for the appointment of a non-white as a non-resident teacher in such a school, nor for the occasional use by non-whites of school amenities such as playing fields, halls, and chapel. Furthermore, non-whites could with government permission be admitted to such a school, except in the Transvaal, whose Ordinance No. 29 of 1953 totally forbade this.[14]

Such permission has been given in the case of a few Chinese and Japanese pupils, of whom there are not sufficient numbers—in most parts of the country—for separate schools. But, as R. F. Currey has pointed out, what is required is

a separate permit in each individual case in terms of the Group Areas Act and its various amendments; and in the case of African pupils the approval, in addition, of the Minister of Bantu Administration has to be obtained. The meshes of the net, in fact, are extremely closely woven; and one does not need to be a political prophet to guess that anything faintly approaching a large scale granting of permits required is hardly to be included in the list of things likely to happen in South Africa.[15]

The same observer, expressing himself in sympathy with the abandonment of ethnic restrictions upon admission to church schools, drew attention to a number of difficulties that might be expected, quite apart from the question of whether the necessary government permits would be given. For instance, the number of African parents who were likely to be able to afford the school fees was very limited,

so limited, indeed, that the number of African pupils who would enter by the normal door would never amount to anything near "integration" in the schools.[16]

In the comparably placed Rhodesian church schools, he noted, the fees of the Africans were heavily subsidized by generous benefactions.

Furthermore, the admission of a group of children from a different background from that of the majority in the school might present substantial difficulties of relationships and of teaching.

[14] *Ibid.*, p. 7.
[15] "Can the Races be Educated Together?" Paper read at Faith in Action Conference, Grahamstown, August 1, 1964. Mimeographed. P. 3.
[16] *Ibid.*, p. 4.

He quoted with approval the following resolution taken by the principals of the Rhodesian church schools:

It is the responsibility of the Heads of the Schools to see that every pupil admitted is able to take his place happily and congenially in the corporate life of the school, and that on returning home for the holidays he will be able to do so happily and congenially in the family circle.[17]

In the light of these considerations, Currey suggested

that it is every Christian's duty to make it clear that he is opposed to the legal enforcing of apartheid in our schools and universities—however futile such protest may appear; that every possible attempt should be made to introduce a small number of non-white pupils into our Church schools, despite the legal, educational, and economic difficulties of doing this; that finally any attempt to do this without going most carefully into the circumstances of each particular case, or without full consideration of the formidable difficulties involved, is to invite certain disappointment.[18]

Reporting in October, 1964, to the Orange Free State Synod of the (Anglican) Church of the Province of South Africa, N. H. C. Ferrandi, principal of one of these schools (St. Andrew's, Bloemfontein), indicated that he was aware of his school's duty to take the lead in non-racialism, and claimed some degree of progress in that connection. Much had still to be done, however, before the stage was reached when non-white South Africans could attend St. Andrew's without embarrassment or prejudice on either side. Most heads of church schools, he maintained, regarded integration at school as an ideal to be attained not by hasty action but by friendly cooperation and the breaking down of racial barriers over many years.[19] This called forth immediate editorial comment in the local pro-Government newspaper; translated extracts follow:

If the principals' ideal be realised, it will not end there. Children who grow up together in this way will want to know why a mixed social and marital life is not possible. And this in a society which in the main is moving away from mixing. . . . How will the products [of such a school] feel in a community which rejects their colour feeling? [20]

If you decide upon and work towards school integration, you decide

---

[17] Cited in *Ibid.*, p. 5.
[18] *Ibid.*
[19] Reported in *Volksblad*, October 6, 1964.
[20] *Volksblad*, October 7, 1964. Translation by A. P. H.

upon and work against everything which the policy of separate development in South Africa has achieved and still seeks to achieve.[21]

If, for religious or any other reasons, teachers and ecclesiastics are convinced that ultimately the racial situation in the country should and will develop differently from the direction in which national policy is at present leading it, they are at liberty so to believe, but if they actively begin working and preparing for the situation of which they dream, they must be willing to clash with the community which judges and acts otherwise. . . . The essence of separate development is against a unitary state, recognises natural barriers, seeks to escape discrimination by preventing or removing points of friction—such as at school desks; and would have the races co-exist by according each one, in its own country, full rights and if necessary full independence.[22]

In a subsequent circular to parents, the school's board of governors stated that the school authorities were resisting the pressure exerted by some people in the country who believed that private schools should be integrated. The board saw the school as a reflection of the social milieu rather than as an agent of social change, and maintained that no attempt to integrate the school should be considered unless there were to come about a significant change in the climate of opinion in the country.[23]

By the end of 1964 no "white" church school had sought government permission to admit non-whites—apart from the few Japanese and Chinese mentioned earlier. Late in that year, however, a Coloured member of the Anglican Church made public his intention to apply for the admission of his son to the white St. George's School in Cape Town. According to reports in *Dagbreek* (December 6, 1964) and the *Sunday Chronicle* (December 13, 1964), the same man stated that a year earlier he had sought the admission of another son to Bishops, an elite Anglican secondary school. He was then told that Bishops was full for many years to come. The man expected that the government would permit St. George's to admit his child—in order to test Anglican reaction. It is commonly recognized that the white communities which support these church schools are likely to be far from eager to approve so radical a venture as integration.

21 *Volksblad,* October 8, 1964. Translation by A. P. H.
22 *Volksblad,* October 9, 1964. Translation by A. P. H.
23 *Volksblad,* December 14, 1964.

The Council of Governors of St. George's School refused to admit the Coloured pupil. The council's decision reads:

> Ever since the founding of the school, over 100 years ago, the boys entering St. George's Grammar School have come from the White group, although there is nothing in the constitution to control this. The majority of members of the council are of the opinion that, having regard for those supporting the school financially, and while having every sympathy for the applications now before the council, the custom and practice of the community, together with the trend of legislation, makes the immediate admission of these boys unacceptable and it is premature to try an experiment of this nature.

The Dean of Cape Town, who is chairman of the school council, disassociated himself from this statement and maintained that "Anglican Church schools should be pioneers and moulders of opinion rather than conformists to a policy we believe to be discriminating and unjust." [24]

One anti-government newspaper commented editorially:

> There can be no doubt that the majority decision will expose the school, and indeed the whole Anglican Church, to a charge of hypocrisy. That charge is not altogether fair; opposition to apartheid, as it is applied by the South African Government, may take many forms, and it is a gross over-simplification to argue that a reluctance to admit, in present circumstances, one non-White boy to a White school makes nonsense of that opposition. But it is more difficult to answer the allegation that the Anglican Church in South Africa is divided on these important issues. The St. George's affair shows that there is a considerable gap between clerical opinion and lay opinion within the church. The clergy say that Christian principles must at all times apply. A substantial section of the laity argues that it is no good attempting to defy Government policy and so-called national sentiment. But in following this reasoning many of the church's ordinary members are, of course, merely evading the agonising decisions, and are doing so by sheltering under policies which are regularly denounced from Anglican Church pulpits. There are many practical hazards in deciding to admit a non-White to a hitherto White school. The Government might intervene. Social problems would arise and have to be faced and solved. Parents might withdraw their children from the school, which might collapse financially. Is it worth while risking the entire future of an Anglican Church school (there are not too

[24] *The Friend,* January 29, 1965.

many of them, and they perform a valuable function in South Africa) for the sake of one Coloured boy? In this case the answer, we think, is yes. The Cape has a long tradition of tolerance, and it seems that the resistance of white parents may well have been over-estimated. More important, those who believe that apartheid in its present form will eventually break down must recognise that a start must be made somewhere. And what better starting point in a new deal for South Africa's wronged and patient Coloured community than an Anglican Church school? [25]

On the other hand, the boy's sister was subsequently accepted by the council of the Herschel School, a local private white school for girls. The school's announcement of this decision noted that the pupil's admission was dependent upon the securing of the necessary government permit. According to the pro-government newspaper *Dagbreek,* government spokesmen maintained that before applying for such a permit, Herschel should ascertain whether most of its pupils' parents were in agreement with the school council's decision. Those parents who do not support the decision should, if they find themselves in the majority, repudiate the council. The girl in question subsequently failed the school's entrance examination. [26]

Many Afrikaners have claimed that private schools tend to isolate their pupils from the main stream of young (white) South Africa, and that South Africans are best educated in state schools. In this connection it is interesting to note the establishment in 1960 of the *Vereniging vir Christelike Onderwys* (Association for Christian Education) , formed for the purpose of opening a series of private schools whose spirit would be that of the Dutch Reformed Church. In the view of the association, the state schools were inadequate for Christian education because they could not follow a definite dogmatic direction. [27] The project had a mixed reception in the Afrikaans press, many ecclesiastical bodies maintaining that private Christian schools were justified only when the Christian education of the child was threatened by alien control of the state school system. [28] Late in 1964 the association announced the opening of its first school—in Pretoria—and indicated its hope

[25] *The Friend,* January 30, 1965.
[26] *The Friend,* March 15, 1965; *Dagbreek,* March 14, 1965; *Cape Times,* July 6, 1965.
[27] *Die Transvaler,* August 1, 1960.
[28] *Die Voorligter,* November, 1960; *Die Transvaler,* March 22, 1961.

that this would be the beginning of a series of state-aided schools catering to particular religious groups.[29] In the meantime an elementary school controlled by members of the Free Reformed Church had opened in Pretoria early in 1964.[30]

A comparable movement at the university level is the *Verenig-ing vir Christelike Hoër Onderwys* (Association for Christian Higher Education). As stated in its leaflet of general information, its purpose is

the promotion of Christian education, Christian teaching [instruction] and Christian science, i.e. [the Association] seeks to do what it can to ensure that our [i.e. Afrikaans] children receive at university and at col-lege (and thus also at school) an education founded upon and in con-formity with the truth of the Word of God. [Translation by A. P. H.]

Among its objectives is the removal of the "conscience clause" from the charters of the universities with which it is concerned, the Afrikaans-medium institutions. This clause, quoted below, was until 1950 included in all those Acts of Parliament by which new universities were established.

No test of religious belief shall be imposed on any person as a condi-tion of his becoming or continuing to be a graduate of the University or a professor, lecturer, teacher or student at the University, or of his holding any office or receiving any emolument, or exercising any privilege therein, nor shall any preference be given nor advantage be withheld from any person on the ground of his religious belief.[31]

As the Association for Christian Higher Education puts it (in the same leaflet),

This clause forbids the Council of a university to make enquiries in any way about the religious convictions of an aspirant professor or lec-turer. Consequently any person who is only academically qualified may be appointed. It is therefore quite possible that the baptized children of orthodox parents may be surrendered to instructors who are unbelievers or are e.g. oriented towards Roman Catholicism. In this way it is impos-sible for the believing parent to meet the obligations of his church mem-bership in respect to the education of his child.

In 1950 the charter of the Potchefstroom University for Christian

29 *Dagbreek,* September 27, 1964.
30 *Ibid.*
31 E.g., Rhodes University Act No. 15, 1949, Sec. 30; University of the Orange Free State Act No. 21, 1949, Sec. 31.

Higher Education included the conscience clause in a modified form:

(1) In appointing teaching, research and administrative staff the Council shall ensure that the Christian historical character of the University shall be maintained: Provided that no denominational test shall be applied to any person as a condition of his becoming or continuing to be a graduate of the University, or a professor, research worker, lecturer, teacher or member of the administrative staff of the University, or of his holding any office or receiving any emolument or exercising any privilege therein.

(2) No person shall be prevented on the ground of his religious belief from becoming or continuing to be a student or graduate of the University.[32]

The Extension of University Education Act. No. 45, 1959, providing for the establishment and maintenance of the Bantu university colleges, did not include a conscience clause in any form.

An attempt by the University of the Orange Free State to re-place the traditional conscience clause by one permitting applicants for academic posts to be assessed in relation to the university's Protestant Christian principles as well as on academic grounds (Bill No. 13, 1961, sec. 3) was abandoned—at least temporarily—after the proposal had engendered considerable public controversy. In the course of this controversy the Minister of Education, B. J. Vorster, stated that though South Africa was accused of many things, it was never accused of intolerance; and the conscience clause was therefore not necessary in South Africa.[33]

The general trend, then, has been towards a proliferation of ethnic distinctions applicable to school admission. In certain sectors of the educational system there have been moves towards greater religious homogeneity within institutions.

The Allocation of Resources

The way in which the resources available for education are deployed illustrates the problem of inequality in separate development and the general increase in the state's direct power in education. The principal features of this deployment are:

---

[32] Act No. 19, 1950, Sec. 31.
[33] *Die Burger,* October 5, 1961.

(a) the reduction or pegging of state funds available for schools not under state control;

(b) the emphasis, in the education of Africans, upon the provision of elementary education rather than secondary education;

(c) the inadequate provision of complete high school programs for Africans in urban areas (even where there are large concentrations of African population with many qualified candidates) and the placing of such programs in the rural "homelands";

(d) most significantly of all, a very great discrepancy between the per capita expenditure on white pupils and that on non-white pupils.

In the African sector, state funds which before 1953 were available for mission schools are now used for those schools which the state controls directly or through local school boards. (The form of this control will be described in the final section of this chapter.) Regarding white schools, most provinces have decided not to add any new private schools to the list of state-subsidized schools (e.g. Cape Ordinance No. 26, 1956, sec. 69). The general tendency, therefore, is toward a smaller share of the public purse for non-state schools.

In 1953, when the Bantu Education Act was passed, the African pupils in elementary and secondary schools were distributed as follows: 72.3 per cent of them in the first four years of school, 24.1 per cent in the next four years, and 3.5 per cent in the final four (high school) years. In 1963 the corresponding figures were 71.8 per cent, 25.2 per cent, and 3.1 per cent (Assembly, 1964, col. 713). Though there has been a substantial increase in enrollment—from 858,079 in 1953 to 1,770,260 in 1963[34]—the proportions have not altered significantly.

At a time when the planners of educational systems serving comparable "developing" societies are generally agreed on the importance of a rapid expansion of secondary facilities, even at the expense of universal primary education, the South African policy in this matter calls for explanation.

Some indication of the reasoning behind this approach may be obtained from a policy speech made in the Senate in 1954 by Dr. Verwoerd, then Minister of Native Affairs. The contributions

---

[34] F. J. de Villiers, *Financing of Bantu Education* (Durban: South African Institute of Race Relations, 1961, mimeo.), p. 2; Assembly, 1964, col. 713.

of white and Bantu taxpayers to Bantu education should be so deployed, he maintained, as to be of greatest benefit to the greatest possible number; each Bantu taxpayer should have equal access for his children to such basic educational facilities as available funds could provide. Such facilities, said Dr. Verwoerd, would probably be between two and four years of instruction in the reading and writing of the vernacular, in arithmetic, in English and Afrikaans, and in the cardinal principles of the Christian religion. Secondly, a Bantu pupil should obtain such knowledge, skills, and attitudes as would be useful and advantageous to him and to his community in the social and economic circumstances of South Africa.[35]

The geographical distribution of school facilities reflects the state's view that in the cities the Africans are merely visitors: the foci of development (and therefore of educational development) are the reserves. As Dr. Verwoerd put it in 1954:

> It is the policy of my department that education should have its roots entirely in the Native areas and in the Native environment and Native community. There Bantu education must be able to give itself complete expression and there it will have to perform its real service. In the Native territories where the services of educated Bantu are very much needed, Bantu education can complete its full cycle by which the child is taken out of the community by the school, developed to his fullest extent in accordance with aptitudes and ability, and thereafter returned to the community to serve and to enrich it.[36]

And in 1959 the Minister of Bantu Education made it clear that although lower primary schools (covering the first four years) would as far as possible be provided wherever there were African children of schoolgoing age, in relation to schooling beyond the primary level

> it is the intention to give preference to Bantu areas because this is in the first place where Bantu development must be promoted generally. . . . For this reason it is our policy to restrict higher primary education, and particularly post-primary education, in the urban locations, but not in the Native areas; preference is given to the Native areas in regard to the establishment of that type of school.[37]

[35] South Africa, *Senate Debates*, 1954, cols. 2606-2607. Hereafter cited as Senate.

[36] Senate, 1954, cols. 2618–2619.

[37] Senate, 1959, cols. 2340–2341.

Furthermore, as the Secretary for Bantu Education put it, the African matriculant's field of activity would be mainly in the Bantu territories, and it was desirable that he should have studied in the environment where he would serve.[38]

The state spends R155[39] per pupil per annum on the schooling of white children and R12.11 per pupil per annum on Bantu education.[40]

A rationale for this discrepancy is provided by a speech by the Minister of Finance in 1958:

> We do not have one homogeneous community in which the prosperous people can be taxed to provide services for the less prosperous, but we have various communities which must be economically sound individually. The White guardian community must provide the funds for the essential development services, and it is the duty of the state to see that the necessary development is planned and carried out, but thereafter the community concerned must itself see to the extension of those services in accordance with its capacity, and that capacity must be determined with reference to the essential benefits that community will derive from such development. If the State is simply continually to give money it will undoubtedly undermine sound development of the Bantu community, and the White guardian would be failing in its duty.[41]

This approach had already been embodied in the Exchequer and Audit Amendment Act. No. 7 of 1955 (see above, p. 255). A more recent elaboration of the official position in this matter, and comment upon it by the South African Institute of Race Relations, is provided in Appendix III, pp. 303–306.

In a memorandum dated August 31, 1964, the South African Institute of Race Relations drew attention to some of the consequences. Despite the 76 per cent increase in enrollment between 1955 and 1963, the increase in expenditure in this period was but 50 per cent—despite the increase in the cost of materials, and despite the higher teachers' salaries introduced in 1963.

[38] *Star,* September 11, 1959, cited in Joy Skinner (ed.), *Bantu Education 1949–59* (Durban: South African Institute of Race Relations, 1960, mimeo.), p. 31.

[39] In February, 1962, South Africa's pounds-shillings-pence currency was decimalized with a unit of one rand (R2 = 1 pound; R1 = $1.39).

[40] *The Friend,* October 17, 1964, a report referring to the Cape Province; Minister of Bantu Education, Assembly, 1964, col. 6847.

[41] Assembly, 1958, col. 3878.

As a South African economist put it in 1964,

Bantu education received a serious setback under the new regime; the Bantu population is too poor to undertake investments in their education at an increasing rate in order to speed up the growth of educational facilities. The real incomes and hence the savings of the Bantu are too small to make the present system more elastic in order to increase schools and teachers to accommodate the growing numbers of Bantu pupils. A growing school population and a very inelastic supply of funds have led to an increase in the pupil load per teacher with the resultant decrease in classroom efficiency. It would thus appear that "diminishing returns" in education is a serious factor in reducing still further the low productivity of the Bantu pupil. Nor can the fall in the unit cost of educating a Bantu pupil be viewed with complacency, because the decrease is not due to any increase in administrative efficiency.

The financing of any future developments in Bantu education will bear heavily on the poorest section of the Republic's population. Caught in a vicious circle of low productivity, low incomes, and decreasing economic opportunities in the European sector of the economy, the Bantu household will be forced to carry an increasing burden of real sacrifice. We are thus faced with two alternatives either the cost of Bantu education be borne by the general taxpayer, or the real incomes of the Bantu people be increased to enable them to meet the cost. In short, Bantu education is a national not a sectional problem. Viewed from this point of view the method of administration and control of Bantu education is a moot point to the economist.

The problem of finance looms large in view of the fact that at present only 40% of all Bantu children of school-going age are at school. Again, the social loss of not giving any formal education to some 60% of the Bantu children constitutes a grave indictment of Bantu education, despite the fact that during the past decade the absolute numbers at school have increased by more than 50 per cent. The numbers completing the matriculation examination have been for some decades a mere fraction of the total school population. This is a serious situation when regard is had to the small numbers of the Bantu in the professions, and the need for training Bantu matriculants at the Bantu colleges.[42]

An indication of the human wastage which occurs may be obtained from the following information, elicited from the Minister of Bantu Education by a parliamentary question in 1964.

[42] Nathan Hurwitz, *The Economics of Bantu Education* (Durban: South African Institute of Race Relations, 1964), pp. 73–74.

To illustrate wastage in African schools[43]

SCHOOL LEVEL	YEAR	ENROLLMENT
Sub-Standard A	1951	211,629
Sub-Standard B	1952	145,689
Standard I	1953	134,815
Standard II	1954	107,051
Standard III	1955	90,948
Standard IV	1956	68,528
Standard V	1957	55,224
Standard VI	1958	46,277
Form I	1959	19,970
Form II	1960	14,105
Form III	1961	9,821
Form IV	1962	2,006
Form V	1963	1,040

Of the 1,040 who enrolled in the final year of high school in 1963, 896 wrote the matriculation examination; in some cases that of the Joint Matriculation Board, in others that of the Department of Education, Arts and Science. Two hundred ninety candidates passed the university-entrance form, and 246 passed the "Senior Certificate" form. *(Bantu Education Journal*, March, 1964.)

In view of the generally acknowledged shortage of trained manpower in South Africa, the failure to exploit non-white potential calls for explanation. As another South African economist puts it,

The South African dilemma is that most whites believe that the future progress of the country depends upon the maintenance of white hegemony. Yet in attempting to maintain this white hegemony they find themselves forced to adopt measures which conflict with the very requirements of economic growth. These operate both in the economic and the political spheres. In the economic, white voters have used their monopoly of political power to entrench their economic position by restrictions on the movement and advancement of African workers, by maintaining differentials in educational opportunities and by legislative methods to give the whites a monopoly of certain kinds of jobs. These

---

[43] Assembly, 1964, col. 6850.

contrived scarcities and imperfections in the labour market have a corrosive effect upon economic growth, and prevent optimum resource allocation. Moreover, the existence of these barriers discourages initiative and enterprise in both those protected and those against whom the discrimination is applied.[44]

Furthermore, the scarcity of Africans with an education beyond the rudimentary must hamper the development of the Bantu homelands upon whose viability the whole separate development venture depends.

Curricula

School curricula in South Africa, as elsewhere, have reflected the present or past values of the dominant group in society. Since 1948, school programs in some fields have come to be closely tied to government policy on controversial issues. This integration of schooling with national policy is seen in syllabi, pupils' books, and the statements of those who control the school systems.

In the case of white schools, it is the Transvaal which has led the way in the reorientation. To the high school curriculum—similar, in general, to that of most Western countries—there was added in 1957 a compulsory subject called "race studies." That part of the race studies program dealing with Africans was almost entirely devoted to their rural and primitive state. The only section of the syllabus treating the urban African was expressed as follows:

1. Administration and control.
2. Native locations and Native towns.
3. Compounds and hostels and bachelor Natives.
4. Problems: housing, indolence, juvenile crime, other forms of crime and the deterioration of tribal authority.

Extracts from one of the approved textbooks will serve to indicate the emphasis:

The Bantu had a splendid way of living of their own before ever they came into contact with the culture of the whites. In the cities and towns

---

[44] D. Hobart Houghton, *The South African Economy* (London: Oxford University Press, 1964), pp. 218–219.

they have lost much of their old delightful way of living but fortunately much of this has been preserved in their tribal reserves.[45]

The ideal of every Bantu man . . . is to have more than one wife.[46]

The subject "race studies" was withdrawn in 1965.

The guidance program in the Transvaal has also shown signs of a concern for political orthodoxy. (In this province, "guidance" includes assisting the pupil to develop a philosophy of life.) In October, 1958, at an in-service course for guidance teachers provided by the Transvaal Education Department, Professor P. J. Coertze spoke on "the origins and development of the traditional and legal point of view on race relations" and advocated an approach to education in accordance with the tenets of Christian National Education. After his address the head of the guidance services for the Department moved from the chair an unopposed motion:

> That no matter how important factors such as training and experience may be for the guidance teacher the most important thing is that he/she be a person of Christian-national outlook.[47]

One section of the guidance program suggested for schools reads:

> Race relations, whites and non-whites, according to the legal and traditional South African point of view—how to promote this tradition.[48]

In an address to a group of school principals in Johannesburg in 1961, the Administrator of the Transvaal, F. H. Odendaal, made clear one of the roles prescribed for the school system. Every teacher, he said, should deliberately emphasize the necessity for the two white "races" to stand together in order to meet the rising Bantu nationalism. A white consciousness should be inculcated, and children should realize that they are the bearers of Christian Western civilization. The fight for self-preservation and the right of self-determination of the whites in South Africa was a special task of education:

---

[45] E. Hudson, *et al., Race Studies for Standard VI* (Johannesburg: Nasionale Boekhandel, n.d.), p. 78.

[46] E. Hudson, *et al., Race Studies for Standard VII* (Johannesburg: Nasionale Boekhandel, n.d.), p. 35.

[47] Cited by Mavis Warren, "Guidance and Race Studies," *The Black Sash,* IV (1960), 11.

[48] *Ibid.*

We must strive to win the fight against the non-white in the classroom instead of losing it on the battlefield.[49]

Another facet of the Transvaal program which is related to the overall divisive tendencies in the republic's educational policy is the religious education syllabus. As a result of representations, changes were made in the English version only, with the result that there are now significant discrepancies in content and emphasis between the religious education prescribed for Afrikaans-medium schools and that prescribed for English-medium schools. For example (according to a report in the *Sunday Times,* September 13, 1964), the instruction to teachers in the original syllabus includes this sentence:

Every lesson should bring the child nearer to a living, practising faith in Christ and through Him to the knowledge, love and service of God.

In the English version only, this sentence has now been added:

This faith should inevitably lead to love and service to our fellow men.

In African primary schools, the curricular programs officially laid down have been conceded by critics of the Bantu education policy (e.g. the Institute of Race Relations, in memoranda Nos. 60 and 182, 1955) to be fundamentally sound, rather better than the pre-"Bantu education" syllabi, but one the whole not radically different from them. The rural and tribal emphases in the "environmental studies" have however been considered unsuitable for the large number of urban children involved. These emphases may be seen as a reflection of the two facets of the apartheid policy: the reinforcement of tribal loyalties and the fostering of the notion that the rural reserve is the locus of the tribe's development and of its "separate freedom."

In the case of African schools situated on white-owned farms, adaptations in the elementary program may be made along the following lines (in the words of the Minister of Bantu Education):

We have made it compulsory that where the farmer wants these facilities, part of the school instruction of those children on the farm of the European farmer must be training in the normal activities of the farm, in order to encourage a feeling of industriousness on the part of these children and particularly to sharpen in the minds the fact that education

[49] *Die Transvaler,* March 6, 1961.

does not mean that you must not work with your hands, but to point out to them specifically that manual labour and also manual labour on a farm is just as good a formulative and development level [better translated as "formative and developmental subject"] as any other subject is. In order to do this, we create the opportunity so that if there is any farmer who has a farm school on his farm and who wishes to make use of the school children under the supervision of the teacher to assist with certain farm activities, this can be arranged in a proper manner to fit in with the curriculum and the plan of development which is envisaged or provided for that farm school.[50]

Before the present Bantu education policy, African pupils followed the same secondary programs as white pupils. Now this is true only for the final two years of high school. The Bantu Education Department has instituted its own Junior Certificate examination (tenth grade). It is only in the social studies course that the new syllabi differ significantly from those studied under the old regime. The section on vocational guidance, for instance, reads as follows:

1. Emphasis should be placed on the manner of setting about obtaining a job: correct behaviour when employed; loyalty to the employer; the importance of punctuality, neatness, strict honesty, courtesy, modest demeanour, etc.

2. Stress should also be laid on the social and economic value of obtaining jobs near home, rather than at distant places. Distant employment involves heavy expenditure in travel and usually results in injudicious spending, whereas employment near the home benefits the family and tends to build up family solidarity and pride.

3. Avenues of employment open to Bantu with Secondary School education and ways of setting about obtaining such employment.[51]

In the section on South African history and civics, that part dealing with the Africans before contact with whites is headed "Turmoil among the South African Bantu tribes." One result of industrial development is seen to be the "excessive removal" of Africans to the cities, and provision is made for detailed instruction on the present Government's policy of social, economic and political development for Africans.[52]

[50] Senate, 1959, col. 3463.
[51] Department of Bantu Education, *Syllabuses for Junior Certificate* (Pretoria: Government Printer, 1961), p. 102.
[52] *Ibid.*, pp. 105-106.

In defense of the above features of the curriculum, it could be argued that educational programs must be broadly consistent with state policy, and that in the special circumstances of South Africa (heterogeneity of population, ambiguities in affiliation inherited from the previous regime, and vociferous opposition to the government within and beyond the republic's borders) there is more than usual justification for the inhibition of heterodoxy by means of the school system. And as to the rural and tribal emphases in the African syllabuses, it is necessary, from the regime's viewpoint, that tribal links be reinforced, or in the case of urban children, be forged; and that all pupils be oriented toward the rural Bantu homelands.

This type of argument can be founded only upon a totalitarian premise. Certainly some of the features discussed here are at variance with the principle of democratic education that what is controversial be presented as controversial. Since interpretations of the South African situation differ so widely, the education system could be expected (arguing from a democratic premise) to insure that alternative views were fairly presented. Educationally this dogmatic approach must produce an impoverishment of thought; socially it is calculated to reinforce the in-groupish narrowness of concern promoted by segregated schooling; in both ways the educational system will tend to restrict the vision of the country's youth and so disqualify it for its role in solving the republic's social problems.

In 1963 the "1961 Education Panel" (a group of white men, mostly English-speaking, from various academic and professional spheres, describing itself as "an independent private organization to study the present and future educational needs of South Africa and to make constructive suggestions as to how the challenge of change can be met") put the problem thus:

> If people's beliefs are to be deliberately formulated in the interests of the State we must know what the interests of the State will be throughout the next fifty years, over which the adult lives of our children will extend. Here, surely, is the simple distinction between moral and political teaching. We can foresee with reasonable confidence that honesty, for example, will be as desirable in forty years' time as it is now, but can we say the same of any political attitude or belief whatever?

> The point can be illustrated by two major examples from the last

ten years, the one an extreme case and the other a moderate one. Russia is a country where the view of the supremacy of State interests is taken to its extreme conclusions and is vigorously applied in education. Consequently throughout the reign of Stalin, Russian children were vigorously taught that everything that Stalin did was right, and entirely admirable. Yet today, although there has not even been any ostensible change of government, they have been told that Stalin was a criminal and that much of what he did was vicious. In so far as the previous indoctrination was effective, its only effect today must be to strain loyalty to the present regime.

The other example comes from Western Europe. Twenty years ago, or at any time before that for very many years, scarcely anybody in France, Germany or Italy would have doubted that it was in the interests of the State to inculcate nationalism and that one of the implications of nationalism was an unalterable belief in the sacredness of the sovereign independence of the country. Many people would have regarded the inculcation of hatred or contempt for other countries and the promotion of ignorance of them as legitimate means of achieving this objective.

In recent years we have seen France, Germany and Italy actively engaged in pooling their sovereignty, and this is regarded by their governments, and the majority of their people, as what the interests of the State require. Yet the opposition to this development comes from the people who hold an unalterable belief in the sacredness of the sovereign independence of their country, or who nurse hatred or contempt for the other countries involved. In other words, in so far as the indoctrination of twenty years ago was effective it is today directly injuring the interests of the State, as understood by the governments and the majority of the people.[53]

There will of course be great variation in the fidelity with which the teacher communicates the orthodox view, and also in the degree to which the pupils make this view their own. Objective evidence is not available about the effectiveness of these curricular emphases.

Language Medium

In 1949 the Transvaal Provincial Council passed an ordinance (No. 19/1949) requiring that in all schools, private as well as state, a child's home language—Afrikaans or English—should be the

[53] 1961 Education Panel, *Education for South Africa* (Johannesburg: Witwatersrand University Press, 1963), pp. 51–52.

medium of instruction. This requirement was to apply up to Standard VIII (tenth grade). "Home language" was defined as the one in which the school principal deemed the pupil to be more proficient. The Consolidated Education Ordinance of 1953 incorporated this provision. In the Orange Free State, Ordinance No. 16, 1954, required the medium of instruction up to Standard VII to be the child's home language (defined as the official language best understood) except that where the pupil's facility was equal in both languages the parent might choose the medium. Similar legislation in the Cape Province (Ordinance 20, 1956) included a provision that after Standard V (seventh grade) a pupil might be taught in the other medium if certified by an inspector of schools to be capable of receiving instruction in that language. There has been no corresponding legislation in the United Party-controlled province of Natal, where parents select the language medium.

In the Bantu education system, primary schools were instructed, from 1959, to provide all instruction through the vernacular as far as possible. To promote the development of the Bantu languages as instructional media, the Secretary for Native Affairs appointed five committees, one each for Zulu, Xhosa, Sotho, Venda, and Tsonga. To each of these committees were appointed white and African officials of Bantu Education and representatives of the universities and of the African teaching force. The committees were charged with the drafting of recommendations on terminology, orthography, and school syllabi. They were also to edit articles in periodicals for teachers and children, and "to develop the Bantu languages and to expand them from other sources so that they can be used as media of instruction in schools."[54]

Until the terminologies had been sufficiently developed, and until the teachers had mastered their use as media in the higher grades, exclusively mother-tongue instruction could not, of course, be enforced. Meanwhile, if the teachers could manage it, Afrikaans and English were to be used, in equal proportions, as the media of instruction in subjects not taught through a Bantu language.[55]

To those unconvinced of the suitability of the Bantu languages as instructional media above the rudimentary level, the govern-

[54] *Bantu Education: Handbook of Regulations and Instructions* (Pretoria: Government Printer, 1957), p. 194.
[55] Minister of Bantu Education, Senate, 1959, col. 2349.

ment reply is frequently along the lines of the following excerpt from an editorial in an official publication of the Department of Bantu Administration and Development:

It should be recalled that the Greek of the period before Pericles, the Latin of the pre-Augustan age, the English of the early Elizabethan era, the Afrikaans of 1909 were also not suitable in every respect for these purposes and would also never have been employed for educational purposes if the conservative grammarians of those days had had their way. Fortunately this did not happen and the rapid development of the languages concerned in the educational sphere did not lag behind, so that Greek, Latin, English and Afrikaans each in its proper time and place was able to evolve into a worthy carrier of culture.[56]

The official position as it is presented to Africans may be indicated by the following extracts from an address by Dr. H. J. van Zyl, then Under-Secretary for Bantu Education, at a teachers' conference on mother-tongue medium, held at Umtata, Transkei, in 1961. Extensive excerpts are presented here not only for the specific points made about a number of aspects of the policy, but also to illustrate the tone and approach of Bantu Education Department apologias intended for African consumption.

When the change in Bantu education came in 1954 one of the first new policies to be introduced was mother tongue medium in the primary school. . . . This meant that in the Transkei English had to make way for Xhosa. Some people immediately became suspicious and blamed the Government for a retrogressive step aimed at a decline in the quality of Native Education. What they did not know was that mother tongue medium had already been made compulsory in schools for English and Afrikaans-speaking children. They did not know that mother tongue medium was a generally accepted educational principle observed in all advanced countries of the world and that an enlightened country like South Africa could not possibly expose itself to the criticism of experts for maintaining an unscientific approach to education. It would have been like cultivating our fields by using a primitive hoe while disregarding the much more convenient plough of modern times.

This conference has been called because it is understood that in certain areas of the Transkei there is doubt as to the desirability of mother tongue medium in our Xhosa schools. We must admit that this is an extremely strange phenomenon . . . the least that we ever expected,

[56] *Bantu* (June, 1959), pp. 8–9.

because it is generally known that all over the world the people have a deep-rooted love for their own language. It is the one aspect of their culture from which they refuse to part. While foreign influences may be marked in other respects one gains the impression that people take pride in their language and do all they can for its preservation and development.

I do not want to propose that the Xhosa people are different and that they do not care for their language. In fact, it would be quite impossible to associate such an indifferent attitude with proud and colourful people like the Pondos, the Tembus and the Fingoes. I think there should be no doubt in our minds about the profound affection the Xhosa have for their language. I also think that we can state without the slightest hesitation that they do not like any other language better. It is certainly also their wish that it should be kept as the most valuable heritage for generations to come. I want, however, to blame those who do not believe in Xhosa as a school language for being ignorant of the dangers that threaten a language which is not given its rightful place in the activities of a progressive community, and more particularly if other languages are given pride of place in those activities. Languages, like the human body, must be in constant use lest they deteriorate and ultimately collapse. I wish also to find fault with those who argue superficially that they know Xhosa well and therefore see no reason why at school it should be used to such an extent that the official languages must suffer. . . .

By being taught through the medium of English and Afrikaans in the secondary school, Bantu pupils are placed in a more favourable position to acquire a good knowledge of these languages than white children. Afrikaans-speaking children are taught in Afrikaans right up to matriculation, taking English as a subject only. The same rule applies to English-speaking pupils who have to learn Afrikaans the same way. . . . For the learning of the official languages the Bantu child is therefore better off than white children. White people will soon say they do not like this discrimination.

You may ask what about those who leave school after Standard II or even later? They will not have the opportunities afforded the more fortunate ones who proceed to the secondary school. Again there is nothing to fear. The youngster who is destined to work with whites will make even faster progress in learning an official language than those who remain at school. You should hear your kinsmen serving at hotels and service stations in Cape Town and its vicinity talking to us in Afrikaans almost fluently, and they did not learn that language in the former Cape Xhosa schools.

I hope that I have succeeded in convincing you that there is wisdom and reason in the Government's educational policies—and above all that there is no discrimination.

The Xhosa people are at the crossroads: they must choose whether they wish to destroy what they have inherited or whether they will jealously treasure and guard their true inheritance, their own language.[57]

The use of vernacular medium throughout the primary school has been claimed by the Minister of Bantu Education to be one of the reasons for the increase in the proportion of successful candidates in the Junior Certificate (tenth grade, external) examination: 78 per cent in 1963 as against 57 per cent in 1962, 55 per cent in 1961, 56 per cent in 1960, and 42 per cent in 1959. (The other reasons: better selection of secondary entrants; improvement in equipment; greater availability of handbooks.)[58] As the Minister put it, in January, 1964:

> The group of Junior Certificate candidates who wrote the examinations last year is the first group which received its tuition through the medium of the mother tongue throughout the entire period of the primary school. This must necessarily prove that pupils get a better grasp of the subject-matter and gain a better insight when they are taught through the mother tongue in the primary school. This is particularly noticeable in a subject such as arithmetic, in which the performance of the pupils in the past was usually weak.[59]

There is of course a great difference between the significance of this vernacular medium principle in African schools and in white schools. In the latter, an insistence upon this principle above all others (above, in particular, the parent's right to choose his child's school from among those locally available to him as a taxpayer and to which his child is academically admissable) may serve to restrict (say) an Afrikaans-speaking child to a type of school with a cultural, religious, and political orientation possibly objectionable to his parents. Either official language is, however, a suitable medium of communication for advanced education, and the social function of the mother-tongue policy in this context is to reinforce the separation of groups referred to earlier in this chapter. It cannot be defended on pedagogic grounds: though in the infant classes the vernacular is the obvious medium, this is not

---

[57] H. J. van Zyl, "Bantu Languages at the Crossroads," *Bantu Education Journal,* VII (June, 1961), 247–252.

[58] Assembly, 1964, cols. 389–390.

[59] *Ibid.,* col. 390.

necessarily true at higher levels; and children who learn a second language in their early years may effectively be taught through that language at school. The more efficient methods of foreign language learning currently being developed are likely to make it clear that the argument is not a pedagogic but a social and political one. And with the pedagogic argument out of the way—at least in the higher classes—it might be suggested that the nation's cohesion could be advanced by allowing pupils to spend a portion of their school career in a stream employing as medium the language of another cultural group.

As regards the schooling of Africans, the insistence upon vernacular medium above the lowest classes handicaps the African people in two ways. First, there *is* a pedagogic argument, and it operates *against* the African language as a medium. The work of the British sociologist of language, Basil Bernstein, has drawn attention to the fact that language deeply influences what is learned and how it is learned, and therefore influences future learning.[60] Bernstein's focus has been upon the situation of the working-class child, whose linguistic equipment, the product of his upbringing, severely limits the conceptualizing activity of which he is capable, and therefore the kind and degree of learning in which he will succeed. The middle-class child, on the other hand, acquires from his upbringing the type of language employed by the education system to communicate the skills, knowledge, and attitudes of the modern world. An analogous situation, it may be maintained, exists in relation to the African child. The language with which he grows up is suitable for many cultural and social purposes (its maintenance as a medium for such communication would seem not to require artificial reinforcement), but it is generally conceded to be incapable—at this stage—of mediating the complexities and subtleties of subject matter derived mainly from an advanced economy. The regime hopes to develop the African languages so that they may fulfill this role in advanced education. But, as the 1961 Education Panel has put it,

Just as there is no place for trying to change cultures from outside, so there is none for trying to preserve them from outside. All cultures must and do change and if they did not they would ultimately perish through

[60] See Basil Bernstein, "Social Class and Linguistic Development: A Theory of Social Learning," in A. H. Halsey, *et al.* (eds.), *Education, Economy, and Society* (New York: Free Press of Glencoe, 1961), pp. 288–314.

losing touch with contemporary needs. The decision as to how fast and in what direction a culture shall change, what its attitude should be to other languages, for example, is a decision belonging to the bearers of the culture alone. In our opinion, therefore, White-inspired attempts to insist upon the preservation of Bantu languages are as misplaced as White attempts to eliminate such languages would be. The decision as to how Bantu languages as a medium of culture and learning shall develop belongs to the Bantu; or, to be more accurate, the decision as to each particular language belongs to those whose language it is.[61]

The second handicap implicit in this state policy is the inhibition of communication (and thus cohesion) among the various African groups.

The African desperately strives for unity, and is strongly opposed to any tendency to division among his people. The multipilicity of African languages has always been regarded as an impediment to unity. In an effort to overcome this, the African has accepted English as the lingua franca of the sub-continent, and is glad to see the disappearance of tribal barriers. To him, then, the retribalisation of the schools and the emphasis it lays on the different vernaculars is a retrogressive step. A national awareness that is little appreciated by many has come over the African, and it is perhaps the greatest single reason for his objection to vernacular tuition. He feels he has a right to decide his own destiny. To the stranger, national consciousness and opposition to mother-tongue instruction may seem incompatible; to the African, in his present circumstances, there is nothing contradictory in it.[62]

In 1962 the government appointed the Cingo Commission (three Africans, with two white assessors) to inquire into the teaching of the official languages and the use of the mother tongue as the medium of instruction in primary schools in Transkei. Reporting in 1963, this Commission (RP 22/1963) recommended that the change from vernacular medium be gradual, during the seventh, eighth, and ninth years of school, and that thereafter the medium be one of the official languages, not two as had been the case since the introduction of the Bantu education policy. In January, 1965, the Secretary for Education in the Transkei announced that when the territory's new syllabi (then being drafted) were brought into

---

[61] 1961 Education Panel, *op cit.*, p. 56.
[62] J. C. M. Mbatha, "Vernacular Tuition: Why Africans Object to Compulsion," *The Black Sash*, IV (September–November, 1960), 26.

effect, the medium of instruction after the first four years of schooling would be English or Afrikaans, according to the choice of the parent. By mid-1965, 1,125 of the 1,600 local communities responsible for schools had decided to choose English as the medium from the sixth year of schooling. In the fifth year there would be a gradual transition from vernacular to English.[63]

Control

As was indicated in the opening section of this chapter, the changes in the roles of church and state in education during the present regime have been mainly in the direction of greater power for the state, and, within the political system itself, greater power for the central government as compared with the provincial governments.

The most radical shifts in control have taken place in African education. First, the missions lost their role as educational agents of the state. As Dr. Verwoerd, then Minister of Native Affairs, put it in 1953:

Good racial relations cannot exist when education is given under the control of people who create wrong expectations on the part of the Native himself, if such people believe in a policy of equality, if, let me say for example, a Communist gives this training to the Natives. Such a person will, by the very nature of the education he gives, both as regards the content of that education and as regards its spirit, create expectations in the mind of the Bantu which clash with the possibilities in this country. It is therefore necessary that Native education should be controlled in such a way that it should be in accord with the policy of the State. . . . If the Native in South Africa today in any kind of school in existence is being taught to expect that he will lead his adult life under a policy of equal rights, he is making a big mistake.[64]

In suggesting other reasons for terminating the missions' local management function in the education of Africans, the Eiselen Commission on Native Education (1949-1951) drew attention to the educational results of denominational rivalry, to the overlap and inefficiency, and to the isolation of the schools from the local African communities. It recommended that the conduct of the

[63] *Sunday Chronicle,* January 17, 1965; *Rand Daily Mail,* August 6, 1965.
[64] Assembly, 1953, cols. 3576, 3586.

schools pass gradually from the churches to local and regional
Bantu authorities under the supervision of the central government.[65]

This recommendation was adopted by the government. In
notifying the missions of the introduction of the new form of local
management, the Bantu Education Division of the Department of
Native Affairs (this division subsequently became the Department
of Bantu Education) stressed that the purpose was not the removal
of religious influence

but the enlistment of the energies of the Bantu in the development of
a healthy social and economic life of their own.[66]

The transfer of schools from church to secular control would be
accompanied by reasonable compensation for any plant changing
hands. Where a church did not wish to sell its school, buildings
might be hired. School managers were asked to inform the department whether they wished to hand over their schools to Bantu
community organizations or retain them with a reduced subsidy:
75 per cent of the salaries of approved teachers. (It was later announced that the 75 per cent grant for church schools would be
progressively reduced and would cease after 1957.)

The Dutch Reformed Churches approved of the secularization
of local educational management, but most of the other churches
indicated their opposition to the transfer. Faced with its implementation, these latter churches ranged in their response from an
unwilling acceptance of the only course which would ensure continued state subsidy for the schools at their missions to an outright
refusal to cooperate in any way in a transformation regarded as
fundamentally evil.

The Episcopal Synod of the (Anglican) Church of the Province
of South Africa, for instance, followed its condemnation of the
Bantu Education Act with a statement that

The majority of us are of the opinion that the Church should not
make itself responsible for taking part in such an education system. All
we are prepared to do is to lease certain of our buildings to the State.

[65] Union of South Africa, *Report of the Commission on Native Education,*
1949–51 (Pretoria: Government Printer, 1951), pars. 595, 816.

[66] Department of Native Affairs, "Circular to Grantees, Superintendents or
Managers of State-Aided Schools." FN 262/302, August 2, 1954.

The majority of us think that in any case it would be wrong to refuse to lease our buildings. Such a refusal would throw many teachers out of employment and leave many children without opportunity of any kind of instruction. It is incompatible with our duty to the African people to take action which might lead to such results.[67]

Decisions similarly expressed were taken by the Methodist Church, the Congregational Union, the Presbyterian Church, and certain smaller bodies.[68] While most Anglican dioceses followed the view expressed by their Episcopal Synod, the Bishop of Johannesburg decided that he could not cooperate even to the extent of leasing buildings. He would rather close the schools than have the plant used for the implementation of the new policy. The Roman Catholic bishops resolved to retain their school buildings and to embark upon a fund-raising campaign to make up, as far as possible, for the loss of state aid.

As a result of the reallocation of public funds, the constellation of mission schools was reduced from over 4,000 in 1953 to fewer than 700 in 1961.

Today the African school system is administered at the local level by a series of school boards whose composition varies according to the local administrative context.[69] All Board members must be African, and all nominations must be approved by the Secretary for Bantu Education.

Within its district, each board controls community schools, employs and dismisses teachers, allocates equipment, investigates complaints, supervises school budgets, and advises the Bantu Education Department on all educational affairs within its constituency. Its powers in relation to teachers are limited by an arrangement whereby state grants for teachers' salaries are earmarked for specific teachers whose appointments have been individually approved by the Bantu Education Department. The salary of any such teacher may be cut off by the government without any reason being given.[70]

Primary schools situated on white farms or on mine or factory

[67] *Natal Mercury,* November 11, 1954.
[68] *Natal Daily News,* September 22, 1954; Skinner, *op. cit.,* p. 8.
[69] See Government Notices Nos. 61, 258, 434, 893, and 2459, 1955; 2206, 1956; 158, 1957.
[70] Government Notice No. 86, 1955, regulation 3.

property are managed by the owners of such properties and subsidized under an arrangement somewhat different from that of the community-managed schools.[71] In white farming areas, each school is erected on land owned by the farmer, and its continued existence depends upon his permission. Furthermore, a child resident upon a neighboring farm may attend the school only with the permission of the land owner. This child must also secure the permission of the farmer who employs his (the child's) father. In explaining these requirements to Parliament in April, 1961, the Minister of Bantu Education, W. A. Maree, stated that only by recognizing the farmer as master on his farm land had the government been able to expand the farm school system by 20 per cent between 1957 and 1960 (from 1,400 schools with 143,000 pupils to 1,750 schools with 172,000 pupils). The government was succeeding in winning the cooperation of farmers who had previously suspected the schools of depriving them of their labor. In the absence of farm schools, Bantu children often went to the towns for education, thus denuding the white farms of potential young workers.[72]

The first shift in the control of African education, then, was that in local management: from the missions to the local secular education authorities, normally African school boards. The second shift was the centralization of legislative and executive power: under the Bantu Education Act of 1953 the provincial governments lost the power to legislate upon and administer African schooling; under the Bantu Education Amendment Acts Nos. 36, 1956, and 33, 1959, the Union Parliament greatly increased the powers of the Minister concerned with Bantu education and provided for some delegation of the minister's powers to the secretary of his department. (The latter was given the power to permit or prohibit the registration—hence the existence—of African schools.) Considerable power nominally assigned to local boards is wielded from Pretoria as a result of the fact that state subsidies for teachers' salaries are earmarked for individual teachers who must be approved by the Bantu Education Department.

In other sectors of the education system there are further instances of both these facets of the shift in control.

[71] Government Notice No. 119, 1955.
[72] Assembly, 1961, col. 5506.

Regarding the shift to state control, instances occur of the loss or potential loss of power in education by the churches, by educational institutions, and by individuals. The Coloured Persons Education Act No. 47, 1963, and the Indians Education Act No. 61, 1965, make it possible (clause 5) for the state to take over and administer directly any of the church schools at present run under state subsidy and state supervision. As to institutions, there is the loss of autonomy by the technical colleges under the Vocational Education Act of 1955, the control exercised in the Transvaal (since Ordinance No. 29, 1953) over the curriculum, plant, and calendar of private schools, and the requirement that each teacher in such schools be registered; finally, there is the diminution of university autonomy in three ways. First, the residential universities have lost the right to admit non-whites. Secondly, under the same legislation (the Extension of University Education Act of 1959), a series of university colleges was established which came under direct state control involving, among other things, the state appointment of college senates and a Ministerial veto over student admissions.[73] Thirdly, with effect from the beginning of 1965 persons whom the Minister of Justice has "named" as Communists (no trial nor public enquiry is entailed) are forbidden to teach at state-subsidized institutions.

Individuals, too, have lost some rights previously enjoyed. Mention has been made of the loss of parental choice entailed in provincial legislation on language media. In a very different sphere, control over the activities of students in the Bantu colleges has been made significantly stricter than has been traditional in South African universities. The following examples are taken from the regulations promulgated in 1960 in respect to the University College of Fort Hare:

3. Resident students may not leave the College precincts without permission from the Hostel Superintendent or a representative duly authorized by the Rector.

6. A student may not admit a visitor to a hostel without permission from the Hostel Superintendent.

7. Any student organisation or student activity is subject to prior approval of the Rector.

8. No meetings may be held on the grounds of the College without

[73] *The Friend,* September 5, 1964.

permission from the Rector. Approved student committees may meet according to the rules of the approved constitution of the body concerned.

11. No statement for the press may be given by or on behalf of the students without the Rector's permission.

15. No collection lists may be circulated in the precincts of the College without permission from the Rector.[74]

Within the political system, the shift in the locus of power over education from province to center has occurred in relation to the education of Africans (already noted), of Coloureds and Indians (the 1963 and 1965 legislation gave the Republic's Parliament the previously provincial right to legislate on Coloured education and Indian education respectively), and, to a very much lesser degree, of whites. In 1959 a Supreme Court decision confirmed the right of the national Public Service Commission to control the appointments of administrative officials serving provincial education departments. (Under the complex administration structure relating the Union to its provinces, such officials—but not the teachers—were Union civil servants under provincial jurisdiction.). In previous years the Commission had normally followed provincial recommendations in making such appointments. In 1959, however, Natal protested in vain to the Union government against the commission's decision that J. H. Stander become Deputy-Director of Education, Natal, rather than the province's nominee, H. Lundie.

The second limitation of provincial power in relation to white schools was Act No. 86, 1962, which established a National Advisory Education Council, appointed by the Minister of Education and charged with advising the minister on educational policy. Since section 8 of this act requires provincial councils to consult with this council and with the minister before introducing educational legislation, and since, in the debate on the measure, the minister stated that if the implementation of the Advisory Council's good advice required it, educational legislation would be introduced in the national legislature,[75] there would appear grounds for interpreting this legislation as a step toward nationalization.

---

[74] Government Notice R-1444, *Government Gazette Extraordinary*, September 23, 1960. These regulations appeared in the 1964 yearbook of that college, and identical or similar rules appear in the yearbooks of the other Bantu colleges.

[75] Assembly, 1962, col. 8187.

This interpretation is supported by announcements that the Minister of Education intended to introduce legislation providing for a national education system,[76] and that he had accepted the Advisory Council's plan to end provincial control over white secondary education and develop instead a "national pattern of education."[77] In 1965 it was announced that the National Advisory Education Council had drafted and submitted to the minister, as a basis for further discussion, a bill to remove divided (provincial) control over (white) secondary education.[78]

A special case in the matter of control is the Transkei. In this African state, education is among those matters upon which the territorial Assembly may legislate, subject to a Pretoria veto. It is not yet clear to what extent the Transkei will be permitted by the republican government to evolve an educational policy at variance with that of the republic. In the Transkeian Assembly, a select committee of members of the Government and Opposition has recommended a return to the pre-Bantu Education curricular programs of the Cape Education Department, and, from the fifth year of school, the replacement of the vernacular as medium by the official language of the parents' choice. The Assembly has adopted these recommendations, but Pretoria has not yet been confronted with legislation requiring its consent to a departure from its policy —or its veto—demonstrating the limits of the Transkei's autonomy.

If one accepts, as the regime does, that the educational system must faithfully reflect the state's overall social policy, and that individuals and groups must not be allowed to control or administer sectors of the system if they are likely to act at variance with that policy; then the centripetal tendencies described in this section are but a logical consequence. (Furthermore, a regime committed to the eradication of racial distinctions would be as capable as the present regime of employing centralized state control in the furtherance of its social objectives.) The churches which administered African schools could not be trusted to communicate orthodoxy, nor could an Opposition-controlled province (Natal) be trusted to legislate in accordance with the central government's views, so the churches ceased to be the state's local educational a-

[76] Natal *Daily News,* October 8, 1963.
[77] *Evening Post,* December 11, 1963.
[78] *Volksblad,* September 17, 1965.

gents, and the provinces ceased to have legislative powers in this sphere. In the Coloured schools, though the legislative power has passed from province to center, the churches still act as local agents; but the state has the power to take over and administer directly any schools at present run by the missions. For white schools, the logical step would be national legislation to bring Natal into line on matters such as language medium. This has not happened yet, but such an event would not be incompatible with the trends in white schooling which have been described above. At the university level, too, a segregationist regime which is determined to implement its policy with or without the consent of the governed will insure that behavior at variance with its wishes will be restricted by a system of regulations, ministerial vetos, and direct state control of institutions.

Some of these measures, however, may be justified without the premise of separate development. The churches' near-monopoly of African education, for instance, was long in need of review, and a necessary innovation from any political viewpoint was some provision for the participation of African communities in the local administration of the school system. However, there have been some complaints from teachers about interference in professional matters by ill-educated members of school boards and school committees, and the government veto over membership must prevent them from functioning as representative bodies.

Conclusion

The way in which the regime has allocated roles in education among the various interested parties (parents; local, provincial, and national governmental authorities; and the churches) and the way the Nationalist Government has carried out its own role have produced an educational picture which makes sense, if at all, only in terms of the separate development policy. "If at all," for there are serious contradictions between elements of the educational policy and the regime's long-term aspirations for South Africa. Two which have been discussed earlier may be merely mentioned here: the separation of Afrikaans- and English-speaking white children despite the government's stated wish and clear need for the development of a united white nation; and the relative underspending on African education despite the republic's critical shortage of trained manpower in the republic as a whole and in the Bantu "homelands" in particular.

But is there any real alternative educational policy? Perhaps not, if one argues from apartheid. The contradictions must be tolerated, for their eradication might produce greater evils. The separation of the two white groups is a case in point. The hard core of racialist sentiment is embodied in the Afrikaner group. Though the English-speaking white tags along readily enough, his ethnic consciousness is not so deep-rooted. Furthermore, through his religious and other associations, and through the English-language press, he is a little more susceptible to influences which might lead him to have misgivings about apartheid. A mixing of the two white groups at school might therefore water down the sentiment upon which the regime relies for its support.

The main trends in the present situation are therefore:

(a) in respect to African schooling, the secularization of local educational management;

(b) increasing segmentation of the school population;

(c) an unequal allocation of educational resources among the various groups;

(d) an increasing direct role for the state, particularly the central government, in the control of education.

It does not seem likely that these trends will be reversed in the near future.

Appendix I

Major Legislative Steps
(Chronologically, Within Population Groups)

AFRICAN

    1953   Bantu Education Act
    1955   Exchequer and Audit Amendment Act

WHITE

    1949   Transvaal Language Ordinance
    1953   Transvaal Education Ordinance
    1954   Orange Free State Education Ordinance
    1956   Cape Province Education Ordinance
    1962   National Advisory Education Council Act

COLOURED

    1963   Coloured Persons Education Act

INDIAN

    1965   Indian Education Act

ALL GROUPS

    1955   Vocational Education Act
    1959   Extension of University Education Act

Appendix II

Some Examples of Church Positions on Racial Policy

N.B.: Rank-and-file white members of churches opposing apartheid tend to be a great deal more conservative than these statements by their leaders suggest.

In 1956 the Federal Council of the *Nederduits Gereformeerde Kerk* approved a statement on race relations which included the following:

The N.G.K. can by no means associate itself unreservedly with the general cry for equality and unity in the world today. The motives and aims in this connection can certainly not always be regarded as purely Christian. It is mostly a surrogate unity and brotherhood that men seek to realise without Christ in a world disrupted by sin. It is a futile attempt, because true unity among men can only be realized in Christ. . . . After the Fall . . . God, for the honour of his name, maintained the unity and diversity in creation by His universal grace. He decreed even greater diversity in order to restrict the expansion of power in mankind in its apostacy and insubordination to Him, and to check the effect of sin in this way. In His mercy He decreed a multiplicity of tongues and peoples and dispersed and established the human race over the face of the earth.[79]

In 1960 a group of N.G.K. leaders issued a statement approving the policy of separate development provided it were implemented in a just and honourable manner, but recognizing that particularly in the initial stages, some degree of personal inconvenience would be entailed. Commenting on this, F. E. O'B. Geldenhuys, Moderator of the Northern Transvaal Regional Synod of the N.G.K., stated that

In any well-ordered state, there are many enforcements to which the individual must subject himself.[80]

In 1949 the Bishops of the (Anglican) *Church of the Province of South Africa* stated their conviction that

no policy for the future of Southern Africa is acceptable which does not envisage the extension to persons of all races who have attained an adequate standard of education, of some effective voice in the government of their country, and which does not provide for all its citizens opportunity of making the fullest contribution of which they can become capable to its cultural, economic and industrial welfare.[81]

---

[79] *Statement on Race Relations*, Pretoria: Information Bureau of the Dutch Reformed Church, 1960, pp. 7, 9.

[80] F. E. O'B. Geldenhuys, "Die N. G. Kerk en Apartheid," *Dagbreek en Sondagnuus*, April 24, 1960. Translated by A. P. H.

[81] This and the following paragraphs are based upon documents cited in Lesley Cawood, *The Churches and Race Relations in South Africa* (Durban: South African Institute of Race Relations, 1964) , pp. 50 *et seq.*

The *Methodist* Conference resolved in 1952 that the policy of racial apartheid was not only impracticable but was contrary to the interests of all sections of the South African community, and inconsistent with the highest Christian principles. Legislation which differentiated against particular groups merely on grounds of race or colour was essentially wrong. In 1957 the Conference emphatically rejected the policy of separate development.

In 1955 the Public Questions Department of the *Congregational Church* included the following paragraph in its report to the Church's Assembly:

It is surely the basic tenet of our Christian faith that every individual has a distinctive value in the sight of God and it therefore follows that any policy that seeks deliberately to limit the full and free development of human personality, or discriminates against individuals because of the group to which they belong, or places obstacles in the way of the full fruition of God-given gifts and skills, is morally indefensible and wrong.

In 1957 the *Roman Catholic* Bishops condemned the principle of apartheid as something intrinsically evil, and maintained:

There must be a gradual change: gradual, for no other kind of change is compatible with the maintenance of order, without which there is no society, no government, no justice, no common good. But change must come, for, otherwise, our country faces a disastrous future. That change could be initiated immediately if the ingenuity and energy now expended on apartheid were devoted to making South Africa a happy country for all its citizens. The time is short. The need is urgent. Those penalized by apartheid must be given concrete evidence of change before it is too late. This involves the elaboration of a sensible and just policy enabling any person, irrespective of race, to qualify for the enjoyment of full civil rights.

In the 1964 Yearbook of the *Apostolic Faith Mission,* the following statement on race relations appears:

We believe that in Christ all people are equal [*gelykwaardig*] and in this sense they are also brothers and sisters in the Lord. However, this does not mean that all racial and national differences are thereby wiped out. The Lord himself willed that there should be nations. Acts 17:25-28, Gen. 11:8, Deut. 32:8. A policy of national or racial separation (also known as separate development) may only be followed as long as:

(a) national or racial mixing would mean that one or all groups would be harmed economically and culturally; or
(b) where racial and cultural differences are so great that mixing would inevitably cause friction; and
(c) where separate development is accompanied by justice and fairness towards all.[82]

[82] Translated in Cawood, *op. cit.*, p. 104.

Appendix III

The Financing of African Education: A Ministerial Statement with Comment by the South African Institute of Race Relations[83]

There is a basic difference of approach between the Institute of Race Relations and the Government on the financing of Bantu education, said Mr. W. A. Maree, Minister of Bantu Education, in a letter replying to the memorandum by the Institute on the present inadequate provision of funds for that purpose.

The Institute was apparently concerned, said the Minister, at the fact that the State only provided from Consolidated Revenue a fixed contribution of R13m per annum for Bantu education instead of making an allocation according to the needs, as in the case of White education.

Mr. Maree said that he and his Department knew the implications of this fact, and continued:

As you will agree, education can only be financed from three possible sources: voluntary contributions, payment of school fees by parents, and direct taxation. In any case the parents should be held responsible in the first instance. According to your proposals, the entire population (White and Non-White) must take full responsibility for Bantu education.

The Government's policy is that the State's contribution be fixed at R13m and that the expenditure for all further expansion and development be financed by the Bantu himself.

The State thus adopted a "middle course" covering all three possibilities referred to above, said the Minister.

Alternatively, he went on, the State could have accepted total financial responsibility, but in that case "Bantu taxation would have to be raised immediately from the present R3.50 per capita per annum to R13.37, the per capita expenditure for Bantu education during the financial year 1963/64. In this latter estimate all services to the Bantu people other than Bantu education are excluded."

Replying to the Institute's statement that virtually no expansion in Bantu education would be possible if it had to depend on increases in the yield from direct Bantu taxation, considering the low wages of the mass of Bantu and their restricted employment opportunities, the Minister said:

According to recent information, the considerable improvement in the income of the South African Bantu renders him capable of enjoying a standard of living which is nowhere equalled in Africa.

[83] *Race Relations News* (published by the South African Institute of Race Relations), November, 1964.

In the past four years the Bantu has received an average wage increase of 44%, while his purchasing power has increased by 400% over the last ten years. The Bantu's contribution to the national income at present is R1,085m per annum, or equal to 23% thereof. This is an increase of 46% over the past two years.

Mr. Maree added that in comparison with the above "the Bantu's financial responsibility for Bantu education is disproportionately low—R3.50 per capita per annum in general taxation and about R3.63 annually per child at school in the form of levies, school fees, cost of books and contributions to school building material, as well as salaries of privately employed teachers."

The Minister concluded: "An increase in the Bantu's general taxation may not be unwarranted."

Dealing with several specific points in the Institute's memorandum, Mr. Maree repeated that the decrease in the cost per pupil in Bantu education could be ascribed to the large increase in lower primary pupils —an argument disputed by the Institute. He said that the cost of school books in Bantu schools was much lower than, say, in Transvaal White schools.

Unspent amounts in the Bantu Education Vote were not re-deposited into the Exchequer, as had been maintained in the memorandum, but were preserved for Bantu education, declared the Minister.

While agreeing with Mr. Maree's general summary of the differences of approach between him and the Institute on the financing of Bantu education, it differed from him on his assertion that "education can only be financed from three possible sources: voluntary contributions, payment of school fees by parents, and direct taxation," said the Institute of Race Relations in a letter replying to the Minister of Bantu Education.

Direct taxation is only one of the sources from which the general revenue of the State is derived, the Institute declared. For example, in 1962–63 customs and excise yielded R230,221,285, which was almost two-thirds of the revenue from income tax, including supertax.

Bantu education is the only case where the services rendered by the State are related to direct taxation, instead of to general revenue to which all active elements of the population contribute. Africans make an indispensable contribution through their labour to the revenue of the State.

The gravamen of the Institute's submissions is that the revenue of the country as a whole should be regarded as serving all the people of the country and should therefore be allocated in accordance with what are considered priority needs without regard to the direct contribution made by the people affected.

The Institute also disagreed that the main financial responsibility for their children's education should devolve on the parents. That principle was not applied to groups other than the Africans.

Dealing with the Minister's statement about taxation in the event of the State's accepting total responsibility for financing Bantu education, the Institute said:

Admittedly the minimum tax paid by African men is R3.50 per annum and the present per capita expenditure on Bantu school-children is R13.37 per annum.

But the Institute fails to comprehend on what basis you therefore deduce that if the State assumes full financial responsibility for Bantu education, Bantu taxation will immediately have to be raised from R3.50 to R13.37.

This surely would imply that the number of Bantu taxpayers and of Bantu school-children is the same, that Bantu taxpayers at present contribute R3.50 per child, that, on the basis of full State financial responsibility, Bantu taxpayers would pay R13.37 (or whatever the per capita cost happened to be in that financial year), and that the number of school-children and taxpayers will remain equal.

The Institute expressed alarm at what appeared to be an implied threat that "an increase in the Bantu's general taxation may not be unwarranted."

The Minister's references to Bantu taxation "might well create the impression that Africans are taxed at a uniform rate of R3.50 per annum, whereas in fact this is the minimum tax that male Africans pay on attaining the age of 18 years. All Africans, men and women, earning more than R30 per month pay on a graduated scale, any amounts paid in normal income tax being deductible."

While noting with satisfaction that Africans had benefited to some extent from the country's prosperity in the past two or three years, the Institute said that the comments by the Minister on the economic situation of the Bantu "tend to obscure the fact that poverty remains the most important factor in the lives of the majority of Africans in the country."

Admittedly, the Institute continued, there was greater poverty in other African countries on an incomparably lower economic level but relative need was not the subject under discussion.

In Johannesburg, the Institute recalled, the average income of family heads in Soweto is R42 per month; 48% of families depend entirely on the earnings of the head of the family; 60% have incomes below the Poverty Datum Line, calculated by the Johannesburg Non-European Affairs Department at R48.24 per month for a family of five.

Ten years ago it was 80%, an improvement attributable to a rise in wages.

The Africans in Soweto were probably more favourably situated than many other urban communities, said the Institute, and added: "That there is an acute and pressing poverty in the Bantu areas and a grave problem of unemployment there is a matter of common knowledge."

The Institute repeated the views it had previously voiced on several other details in the Minister's statement. It concluded:

It is because of these many considerations, and the urgent desire to enable the quality of Bantu education and consequently the human quality as well as the skills of its products to be raised, that the Institute has addressed its earnest request to the Minister to increase the financial contribution of the State to Bantu education.

Commentary

PROFESSOR J. J. FOURIE

Dean of the Faculty of Education of the University of the
Orange Free State, South Africa, and a member of
the National Advisory Education Council

INTRODUCTORY REMARKS

The author of this chapter states that he will make an attempt
to assess the situation in South Africa in the light of educational
criteria and in terms of probable social consequences. To this we
have to reply: which criteria? Bias, or a true knowledge and understanding of the traditional situation in South Africa as it has developed in this country over a period of 300 years?

In order to give a fuller perspective and to eliminate the mis-
representations, false and misleading statements, and lack of understanding of our country's policy and circumstances, it would be
necessary to recollect certain historical facts, comment on geographical factors involved, and give a fuller exposition of universally accepted educational principles—like mother-tongue instruction—for which South Africa is criticized in this chapter. This
would, however, entail a more extensive commentary than the
author's contribution. I shall therefore have to confine myself to
a few major points.

HISTORICAL AND GEOGRAPHICAL FACTORS IN PERSPECTIVE

I should like to make it clear at the outset that our country's
policy is based on a solemn conviction that has come to us from the
lessons of the past and our belief in the future of this country. It is
based on a more realistic understanding of the problems of our own
than that which the outsider—under the influence of liberalist and
communist propaganda—would like to have for us: "one man, one
vote," and "Africa for the Africans"—i.e. the capitulation of the
whites in a country which they have built up from a desolate and

deserted state in the days of annihilating wars among the barbarian Bantu tribes before the dawn of Christian civilization, to one of the most developed and civilized countries in the world. Where the author of this chapter finds fault with the heading "Turmoil among the South African Bantu tribes" in that section of the South African history syllabus dealing with the Africans before contact with the whites, we have to advise that nobody who is well acquainted with the facts of South African history will ever question that part of our history syllabus. Moreover, the true historical facts regarding the beginning of Western civilization at the Cape, the occupation of vast stretches (thousands of square miles) of deserted country and no-man's-land by the whites, the "turmoil" that opened up this country for Christian Western civilization, and, in consequence, the claims of the whites to this country as their only fatherland are very often overlooked by "outside" observers who are more concerned with so-called humanitarian ideals than with matters of truth.

By quoting the Administrator of the Transvaal that "a white consciousness should be inculcated and children should realize that they were the bearers of Christian Western civilization," the author inadvertently stresses the issue and endorses the fact that the fight for self-preservation and the right of self-determination of the whites in South Africa—and I should like to add: on a basis of non-intervention and in the interests of whites and non-whites alike—is a special task of education in this country.

Reference to the fact that the African homelands will ultimately constitute no more than about 13 per cent of South Africa's land surface, despite the fact that the Africans form 68 per cent of the total population, lacks true perspective for which the author could have consulted the Tomlinson Report. Unfortunately he did not give the world the following facts:

1. 13 per cent of 472,359 square miles (the total area of the Republic of South Africa) equals approximately 62,000 square miles.

2. Three-quarters of the total area of the Republic of South Africa has a rainfall of less than 24 inches a year, including vast stretches of thinly populated country in semi-desert and desert areas.

3. The 62,000 square miles of Bantu homelands are mainly

situated in the remaining 118,000 square miles (the remaining quarter) of South Africa's land surface, which has an annual rainfall of more than 24 inches and forms by far the most productive part of the country.

4. To this must be added the three British Protectorates, Bechuanaland, Swaziland and Basutoland, with a total area of 293,420 square miles of which approximately 200,000 has an annual rainfall of 24 inches or more.

Considering the fact that these protectorates which are in the main surrounded by South African land surface form geographically and historically the natural abodes of the Bantu People, the horizon will expand to a much wider perspective than the figures mentioned in this chapter (i.e. the 68 per cent of the population on 13 per cent of the land surface) can ever reveal.

ETHNIC GROUPING

Although the notion of separate development of whites and non-whites may seem strange to the outsider, the underlying principle has proved itself to be sound practical policy in this country. In fact, it is conceded in this chapter that "The long-standing divisions and tensions among the various cultural groups lead one to give serious consideration to the possibility of some form of partition." For this reason the full significance of the report of the Commission on the Separate University Education Bill (the De Wet Nel Commission, 1958) that "to put all African groups together in one institution would be to overlook the profound differences between the various groups, to disregard the importance of common cultural traditions and language in building up a college, and to ignore the university's role in the general development of a particular group" would only be clear from a fuller understanding of the needs of the country.

Again, when the author explains in a footnote annotation that it is envisaged that at an appropriate stage in the development of each of the non-white colleges, the white bodies (councils and senates) would become advisory, and the non-white bodies would assume the powers hitherto exercised by the whites, he unwittingly faces the issue that it is the inclination and the intention of the whites of this country to lead the non-whites to their fullest possible development and self-realization under the guidance and guardianship of the whites. But this may be wrong in the eyes of the world which has not yet come to understand fully the lessons of Africa.

ALLOCATION OF RESOURCES

The author comments at length on the alleged discrepancy in financial provision for African and European education and blames the South African Nationalist government for the relatively low level of education of the African teacher. This is, however, a distorted picture which fails to make any allowance for the basic differences in the educational needs of the two groups according to their present degree of development and civilization. Why pick on the South African Nationalist government, which has done more for the education of its non-white masses than most other governments in Africa can boast of? Had the author been more realistic in discarding the idea of comparing education for whites and non-whites in the Republic of South Africa and in submitting sufficient statistical evidence for a fairer basis of comparison, namely that of non-white education in the republic and the three British protectorates respectively, a much truer perspective would have been given to emphasize the favorable position of non-white education in the republic in comparison with that of other territories in Southern Africa. The latter would be a much fairer basis of comparison. It would also emphasize the truth that only a very small percentage of the non-white masses is beginning to find its way into the intellectual standards of the whites, making it practically impossible to find an adequate number of fully qualified teachers for African education, especially in view of the fact that—as Dr. Hunter correctly points out—the school enrollment for Bantu children has shown an increase of 100 per cent in the past ten years (from 858,079 in 1953 to 1,770,260 in 1963) —and that "in spite of" the South African Nationalist government. I fully realize how difficult it could be, sometimes, to see the truth; but let us face the "To be or not to be" issue. For if the intellectual standards for qualification to the teaching profession would have to be the same for non-whites as for the whites, there would be very little African education at all in this country, as in other parts of Africa—unless some philanthropic dreamer could use a magic wand to solve all the problems of darkness which will still exist in the African con-

tinent for a long time to come. To blame the South African government, which is doing its level best to encourage the awakening of
non-white civilization and to meet the needs as they arise, would
therefore be an error of judgement.

The following facts should be noted in particular:

A strongly centralized state control in educational matters is
not necessarily at variance with democratic ideals. We find a much
more strongly centralized system in some European and other democratic countries today than the one which has developed in South
Africa under the Nationalist government.

The author of this chapter is very much concerned about a so-
called shift in the locus of power over education from province to
the central government and mentions Act No. 86, 1962, "which
established a National Advisory Education Council, appointed by
the Minister of Education, and charged with advising the Minister
on educational policy" as one of the significant limitations of provincial power in relation to white schools. As one of the twenty-
nine members of that council, it may be my prerogative to warn
those who want to rouse suspicion against jumping at conclusions
before having fully acquainted themselves with the work of this
council. It is not only correct but also imperative at this stage that
there should be a body of this kind to assist in developing a "national pattern of education," but it would be a mistake to confuse
unity with uniformity and the alleged limitations of provincial
powers. This council of professional men and women represents
all sections and climates and the diversity of interests of our South
African community and will not render itself guilty of irresponsibility in handling such a delicate matter as the education of our
youth for the future of our country.

There is an intimation of state control over the activities of
students in the Bantu colleges, and the instance cited is the Fort
Hare incident of 1960. The author, however, fails to explain
that these were emergency measures that had to be taken as a
result of a series of riots at the Fort Hare college in 1959 and 1960.

The South African government is also criticized for the Bantu
Education Act of 1963, which "took from the provinces and from
the Christian missions the functions they had traditionally exer-

cised in relation to Africans." It is however, conceded that "those missionaries — many of them expatriate — who ran the African schools often did not share the racial views of the average white South African," and again that "the close links which the mission teachers often felt with corresponding Christian groups overseas gave many of their pupils a vision of a world-wide community," with the result that "the African education system was then correctly perceived by the Nationalist Government to be incompatible with its vision of the future South Africa." It is also conceded that this measure

1. "gave to the central government the power to ensure that this enterprise was carried out in accordance with the national racial policy,"

2. "and made provision for some participation by Government-approved Africans in the local administration of their school system."

The fact remains that there were very many good reasons for ending a great deal of the management of African schools by the missions by revising the system of government grants to these schools. To quote the author of this chapter:

> Some African leaders sought a greater say in the schooling of their children, and sectarian rivalry was seen by many as a hindrance to the overall development of African education.

I should like to add that, in spite of the negative reference to the "superficial" way in which the religious spirit is alleged to be carried on in our state schools, there is yet more religion in the schools of this country than in those of most other countries of the world.

MOTHER-TONGUE INSTRUCTION AND SINGLE-MEDIUM SCHOOLS

It is none of my intention to defend a universally accepted educational principle, that of mother-tongue instruction, for which the South African government is criticized severely in this chapter. If it were true that this principle was introduced as a result of the "increasing opposition from Afrikaner Nationalists who were insistent upon the need for compulsory mother-tongue instruction," it would be equally true that this group had then rendered the country an invaluable service, in spite of the accusation that "the hard core of racialist sentiment is embodied in the Afrikaner group." Again, if the writer maintains that "the social function of the mother-tongue policy in this context is to reinforce the separation of groups referred to earlier in this chapter," we have to advocate the separation of party politics from educational policy. To face the issue: where other countries believe in mother-tongue instruction, it is correctly regarded as the only sound educational policy, but when South Africa introduces this policy into our schools, it is state indoctrination and racialism.

The Nationalist government and the Afrikaner Nationalists are also blamed for the policy of single-medium schools. It might be necessary to point out here that if somebody were to blame, the boot would be on the other foot: the English-speaking section of our community which had believed in its traditional English-medium private schools for many years before the so-called "Afrikaner" section advocated the same principle. But there is no blame. The principle of single-medium schools is generally accepted by both language groups as a sound educational policy in this country; and I must add that it must be clear to any unbiased observer who has a sufficient knowledge of the history of this country that the two language groups have never been nearer to each other than under the present regime. (This will also be obvious from the substantially increasing support for the present government at every election and by-election.) For this and many other reasons the author's concluding statement that "a mixing of the two white groups at school might therefore water down the sentiment upon which the regime relies for its support" could be regarded as an insinuation unworthy of an academic treatise.